Designed to Stay

gestalten

The Design Hotels Book

Table
of Contents

Foreword

For more than 30 years, Design Hotels has curated a boundary-pushing portfolio of hotels in all corners of the world, in destinations of discovery and those we know well. As the boutique hotel movement of the early nineties began to flourish, what started out as a small group of ten member hotels has evolved into a global culture platform, where each property tells a singular story defined by its vision and locality.

As a former chef myself, I know that crafting a memorable dish is a true team effort. And just like any great cuisine, our hotel community is a blend of distinct ingredients—shaped by diverse palates and perspectives, the skilled hands that bring them to life, and those who serve them. Constantly evolving, continuously expanding. That's where we come in: thoughtfully selecting new voices to enrich the mix, one flavor at a time. With each new arrival, our community grows stronger and more diverse, as we foster unexpected connections between people and place.

Every hotel is a testament to the Originals—the owners, designers, architects, or artists—behind it, to their teams who breathe life into their spaces, to the locals who enliven our sense of hospitality, and the travelers who join us when the table is set. This publication is our love letter to all of them. We stand beside them, the incubator for futures not yet written.

More than just a book, the following pages offer a moment outside of time, built by the collective imagination of those who dream beyond the known. May this volume spark your own.

Savor every page.

Stijn Oyen
Managing Director
Design Hotels

Designed to Stay

Why Certain Places Never Leave Us

6

A great hotel is not defined by its thread count or star rating, but by its resonance: the quiet, lasting imprint a place leaves upon our memory. This is a quality born from intention. It arises from a soundscape, a scent, the grain of wood beneath a hand, or the precise way light animates a room. Such places do not just host us; they attune us to their surroundings. They shift our perception of time, of place, and sometimes, of ourselves.

The Design Hotels book gathers hotels that are united by this rare sensibility. It proposes a new classification for hospitality, one arranged not by geography but by atmosphere. "Space as Story" explores spaces conceived as narrative performances. "Natural Resonance" examines a luxury rooted in the elemental dialogue between design and landscape. "Rooted in Place" reveals hotels that function as living archives of their immediate cultural context. Finally, "Attuned to the City" redefines the urban retreat as a sophisticated pause within the city's rhythm.

To illuminate these themes, we have invited an ensemble of singular voices. Oliver Jahn, Alexis Dornier, and Eleni Petaloti explore how space itself performs, carrying narrative and shaping cinematic memory. Cultural observers Christina Ohly Evans and Sarah Owen consider the hotel's evolving role as a vital form of social infrastructure. To decode the sensory realm, tastemakers Arman Naféei and Nicola Leigh Stewart investigate how ambiance and scent create a deep emotional connection. Finally, Kissa Castañeda looks at the influence of wabi-sabi minimalism in the creation of calming spaces that nurture authenticity and well-being.

These written reflections are thoughtful interludes. They sit beside the hotels, offering shifts in tone and tempo that provide lenses through which to consider what makes a stay unforgettable. Many of the featured places could, of course, belong to several chapters at once. That is the point. They resist a singular definition, living instead in the overlap between design and memory, beauty and feeling.

They are not just places to stay. They are places designed to stay with you.

Space as
Story

Design can be more than beautiful—it can be bold, emotional, and expressive. These hotels are driven by vision, narrative, and theatricality. They show how architecture, form, and atmosphere can tell stories, shift perception, and provoke certain emotions in unexpected ways.

9

The Whisper of the Steps:

Oliver Jahn

What Spaces Tell Us (and Conceal)

With the lyricism of a seasoned editor and the insight of a cultural historian, Oliver Jahn traces the storytelling force of architecture—where every step, wall, and void is charged with narrative potential.

It was the architect John Pawson who once urged me to visit the famous Cistercian abbey of Le Thoronet, tucked away in the hinterlands of Provence near the Argens River. It is a place that has drawn this master of English minimalism to study an atmosphere etched into stone over nearly a thousand years, an atmosphere shaped by light and shadow, focus and spirituality. On a shimmering hot day one June, I finally did what Pawson suggested. Absentmindedly, my bare feet traced the grooves and scars of the worn, polished corridors and stone steps that stretched out before me like waves patiently rolled into form. Vaulted passages in which centuries of ascetic monastic life found their ideal geometry. I placed my hand on the stone. What have these steps seen? What prayers, doubts, and rituals still echo in their hollows?

Of course, walls can whisper: buildings preserve history not only in a material sense but also as living archives of human action, thought, and emotion. The stairways of Le Thoronet speak of quiet discipline, of repeated rituals, of a community shaped through time and space. Architecture is never a neutral frame. It is an active vessel, a form of embodied memory.

Take, for instance, Goethe House in Weimar. It symbolizes artist homes around the world that attract millions of visitors each year in search of the elusive spirit of genius. This, too, is such a vessel. Every room—from the study to the Juno Room to the bedroom—breathes intellect, design, and meaning. In the furniture, the light, and the palette, Goethe's expansive worldview is made tangible: Enlightenment, order, and sensuality.

The visitor enters a world where each object carries a narrative, and each arrangement reveals a worldview. Here, architecture is not merely evidential, but a finely calibrated expression of someone's mind.

In his groundbreaking book *The Four Walls: A Hidden History of Dwelling,* the German theorist Gert Selle reflected upon these themes. In this title, he also coined the idea of the "living room as a museum of the self," an apt description for what inevitably takes shape in our homes, and

Oliver Jahn

what interior design at its best strives to express: identity made visible. The spaces we inhabit are self-narratives. Who we are, who we wish to be, what stories we tell ourselves and others—and what we choose to keep silent.

Hugo von Hofmannsthal, the Austrian author, also touched on this when he spoke of his literary contemporary Thomas Mann: "He reminds me of an exquisite ten-room apartment somewhere in northern Germany—say, Hamburg. The rugs, the paintings, the library, the silver, the porcelain—everything couldn't be more tasteful, more solid, more refined. And then, there is a little room where no guest is ever shown, and in it lies a dead cat..." Architectural space is personal, not just because of who it is owned or made by, but because it is a physical manifestation of someone's subjectivity.

But unlike humans, spaces cannot lie; they can only hint. Some forms of architecture elevate this self-staging to monumental levels. William Beckford's Fonthill Abbey—a Gothic folly, an artificial ruin in glorious excess built around 1800—was less a home than a theatrical act of eccentric self-invention. The towering spire, inspired by his 1786 novel *Vathek,* collapsed repeatedly, as if reality itself objected to such hubris. Yet the building told a story, a narrative concerning a man who sought to construct, through architecture, a legend of power, isolation, and decadence.

And as Beckford understood, architecture has indeed always been a form of representation; of power, influence, and vision. Louis XIV did not build Versailles merely to house his sprawling court—if such rarefied refinement can still be called "dwelling"—but to reign. The architecture of representation is never modest; it aims for the theatrical. It wants to impress, intimidate, seduce. So too with Charles de Beistegui's Château de Groussay—a stage set for the flamboyant French art collector, whose famous ball at his palazzo in Venice in 1951 went down as "the party of the century." These were not everyday spaces but crafted narratives of cosmopolitan excess. Theater and archive in one.

Another compelling example is the pavilion created by none other than Salvador Dalí, "Dream of Venus," at the 1939 World's Fair in New York. It was a surreal explosion of this idea: architecture as dream image, as subversion of the everyday. Visitors entered through the parted legs of a Venus figure and found themselves in an underwater world where mannequins in fish costumes drifted. Here, interior design was used to stage and *represent* the unconscious.

Edward James's Monkton House offers another example. In this eccentric English aristocrat's hunting lodge, no room was left to chance. A patron and friend of Dalí, James furnished the room with sculptures by the surrealist (including his iconic *Mae West Lips Sofa* and his *Lobster Telephone),* alongside works by Max Ernst and hand-painted walls. In James's architectural vision, everything spoke of a man who lived, dreamed, and created with surrealists. On the other hand, consider Charleston Farmhouse, the home of Vanessa Bell and Duncan Grant, and a sanctuary of the Bloomsbury Group, one particularly associated with Virginia Woolf. There, even today, one can study how rooms become paintings, how furniture can become a carrier of thought and color, and how dwelling becomes a continuous artistic act.

And let us not forget the grand hotels, both past and present—the Ritz, the Chateau Marmont, the Danieli—which have never been *merely* hotels but world theaters conjuring dreams and desires. These places generate narrative in abundance; they are storytelling machines sui generis.

All these examples illustrate what holds true for every space shaped with intention: architects and interior designers are directors. Rooms are their stage, their canvas. It is rarely just about functionality, but about crafting atmosphere, dramatic arcs, and moments of surprise, and recognition. A home is always a story, with rhythm, climax, rupture, and resolution. These spaces are palimpsests, inscribed with the lives of their owners, staff, and—of course—guests. Thinking in this way, seeing a room as a narrative gesture can make sense. A vaulted passageway is a way to welcome people. A narrow stairway, a trial. A great hall, a proclamation of power. Architecture speaks. It does so through proportion, material, light, sound. It inscribes itself in our bodies, influencing our movements and thoughts.

And sometimes it speaks simply through wear, like the immovable steps of Le Thoronet. No grandeur. No staging. Only the quiet, rhythmic passage of feet across centuries. No words are needed. Just the sound of soles forever preserved in stone. They whisper of silence and permanence, of ritual and change, of fleeting traces of life. Architecture is never mute. To those who listen, it reveals not just space but narrative; not just form but meaning.

Just as I heard that June afternoon—barefoot on sun-warmed stone—the voices of time. Rooms speak. Always.

Oliver Jahn is a cultural strategist and creative director based in Switzerland. Formerly the editor-in-chief of *Architectural Digest Germany* and deputy global editorial director for *Architectural Digest,* he is now the CEO and chief creative officer of House of Manus, a platform dedicated to preserving and advancing craftsmanship through cultural investment and creative consulting.

La Purificadora

Once a 19th-century factory, this former water-purification and ice factory now houses a chic hotel that prioritizes natural materials with a restrained palette. Located in Puebla, the building's colonial heritage required special protection during the design process—a challenge that renowned Mexican architect Ricardo Legorreta was happy to take on for owners **Carlos Couturier** and **Micha Moisés**—pioneers of Mexico's boutique hotel scene through Grupo Habita. With a bare-bones tool box of natural materials and black and white, Legorreta allowed the original, raw materials to shine. The designers even incorporated historic bottles and glass fragments into the structure. Internally, rich timbers, exposed walls, and patterned tiles also feature, balancing minimalism with industrial history. This balance appears again on the roof terrace, where the glass walls of a 30-meter heated pool contrast with the building's antique walls. As the self-proclaimed birthplace of *molé,* the city has a rich culinary history. Honoring this heritage, chef Nanyely Pastrana's menu offers a contemporary approach to authentic Mexican cuisine.

Destination
United Kingdom

Location
London

Rooms
81

Themes
City, History

Sir Devonshire Square Hotel London

Liran Wizman adds a redbrick classic dating back to 1768 to his Sir Hotels portfolio, this time in the heart of east London. Since launching in 2013, Wizman's vision of combining luxury, clean design, and a distinctive neighborhood feeling now extends beyond Amsterdam, Berlin, Hamburg, and Ibiza to this prime London location. Perfectly positioned between the Square Mile and Shoreditch, with a buzzing market to the east and towering skyline to the west, the 81-room boutique property offers both quiet seclusion and on-the-pulse action. Inside, multiple spots invite guests to linger: a glorious plant-filled courtyard provides sanctuary from the urban hustle, while newly installed fireplaces create intimate lounging spaces throughout. Seven North restaurant serves as a culinary launch pad, drawing inspiration from Mediterranean, French, German, and Italian cuisines. Just steps from Liverpool Street station and Spitalfields Market, guests can easily explore the neighborhood's distinctive sights and sounds, while The Cover private members' club provides an exclusive retreat for those keen to stay on-site.

Destination
Greece

Location
Athens

Rooms
47

Themes
Art & Culture, City,
History, Sustainable

Perianth Hotel

A sleek, dark palette of charcoal marble, brass, and timber define the conversion of this 1930s modernist structure. Siblings **Alexandra, Anastasia,** and **Konstantinos Sgoumpopoulou** wanted guests to experience all that Athens has to offer, while instilling aspects of their individual characters into the hotel. One is an arts advocate, one a DJ, and one a Zen monk and tae kwon do master; to achieve this, the trio asked architects and designers K-Studio to help establish the hotel as a place of art, mindfulness, and modern design. The trapezoidal building embodies Athenian modernism, which K-Studio looked to when considering the fit-out, incorporating terrazzo floors, black metal frames, marble furniture, and glass-brick walls into the design. The rooms are chic, balconied havens, featuring custom-made walnut furniture with brass details and charcoal marble benches. The restaurant serves Greek-inspired cuisine in the evenings following an all-day brunch, all in sight of the Acropolis.

Destination
South Africa

Location
Johannesburg

Rooms
10

Themes
City

Destination
Mexico

Location
Mexico City

Rooms
40

Themes
City, History

Ten Bompas

The zenith of contemporary luxury, the suites in this boutique hotel, created by architects Luc Zeghers and Enrico Daffonchio, are each designed by a different designer. Here, owners **Christoff van Staden** and **Peter Aucamp** collaborated with both on the blueprint, which is replete with distinct materials such as cement, bronze, burnished brass, and gunmetal. Local art lines the lobby, conference rooms, and the walls, creating an inspired atmosphere. Set in a commercial district, the hotel is suitable for business and pleasure, with three meeting rooms and an outdoor pool.

Condesa DF

In Mexico City, Condesa DF transforms a French building of 1928 into a statement. Here, owners **Carlos Couturier** and **Moisés Micha,** architect Javier Sánchez, and designer India Mahdavi have created a space enlivened by Mexican vibrancy and high-tech chic. The hotel centers around a patio where three floors of shuttered windows create geometric patterns leading skyward, culminating in a roof terrace and restaurant serving Japanese-Mexican dishes. The property integrates with its surroundings: a place where people gather to celebrate local creativity.

Destination	Location	Rooms	Themes
United States	Santa Monica, CA	267	City, History

Santa Monica Proper Hotel

Glittering tiled columns, towering archways, designer lounges, and grand potted palms foster a uniquely Californian atmosphere in the public spaces of Santa Monica Proper Hotel. Owners **Brad Korzen, Brian De Lowe,** and **Kelly Wearstler** aimed to embed a looser kind of luxury into the premises, calling on the area's coastal lifestyle for the aesthetic. Wearstler handled the hotel's design alongside Howard Laks Architects. The hotel connects two separate buildings—one a 1928 Spanish Colonial Revival building, the other a new build—via a suspended bridge. To cohere the different buildings, Wearstler employed synchronizing aesthetics throughout, including

Moorish detailing, baroque ornamentation, artworks from Ben Medansky, and ceramics by Morgan Peck. A rooftop playground featuring an Ayurvedic spa, pool, and indoor-outdoor bistro, alongside Pacific views that deepen to a mood-enhancing glow at sunset, crown this singular place.

Destination
Mexico

Location
Mexico City

Rooms
17

Themes
City, History

Downtown Mexico

Housed within a 17th-century palace in Mexico City's Centro Histórico, Downtown Mexico—created by hoteliers **Carlos Couturier** and **Moisés Micha**—brings a raw, industrial edge to viceregal grandeur. Couturier and Micha, the visionary minds behind Grupo Habita, bring their signature blend of design-forward thinking and attention to local authenticity to every detail. The 17-room property also brings a bohemian touch to elegant minimalism, with volcanic stone walls, high-vaulted brick ceilings, and a dramatic stone staircase. Interiors by Paul Roco highlight local craftsmanship and indigenous influences in the Aztec-red upholstery, for stripped-back yet luxurious spaces. On the rooftop, a terrace with a pool and cocktail bar offers panoramic views of the city's historic skyline. Designed by Serrano & Cherem Arquitectos, the hotel honors its UNESCO World Heritage surroundings while offering modern comfort within. Complimentary bike hire makes exploring easy as well as sustainable. Steps away from museums, galleries, and cobbled streets, Downtown Mexico is a stylish, soulful retreat at the cultural heart of the capital.

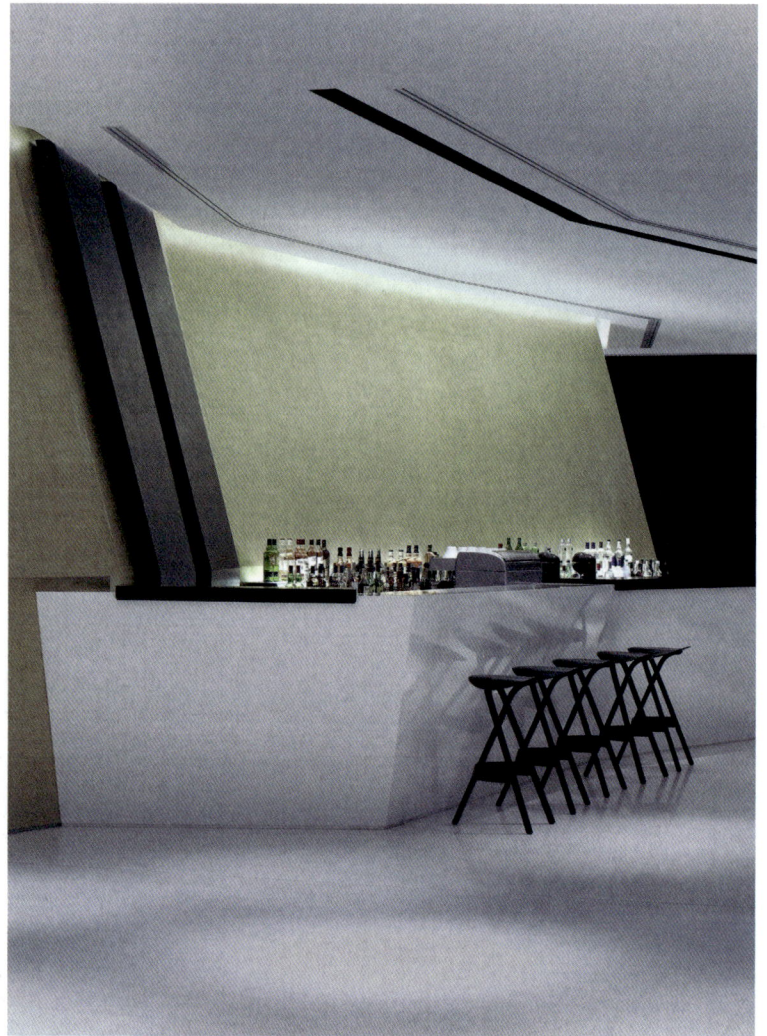

Destination
Greece

Location
Athens

Rooms
148

Themes
City, Sustainable

Destination
Greece

Location
Thessaloniki

Rooms
212

Themes
Art & Culture, City, Sustainable

Fresh Hotel

Fresh Hotel is a charming Hellenic sanctuary. Owner **Ada Yfanti** and designer Paola Navone reimagined the property via modernist, neoclassical, and folkloric influences. Minimal geometric motifs adorn the interiors, while wooden fittings and pops of color make for a clean aesthetic. A rooftop pool, the Air Lounge Bar, and a new extension add depth. The façade's signature glass panels pay tribute to the building's origins, while the Acropolis is visible almost throughout. Fresh and inspiring, authentic and forward thinking, this is Athens, old and new.

The Met Hotel

The Met Hotel, a bold statement of contemporary luxury, sits in Thessaloniki's vibrant New Harbor, an emerging cultural hub minutes from the historic city center. Against an industrial-chic backdrop, it offers refined comfort and cutting-edge design, with modern artworks animating interiors. Guests unwind in sleek rooms, enjoy 360-degree views from the rooftop Sky Bar and Restaurant, and relax at the rooftop pool bar. A full-service spa, high-tech conference spaces, and complimentary shuttle redefine this dynamic urban resort.

Destination
United States

Location
Beverly Hills, CA

Rooms
84

Themes
City

Avalon Hotel
Beverly Hills

Within short distance of Beverly Hills' shopping and dining "Golden Triangle" is a midcentury modern boutique hotel offering comfortable luxury with a retro touch. **Brad Korzen, Brian De Lowe,** and **Kelly Wearstler** repurposed the property, originally conceived of by legendary graphic designer Alvin Lustig in the 1940s. Wearstler's thorough research of the original design allowed her to preserve much of the 1949 building's midcentury features, while giving it a much-needed facelift. Now, custom-glazed European white oak hardwood flooring, bespoke furnishings, and floor-to-ceiling windows complement views of the hourglass pool. Nods to the property's heritage appear on the menu at Viviane, the hotel's poolside Euro-American restaurant serving 1950s-inspired seasonal cocktails. Chef Michael Reed is in charge of the menu, highlighting organic produce, sustainable dining, and boutique wines.

The Ludlow Hotel

Located in New York's Lower East Side, The Ludlow is a love letter to the iconic neighborhood's ever-evolving history. Created by hotelier **Sean MacPherson** along with **Ira Drukier** and **Richard Born,** this 175-room sanctuary—once an abandoned building—is now a living tribute to Downtown New York's creative spirit. Industrial elegance is the overarching theme. Exposed brick walls, factory casement windows, and a stunning distressed limestone fireplace make for an authentically raw backdrop. Rooms boast loft-like comfort and artful touches, including plush throws, leather furniture, lavish bathrooms, and expansive windows that capture the area's dynamic, mercurial character. The hotel speaks to the area's reputation as an artistic haven for parties and "happenings," from its marble mosaic floors to the eclectic mix of vintage furniture and handpicked art. The lobby lounge feels like a private living room for creatives to gather, while the Terrace suites offer sweeping views of graffitied walls and urban roofs.

Charlotte Street Hotel, Firmdale Hotels

Charlotte Street Hotel is a celebration of creativity rooted in Bloomsbury's rich artistic legacy. Conceived by **Kit Kemp,** this central London gem occupies a former warehouse and pharmacy just north of Soho—once frequented by writers and artists of the Bloomsbury Group. Inside, sumptuous fabrics, eclectic furnishings, and handpicked art—including original pieces by Vanessa Bell, Roger Fry, and Duncan Grant—evoke the group's spirit in a blend of vintage and contemporary London style. The centerpiece is Oscar Bar & Restaurant, whose vibrant mural by Alexander Hollweg references Roger Fry's *Scenes of Contemporary London Life.* In summer, Oscar spills onto Charlotte Street; in colder months, its cozy charm and fireplace set the stage for relaxed gatherings. From the stylish rooms and screening chamber hosting a weekend film club to drawing rooms, a library, and comfortable lounge areas, every corner of Charlotte Street Hotel is designed for creative exchange and immersive comfort.

Bursa Hotel

Despite being sought-after among hoteliers in New York, **Vasily Grogol** decided, after graduating in hospitality management, to open his own venture back on European soil. He envisioned a hotel that would host a creative "it" crowd like New York's Chelsea Hotel in its heyday, and the result is Bursa, a Bauhaus-inspired hotel in Kyiv's bohemian Podil neighborhood that brings film and art to the fore. The hotel has its own cinema, Kino42, which presents curated independent films, alongside an art gallery, bistro, and two bars. Building on Vasily's goal of encouraging and drawing a flourishing new generation of artists to the venue, Bursa Gallery supports the city's emerging artists and projects. The hotel is an amalgamation of two new structures and two 19th-century buildings, cohered via a design language incorporating glass, concrete, and brick. Bauhaus minimalism runs throughout the venue, and each detail—from custom lighting to the cubist-style canvas by artist Masha Reva in the lobby—is considered, attracting a young, stylish, and creative crowd.

Destination	Location	Rooms	Themes
France	Saint-Saturnin-lès-Apt, Provence	19	Countryside, Gastronomy, Offbeat

Domaine des Andéols

Domaine des Andéols is as much a gallery of art and design as it is a hotel. Knoll, Breuer, and van der Rohe furniture, art by Isamu Noguchi, avant-garde architectural design, and elevated French gastronomy define this idyllic escape in the Provence countryside, an hour outside Avignon. **Olivier** and **Patrizia Massart** transformed 59 acres (24 hectares) into an art foundation, converting 11 stone farmhouses and eight nature suites into modern accommodation with discrete identities. Different colors, themes, or artworks—such as *Maison Toujours,* with its delicate pastel palette and art celebrating the female figure—inspire each room, ensuring guests enjoy a bespoke stay. Art falls at the heart of the escape, with over 250 artworks, photographs, and furniture pieces decorating the halls, and exhibitions organized in collaboration with Parisian gallery Kamel Mennour. The on-site restaurant, Le Platane, serves up healthy and seasonal dishes using ingredients from the property's farm.

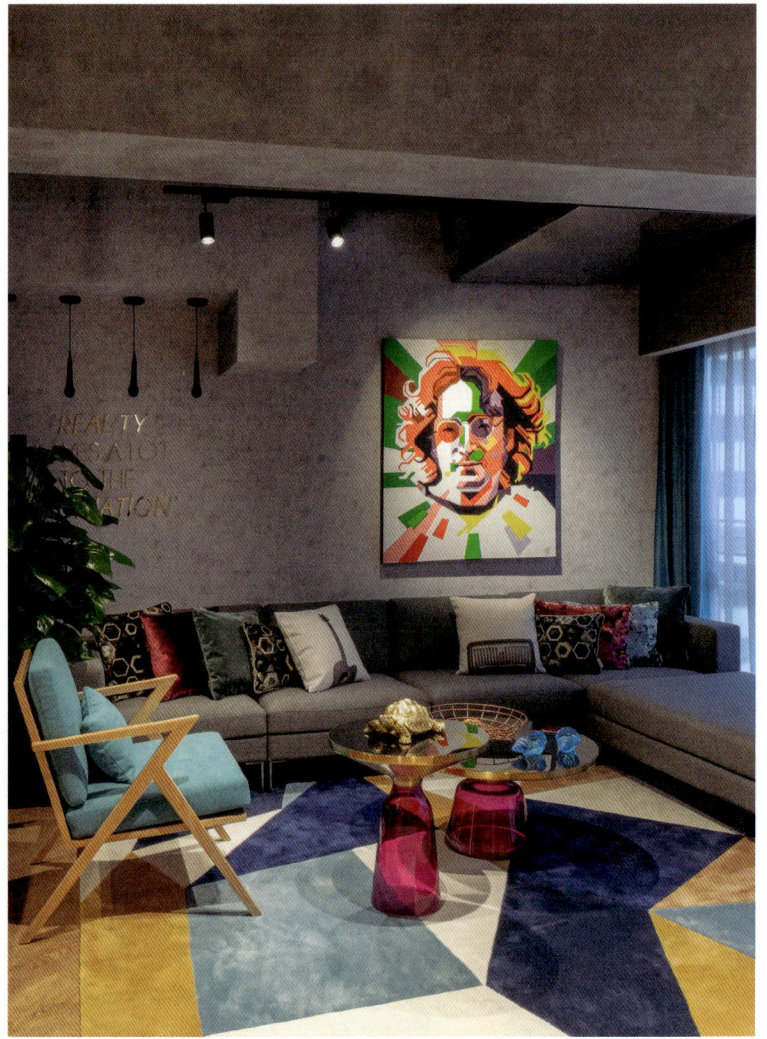

Destination
Canada

Location
Montréal

Rooms
119

Themes
City

Destination
China

Location
Hong Kong

Rooms
160

Themes
Art & Culture, City

Hotel St. Paul

At Hotel St. Paul, guests have direct access to the beating heart of the city's old town. Its creative director, **Ana Borrallo,** founded the hotel within the walls of an historic eight-level Beaux-Arts building, establishing it as a design hub replete with sumptuous fabrics and abstract paintings. Yubari restaurant explores Japanese cuisine, with a focus on sushi, in a high-ceilinged setting. Lovers of daring design will appreciate the hotel's use of contrasting textures and tones in rooms with dark-wood floors and velvet upholstery in jewel tones.

Southside by Ovolo

Southside by Ovolo, owned by **Girish Jhunjhnuwala** and designed by Paul Kember, is Hong Kong's first-ever warehouse conversion hotel. Combining raw concrete, exposed piping, steel furniture, and vibrant colors, the 160-room hotel's floor-to-ceiling windows and graffiti-lined corridors reflect the city's creativity. In other quarters, the rooftop bar Above by Komune and lively Komune restaurant present inventive cocktails and vegetarian fare. At Southside, innovative hospitality is folded into this striking celebration of Hong Kong's past and present.

SIDE

In Hamburg's Neustadt district, **Gregor Gerlach's** urban-chic hotel captivates immediately on entry with its soaring eight-story atrium, backlit by iconic light choreographer Robert Wilson's spectacular pulsing installation. Moving through Jan Störmer's 11-story glass and steel structure, Matteo Thun's quiet minimalism plays against voluptuously curved furnishings. The aptly named sky lounge appears to hover above the atrium, sustaining the illusion of weightlessness with floating disk lighting. Guestrooms offer sanctuary to the senses in soothing creams and careful accents, including colorful freestanding bathtubs, while public areas and the spa are enlivened by blocks of joyful color. After exploring nearby attractions like the Town Hall or shopping along the Grosse Bleichen, guests can unwind in the indoor pool, rejuvenate with a massage, or alternate between the invigorating sauna and Jacuzzi, with the tranquil Inner Alster Lake just beyond.

Destination	Location	Rooms	Themes
United States	New York, NY	69	Art & Culture, City, Interior Design

Warren Street Hotel, Firmdale Hotels

Boldly colorful and artfully maximalist, **Kit Kemp's** stylish sense of fun is on vivid display in Warren Street Hotel, Firmdale Hotels. Located in the creative heart of Tribeca, the hotel's vivid aesthetic—teal blue exterior crowned with a yellow roof—is in stark contrast with its sleek and serious New York City competitors. As per Kemp's signature style, art abounds on the hotel's walls. In the bright-yellow lobby, a sculptural black Wendell Castle chair and Tony Cragg sculpture stand beside a beaded Sanaa Gateja work, immediately setting the tone for what lies in store. Rooms are plush and vibrant, with contrasting textures and colors across the wallpaper, curtains, upholstery, and bedding. In Warren Street Bar & Restaurant, seasonal menus pair with anarchic patterns and framed art. The Michelin Guide recently awarded Kemp's Tribeca spot One Michelin Key, acknowledging the hotel's uniqueness and inaugurating it into a small handful of recognized American hotels.

31

Hotel Matilda

White walls crowned with bountiful bougainvilleas and towering cacti define the exterior of **Bruce James** and **Harold Stream's** artistic and cultural hub, Hotel Matilda. Named for the owner's mother—immortalized in a portrait by none other than Diego Rivera that hangs in the lobby—the hotel fittingly prioritizes art and gastronomy. In the restaurant, Michelin-star chef Vicente Torres—known for his Ibiza kitchen—serves bold Mediterranean dishes with a Mexican twist. James designed the space, with custom lighting and art from the likes of Bosco Sodi. In the lounge, shelves of books, photographs, and comfortable settees build a space that is both chic and homely.

Color reigns in the courtyard, where the glistening pool welcomes guests beneath a large-scale mural. Comfortable, plant-shaded nooks make for cozy and convivial social spaces.

Destination
Germany

Location
Offenburg

Rooms
38

Themes
Art & Culture, History, Interior Design

Destination
Netherlands

Location
Amsterdam

Rooms
108

Themes
Art & Culture, City,
History, Sustainable

Hotel Liberty

Once a 19th-century jail, this hotel is composed of a glass structure uniting its former wings. Elsewhere, 38 rooms have been created by combining cells. Parquet, arches, and concealed lighting enlarge its rooms' scope. The Rooftop Suite features exposed beams, a separate living area, and a free-standing bath. At WASSER & BROT restaurant, guests can enjoy an open grill and a modern, scintillating menu. From this central location, the treasures of Ortenau, Strasbourg's Gothic cathedral, and the Black Forest's walking trails lie within easy reach.

Sir Adam Hotel

Located next to cutting-edge restaurants, galleries, and music venues, the equally avant-garde Sir Adam Hotel is a welcome addition to the neighborhood. Owned by **Liran Wizman,** here, music comes to the fore via in-room vinyl players, rock 'n' roll decor, a music library and studios, and guitar lessons. Rooms feature industrial concrete columns and exposed ceilings, while communal areas include a state-of-the-art gym, The Hub—a social space for guests and locals—and The Butcher Social Club, an all-day spot for burgers, cocktails, games, and DJ sets.

Destination	**Location**
Italy	Milan
Rooms	**Themes**
64	City, History, Interior Design, Sustainable, Well-Being

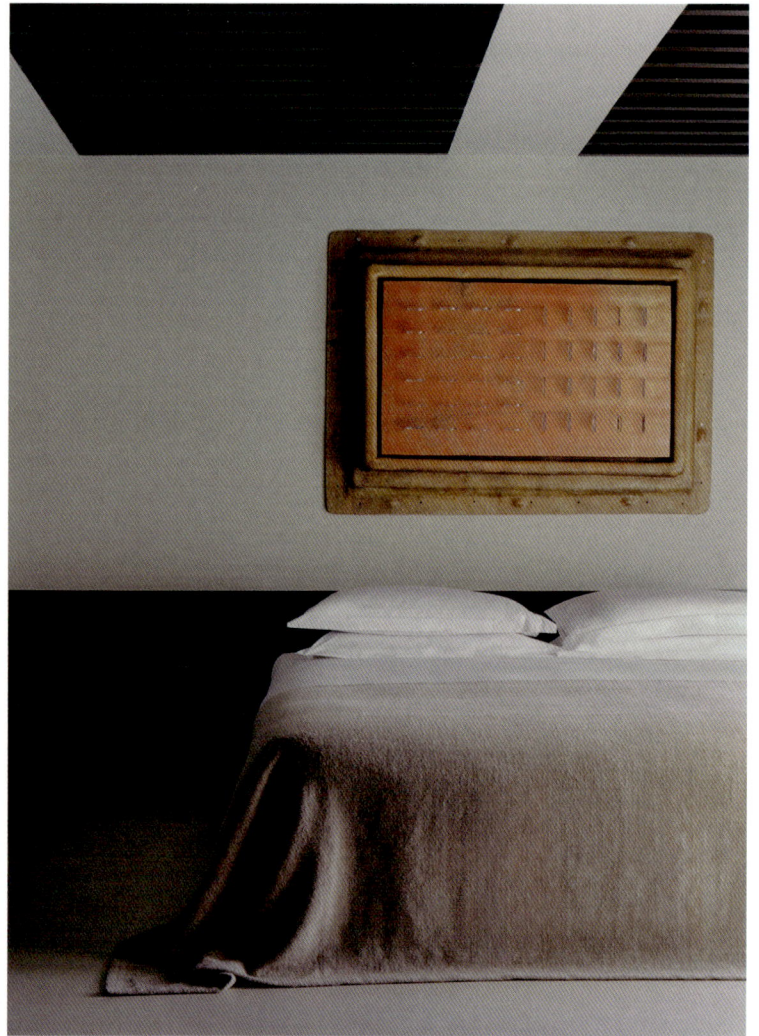

STRAF

In Italy's fashion capital, fashion designer and architect Vincenzo de Cotiis has transformed a 19th-century palazzo into a stylish, eco-conscious space for seasoned aesthetes. Along with **Daniela Bertazzoni,** and **Alissia** and **Sarah Mancino,** he has created a striking alternative to standard hotel aesthetics. This minimalist installation within classical walls uses cement, earthy metals, and raw materials for a warm and inviting atmosphere. The hotel's industrial style recalls Italy's Arte Povera movement of the 1960s and 1970s, with non-traditional organic materials including slate and iron, and a focus on simplicity that doesn't sacrifice comfort. Atmospheric paintings and rich textures provide a sense of luxury in stripped-back spaces. At STRAFbar, hung with Arte Povera artworks, worn leather sofas invite relaxed socializing to curated soundtracks. In the sleek wellness area, a countercurrent swimming pool shimmers amid mirrored surfaces. At STRAF, guests experience a perfect fusion of raw materiality and refined luxury.

San Francisco Proper Hotel

Brad Korzen, Brian De Lowe, and **Kelly Wearstler's** high-ceilinged San Francisco landmark is a rich canvas of colors, textures, and design styles. Set in a Flatiron-style building that is marked on the United States' National Register of Historic Places, the hotel's 1904 building epitomizes Beaux-Arts architecture. Wearstler painstakingly restored the building to what it is today, drawing on French and European Romanticism to cubism and more to create a timeless, cross-era marvel. Wearstler executed the design with her signature attention to the finest details, from patterned wallpapers to plush upholstery. Inherently cosmopolitan, the guest rooms provide sweeping city views from sumptuous comfort. The hotel features a variety of food and beverage options: Charmaine's Rooftop, which offers 360-degree city views; Villon, with its contemporary American cuisine; and streetside cafe, La Bande. Gilda's Dining Room, an intimate hideaway, pays homage to Italian modernism while offering custom menus and boutique wines.

Destination
Germany

Location
Münster

Rooms
50

Themes
City, Gastronomy

Mauritzhof
Hotel Münster

Mauritzhof Hotel Münster fuses cosmopolitan flair with a design language uniquely its own in Münster. Located minutes from the city's historic center, the hotel sits on a peaceful promenade, with shops, restaurants, and bike paths all within easy reach. Following the vision of **Dr. Stefan Reckhenrich,** the 1958 structure was renovated to create open spaces, including a terrace with a chef's table and bar. The interiors are classic and comfortable, featuring oiled oak-parquet floors, Westphalian limestone, and a warm palette. Local art is featured throughout, including atmospheric, black-and-white scenes by the late photographer Berthold Socha. The open-plan lobby includes a fireplace, with stylish furnishings by Gubi and Fredericia in the relaxed lounge. The hotel's renovation also introduced a sandstone façade, floor-to-ceiling windows, and a third and fourth floor. Reckos Restaurant serves locally inspired dishes that celebrate the region's finest produce and changing seasons. The outdoor terrace is the perfect spot for a sunset cocktail surrounded by lush greenery.

Destination
Iceland

Location
Reykjavik

Rooms
46

Themes
Art & Culture, City

Destination
Australia

Location
Melbourne

Rooms
34

Themes
Art & Culture, City, Gastronomy

101 Hotel Reykjavik

Located near Reykjavik's main street, 101 Hotel is a doorway to the city's cultural heart. Constructed in the 1930s, the building's interior designer, **Ingibjörg S. Pálmadóttir,** re-envisioned the space in 2023 with a Nordic, minimalist aesthetic. Featuring work by a range of contemporary Icelandic artists throughout, the hotel also hosts furniture by Eero Saarinen and Philippe Starck beside a fireplace in its lounge. Shopping, dining, nightlife, and culture are all close by, with the Icelandic Opera House and Pálmadóttir's cooperative 101 Gallery steps away.

Adelphi Hotel

A sweet tooth inspires the colors and textures at Adelphi Hotel, with a palette that's joyful yet sophisticated—never saccharine. Set in Flinders Lane in Australia's gastronomic capital, the candy-focused inspiration is fitting. The interior design adds layers of whimsy with rich, chocolate-toned furnishings, carpets with zig-zagging geometric patterns, and stools inspired by licorice. Bold, artistic elements are prominent, including a wire horse-drawn cart that acts as the reception desk, and artworks that evoke the city's laneway mural culture.

Destination
Germany

Location
Göttingen

Rooms
118

Themes
Art & Culture, City, Family-Friendly,
Gastronomy, Sustainable

Destination
Mexico

Location
Guadalajara, Jalisco

Rooms
37

Themes
City, Offbeat

FREIgeist Göttingen Innenstadt

Georg Rosentreter's sandstone haven
is inspired by the brickwork of the surrounding university town. Inside, Frank
Kassner's Basquiat-inspired works
animate public spaces, while guestrooms
feature motifs nodding to the city's
academy. Moroccan tiles complement
blue-velvet textures and wood finishes
and flooring. The Herbarium bar, where
ingredients come from a vertical herb
bed, sits beside Intuu's Japanese–
Peruvian restaurant. As the surrounding
greenery matures, it will link the entire
district—an expression of Rosentreter's
holistic ethos.

Casa Habita

Casa Habita is an early 20th-century,
37-room residence renovated by owners
Carlos Couturier and **Moisés Micha**
in collaboration with Estudio5 architects.
Inside, Dimorestudio infused the interiors
with Mexican and European influences,
combining marble, brass, wood, and
glass. The original structure now houses
a library and restaurant serving U.S.
cuisine with Mexican savoir-faire. On the
tower's upper level are a rooftop pool,
movie theater, spa, and a sunbed area
offering panoramic views. Thoughtful
and innovative, the hotel is now a local
landmark.

Periscope

High above Athens's Kolonaki district—located at the southern foot of Lycabettus Hill—art collector extraordinaire, **Dakis Joannou's** aptly named Periscope Hotel transforms a 1950s concrete structure into a meditation on the art of seeing. Moving through the space, guests encounter contemporary artworks and interactive installations contemplating what it means to observe and be observed. Sandblasted-glass doors open to reveal rooms with ingenious fold-away mirrors, while junior suites showcase panoramic cityscapes through ceiling-mounted light boxes. After dinner, visitors can use the bar's custom-built rooftop periscope and joystick-controlled screens to explore the city's urban tapestry, before unwinding in the Jacuzzi with fresh perspectives on the Greek capital.

Destination	Location	Rooms	Themes
Switzerland	Zurich	132	City, Interior Design

The Home Hotel Zürich

Culture, cuisine, and nightlife intersect in this Dada-inspired hotel, encouraging guests to expect the unexpected. Aimed at a youthful, creative crowd from Zurich and beyond, the hotel blends modern luxury with artistic flair in a collage composed of multiple layers of textures and colors. Architect Theo Hotz renovated the former paper mill, respecting conservational requirements and honoring features like glass bricks and high ceilings—even transforming the hotel's columns, which couldn't be removed or covered, into tree-like structures. Zurich-born Dadaism inspired the interior design, with the hotel mirroring the movement's experimentation and playful juxtapositions. Bold wallpapers and custom sofas upholstered in copper velvet contrast with soft-toned areas and rich walnut veneer. The hotel's LivingHome&Bar is a hub for creatives, drawing a fun crowd with DJ sets, comedy nights, and cocktails. At LouLou, guests can enjoy French cuisine and a popular raw bar.

Destination	Location	Rooms	Themes
Greece	Athens	79	City, Sustainable

New Hotel

Industrialist and art collector **Dakis Joannou** enlisted the help of pioneering Brazilian designers Fernando and Humberto Campana to reimagine the modernist Olympic Palace Hotel, which has been part of the Athens skyline since 1958. The result is a meeting of the senses, featuring visual art, cult design pieces made from cast-off materials, as well as views of the Parthenon over a sea of urban rooftops. Sharp lines and bold geometry flow throughout the hotel, creating visual interest in otherwise subtle spaces. A recurring motif of jagged shapes appears in the reflective, angular reception desk, the guestroom bathroom basins, and mirrors. The New

Lobby Bar promises the finest cuisine in the city center, serving Greek-style brunch and Mediterranean dishes crafted from local, organic ingredients.

Mason

Set on a tranquil stretch of private beach, Mason was envisioned by **Nirut Ngamchamnanrith,** with building design led by award-winning architect Vasu Virajsilp of VasLab. This beachfront private pool villa resort was crafted to both contrast with and reflect its unique setting in Pattaya's Na Jomtien. The sophisticated retreat features sculptural granite formations that honor the storied stone carvers of the Ang Sila community, complemented by lush, tropical greenery. A curated collection of one- and two-bedroom pool villas is appointed with terrazzo floors, expansive bathtubs, mirrored surfaces, and broad windows offering uninterrupted sea views. Every element, from architecture to interiors, reflects the bold vision of its founder, who oversaw the entire process to ensure a seamless blend of artistry, luxury, and wellness. This same confident design philosophy extends to the resort's dining and lifestyle venues—including Zila Street Bistro & Bar, Krok-a-Café Espresso Bar, and the Beachside Bar—as well as the signature treatments at Mason Spa, creating a unified and immersive guest experience.

Destination
Bulgaria

Location
Sofia

Rooms
71

Themes
City, Interior Design

Destination
Germany

Location
Berlin

Rooms
58

Themes
City, Gastronomy

Sense Hotel Sofia

Modern, clean lines and a glass-and-steel façade make this hotel in Sofia's city center, owned by **George Chopev,** a suave option. Located near St. Alexander Nevsky Cathedral and the National Gallery, its rooms are chic and contemporary, featuring hardwood floors, leather upholstery, Lutron mood lighting, and pivoting brass panels. On the ninth floor, guests can discover Sense Gastro Bar, a sophisticated restaurant with views over the city. The all-day menu combines fresh, healthy ingredients alongside a comprehensive selection of wines and cocktails.

Provocateur

Alex Urseanu, Micky Rosen, and **Liran Wizman's** hotel is a tribute to the glamour of 1920s Paris. Located near Berlin's shopping district, its art nouveau building is typical for the area. While much of its original form remains—courtesy of TSSB Architekten Ingenieure, who updated the façade—designer Saar Zafrir has added opulent materials like velvet, marble, brass, and chandeliers. Chef The Duc Ngo leads the French-Chinese fusion restaurant, and the hotel's award-winning bar offers low-lit ambiance, classic cocktails, and 18th-century-inspired punches.

The Design of Stillness:

Kissa Castañeda

A Language of Texture, Light, and Presence

With an eye honed by her work covering the intersection of design and travel, Kissa Castañeda traces how the timeless wisdom of Japanese design redefines luxury by prioritizing a soulful connection to nature over extravagance.

Soft sunlight filtering through shoji screens, the relaxing aroma of hinoki wood permeating the air, the rustling of *momiji* leaves framed by a perfectly positioned window—there's something about the soulful simplicity of Japanese design that makes you feel grounded.

Here, nature is undeniably the star. Be it the centuries-old *ryokan* inns along the Nakasendo Way or in the ancient temples of Kyoto, these structures sit lightly on the land, providing respite from nature, yet shaped by its surroundings.

It starts from humble materials: wood, paper, stone, straw, bamboo, and more come together to create spaces that honor the Earth's majesty. For humans, the connection is intimate, and the welcoming feeling immediate. "To bring nature into everyday life, we prioritize natural materials chosen not only for their aesthetic qualities but for how they resonate with

our biological organism. These materials foster a tactile connection to the world and ground the user in something real, enduring, and evolutionarily familiar," says Jonas Bjerre-Poulsen of Norm Architects, an award-winning Danish design firm renowned for their aesthetic of "soft minimalism."

Imagine entering hotel grounds and being enveloped by towering trees that mimic a forest. You take off your shoes and lay your bare feet on a warm, wooden floor smoothened by time. In what looks like a spartan setting, you take in the distinct smell of tatami matting—similar to freshly cut grass. When the sun sets, you soak in a mineral-rich *roten-buro* (a hot bathing spring) dotted by rough-hewn stone. You retreat back to your room and put on an oatmeal-hued linen robe. In places where nature is allowed to shine, you feel an instant sense of belonging, of ease. This is true luxury.

"Natural materials carry a quiet wisdom. They are never static. They shift with temperature, absorb scent, and catch the light differently," says Ed Ng, cofounder of leading hospitality design firm AB Concept. "There is deep emotional comfort in being surrounded by nature indoors. It reminds

Kissa Castañeda

us that we are not living in a fixed scene but within something breathing and evolving," he adds. Ng speaks from experience, having left frenetic Hong Kong to live full-time in the resort town of Karuizawa in the Japanese Alps, where he built his home, Itsu Sho Sha, ensconced in nature.

Pride of Place

One of the greatest defining features of Japanese architecture are its walls, which are found in traditional *machiya* (town-houses) as well as grander buildings like teahouses. Called *tsuchikabe* (earthen walls), these walls are crafted by trained artisans using a mix of clay, straw, sand, and naturally derived pigments. They are renowned not only used for their durability and insulation but for their perfectly imperfect appeal too.

Polish is often equated to superior craftsmanship, but the Japanese philosophy of *wabi-sabi* invites us to celebrate life's inherent imperfection. It's that maker's mark, that slight difference that really imbues something with a special character.

"The idea of wabi-sabi has quietly transformed the way I design, and, more importantly, the way I live. I began to feel it more deeply after I moved to Karuizawa," says Ng. "Every morning, when I draw open the curtain, the view of the forest and the mountains is different. None of it is arranged. Nature, left entirely on its own, always manages to create moments of perfect balance. It taught me to let go of the idea that everything must be refined or resolved."

The concept of wabi-sabi can be applied to things both big and small—from the asymmetrical placement of furniture down to the way broken ceramics are put back together with urushi lacquer, a craft called *kintsugi.* Its entire premise is to find beauty in what's impermanent, imperfect, and incomplete. It's a call to be more authentic.

Space for more

In a world defined by excess, can less really be more? In the school of Japanese design, the answer is a resounding *yes.* Whether or not you're partial to a more lavishly decorated interior, one cannot deny the clarity that a clean, considered space brings. In effect, the existence of negative space is, in fact, a positive.

"Minimalism is often misunderstood as mere emptiness or a lack of character," says Bjerre-Poulsen. "For us at Norm Architects, it's not about absence but presence. It's about creating spaces that support human well-being through a calm and deep connection to the sensory world."

One thing most of us can agree on is that there is too much noise around us today—the literal hum of a city, the constant pings from work, the endless distractions on our devices. It's no wonder many of us crave spaces that feel like a refresh button. As the desire for quietude has become more crucial, these minimalist, nature-centric spaces serve as a balm. This is why timelessness and the natural ethos of Japanese design resonate far and wide.

"Japanese architecture," stresses Bjerre-Poulsen, "has long been a subtle yet significant source of inspiration, as it reflects values we share: simplicity, restraint, naturalness, and a deep respect for craftsmanship and context. Rather than stripping interiors of life, we focus on what is essential—materials that age beautifully, proportions that feel balanced, and a palette that soothes rather than overwhelms."

While traditional Japanese design follows time-honored techniques, it was originally conceived as being in harmony with nature—something that is still evident today via Zen gardens and stylish boutique hotels alike. "Nature is a great storyteller," concludes Ng. "It surprises, it changes, it never repeats itself."

Kissa Castañeda is a lifestyle journalist, based between Europe and Asia, who has, since 2005, covered the interstices of travel and design. Formerly the editor-in-chief of Tatler Singapore and editorial director of *Tatler Travel,* she contributes to *Travel + Leisure, Forbes,* the *Daily Telegraph,* and more. In 2025, she cofounded Two Keys, hich unlocks, through human-powered insight from global creatives, the world's best boutique and luxury stays.

Destination		Location
United States		Oklahoma City, OK

Rooms		Themes
36		City, Family-Friendly, Gastronomy, History, Interior Design

Bradford House

At Bradford House, a contemporary structure joins a restored 1912 building in the heart of Oklahoma City. **Sara Kate** and **Jason Little** curated a sophisticated haven where period features are put into relief by bold design. The guest rooms were conceived according to minimalist aesthetics, accented by vibrant color palettes and handpicked treasures: vintage Italian furniture, French medicine cabinets repurposed as end tables, and Stilnovo chandeliers. Altogether, these idiosyncratic touches make for a space that feels like a beloved family home influenced by generations of residency. The intimate dining room serves interpretations of French, Italian, and American classics. The gilded bar has become a local gathering point for appreciating traditional cocktails with modern riffs and boutique wines. From relaxing in the landscaped courtyard to socializing on the wrap-around porch, guests experience the American heartland through a cosmopolitan lens.

Destination
Germany

Location
Göttingen

Rooms
123

Themes
City, Family-Friendly,
Gastronomy, Sustainable

Destination
Netherlands

Location
Amsterdam

Rooms
90

Themes
City, Gastronomy,
History, Sustainable

FREIgeist Göttingen Nordstadt

Georg Rosentreter lends his aesthetic
to this former factory in Göttingen.
The building's heritage remains through
lattice windows, corrugated iron, and
black steel, while upcycled items honor
the site's roots. Burnt larch backboards
on beds and kilim carpets soften the
look. The hotel's rooftop and indoor
communal areas provide places to socialize. Culinary highlights include an on-
site deli and East of Italy, which fuses
Italian and Middle Eastern cuisines.
The Weights & Measures bar completes
things, serving cocktails in a relaxed
atmosphere.

Sir Albert Hotel

Liran Wizman has transformed a 19th-
century diamond factory into a captivating hotel. This monumental redbrick
structure speaks to its storied past
while connecting guests with its present-
day surroundings. Interiors feature pieces
from Italian brands Maxalto, Moroso,
and Ceccotti alongside limited editions
from Dutch designers Piet Hein Eek
and Joy van Erven. Locals come for the
top-notch Japanese experience at
Izakaya Asian Kitchen & Bar, while guests
can use the hotel as a launchpad to
explore the nearby Albert Cuyp Market
and Rijksmuseum.

La Maison Hotel

After retiring from his role in his family's food company, Saarland native **Günter Wagner** purchased a disused officer's casino and began plans to create a chic, adults-only hotel. La Maison now has 50 rooms split between a historic mansion and two contemporary extensions, one clad in bronzed, folded aluminum, the other in wood, echoing the surrounding trees. A separate *Gästehaus* offers further accommodation. The Louis Bar and Library occupies a former courthouse with park views, while a glass-enclosed terrace houses a delicatessen and the Pastis Bistro. Dishes like Bouchot mussels and Burgundy truffles grace lunchtimes, while LOUIS restaurant showcases chef Sebastian Sandor's gourmet innovations. Duly, the restaurant has earned two Michelin stars, three Gault and Millau toques, and eight Gusto pans. Interiors feature herringbone or oiled-oak floors, timber paneling, and lighting mood-pads for the ultimate in casual, considered luxury.

Destination
Kenya

Location
Nairobi

Rooms
128

Themes
City, Sustainable

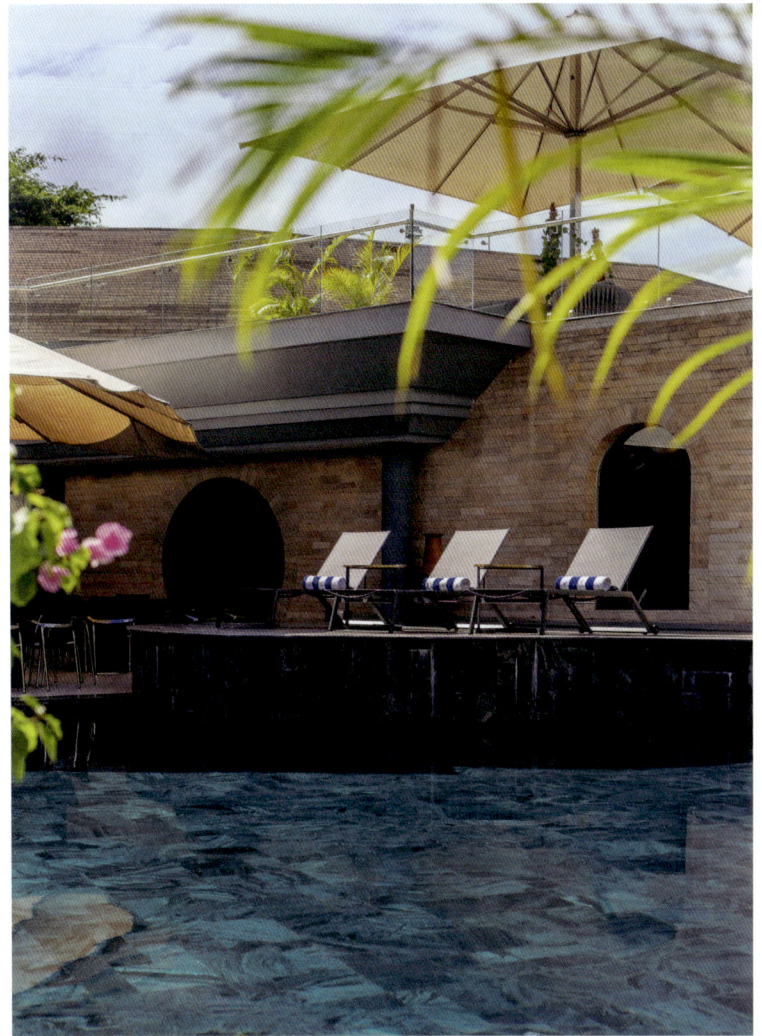

Tribe Hotel

In Nairobi's leafy diplomatic quarter, Tribe Hotel is a bold, geometric vision and a soulful celebration of African artistry. **Shamim Ehsani** and designer Les Harbottle of Plan One envisioned the space, with its soaring four-story atrium, angled sand-colored walls, and stainless steel columns. Throughout the 128 rooms and public areas, tribal crafts and contemporary design objects invite contemplation and discovery—from fold-away mirrors to hand-carved gourds and art by local artists with increasingly global platforms. The Jiko restaurant and jungle-like roof terrace offer moments of reflection in vibrant settings—even more so in the pool itself, which features a submerged granite meeting table. Nature pours in through the lush gardens and waterfall, while the adjacent Maasai market ties the experience to Nairobi's vital culture.

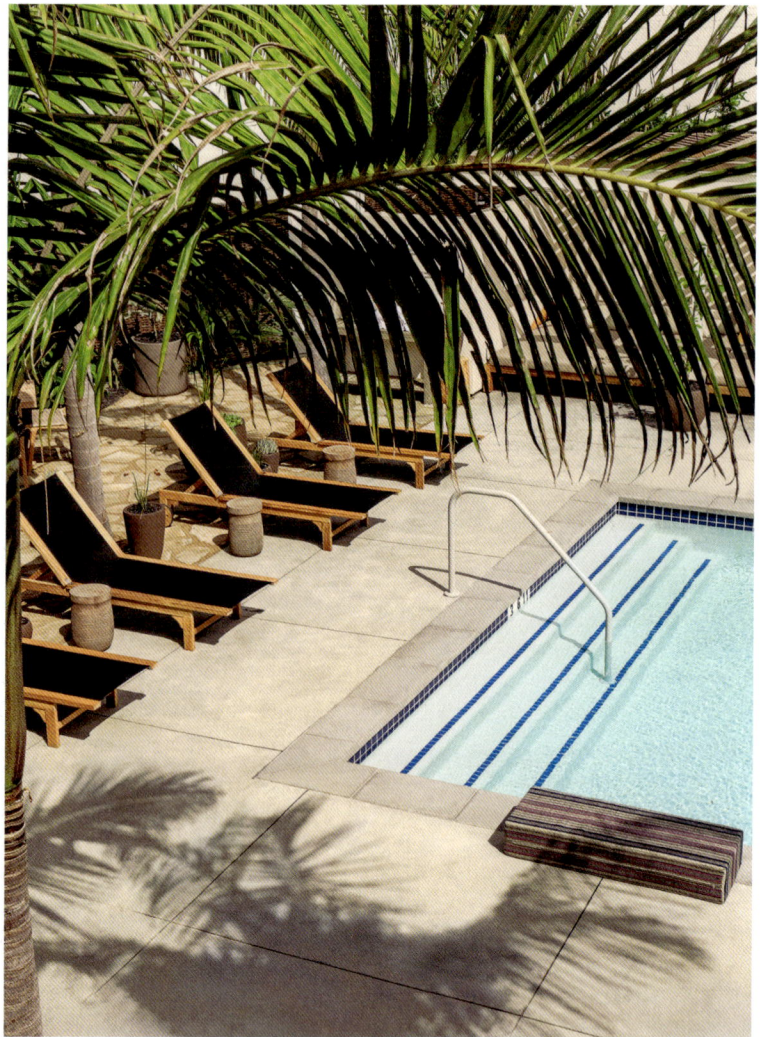

Destination
Spain

Location
Alicante

Rooms
81

Themes
City, History, Sustainable

Destination
United States

Location
Los Angeles, CA

Rooms
250

Themes
City

Hospes Amérigo

This former monastery is now home to modern elegance. The neo-Gothic façade remains, while salvaged stone-work features above the glass and marble lobby. Guestrooms are awash with dark-wood contrasts, flowing curtains, hand-woven rugs, and cream-colored armchairs. Discreet pocket doors open onto serene spaces. Guests can unwind at the rooftop pool, Spa Bodyna, and solarium terrace, or enjoy curated tastings and sailing excursions. Fondillón serves avant-garde Mediterranean flavors, while the rooftop bar and tapas lounge offer laid-back atmospheres.

Hotel June West L.A.

Hotel June West L.A.'s owners **Brad Korzen** and **Brian De Lowe** have re-imagined their establishment as a home away from home. Kollin Altomare Architects and Studio Collective have added quirky touches and California-inspired design to entice youthful guests. The lobby features terrazzo floors, the rooms offer vintage furnishings, and travertine accents and abstract-patterns are ever-present. When not visiting the rooftop pool bar or restaurant (serving vibrant Baja California flavors), guests can enjoy bike access, allowing them to explore the area.

Destination
Germany

Location
Hamburg

Rooms
129

Themes
City, Gastronomy,
History, Sustainable

Tortue Hamburg

In the heart of Hamburg's lively Stadthöfe district, Tortue Hamburg balances French elegance with German precision in a reimagined 19th-century former ministry building. Owners **Marc Ciunis** and **Carsten von der Heide** have created a destination where gastronomy, design, and hospitality intertwine across thought-fully styled spaces. The building's historic bones—high ceilings, grand façades, and heritage features like arched windows—are paired with interiors by designers from Hong Kong, the Netherlands, and Germany, for a sophisticated, multi-layered aesthetic featuring brocade, patterned walls, and concept lighting. Guests dine at Jin Gui for Asian-influenced cuisine,

the lively Brasserie for Franco-German classics, and Chez l'Ami for premium steaks and seafood. The hotel's inner courtyards and rooftop terrace provide beautiful views of the city and harbor, while a curated display of street art reflects Hamburg's creative buzz.

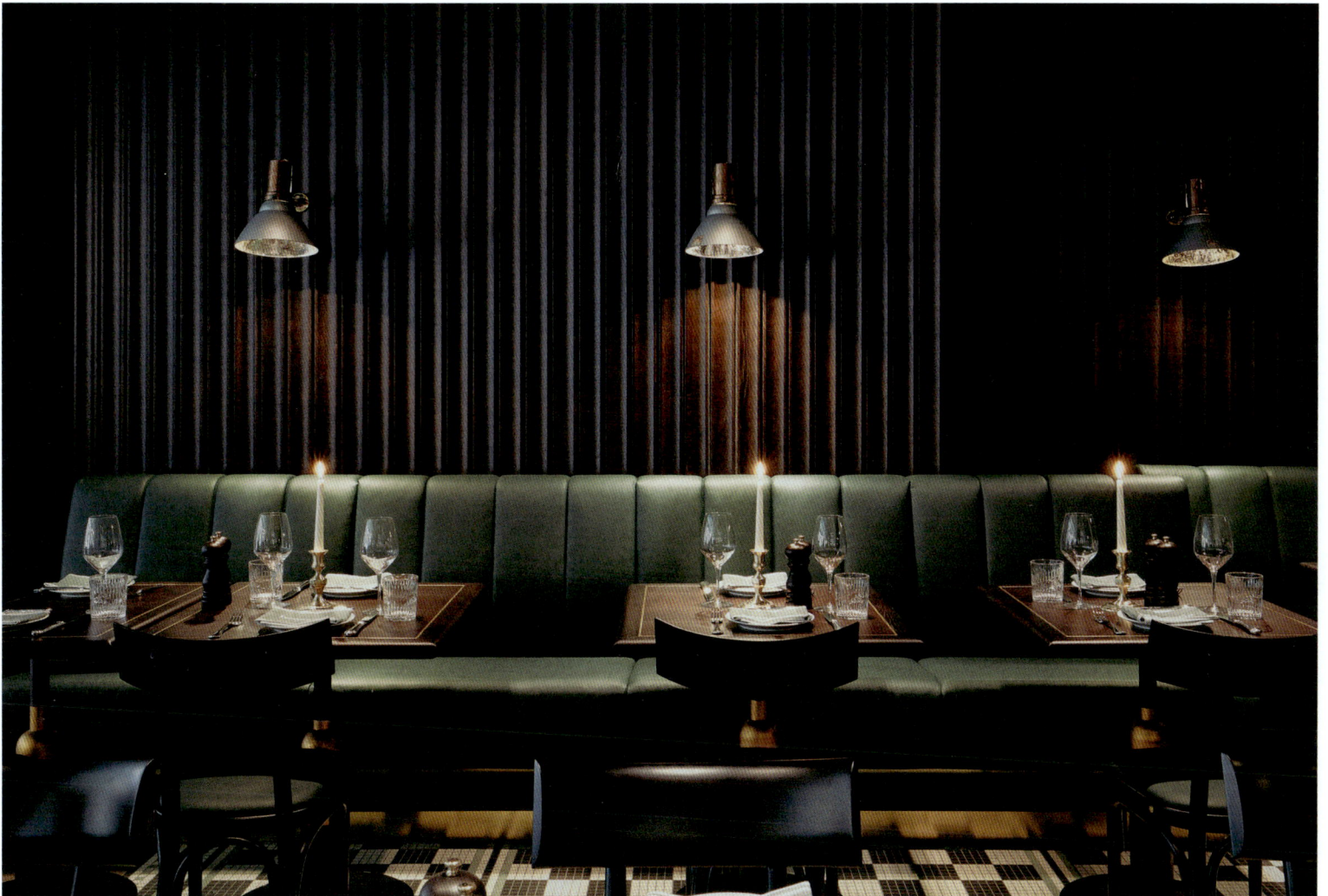

Destination
China

Location
Hong Kong

Rooms
489

Themes
Art & Culture, City, Gastronomy

The Mira Hong Kong

In the heart of Tsim Sha Tsui, The Mira Hong Kong is a world within a world, a place where style and innovation converge. With 489 sleek rooms—including an all-suite floor—the design-forward property with interiors by CAD International takes a futuristic touch to comfort and functionality. Guests can indulge in world-class wellness at MiraSpa or dine at six standout restaurants, including modern European Whisk—named one of the city's 100 Top Tables by the *South China Morning Post*—and Michelin-recommended modern Cantonese favorite Cuisine Cuisine. From the vibrant lobby, with its vinyl-black sculptures and suspended lights, to the indoor infinity pool under a starlit ceiling, each space is crafted for maximum impact and ease of use. The vision of **Dr. Martin Lee,** this shimmering jet-black monolith is a dynamic base for exploring Hong Kong, and a destination in its own right.

Destination
Taiwan

Location
Taipei

Rooms
42

Themes
City, Gastronomy

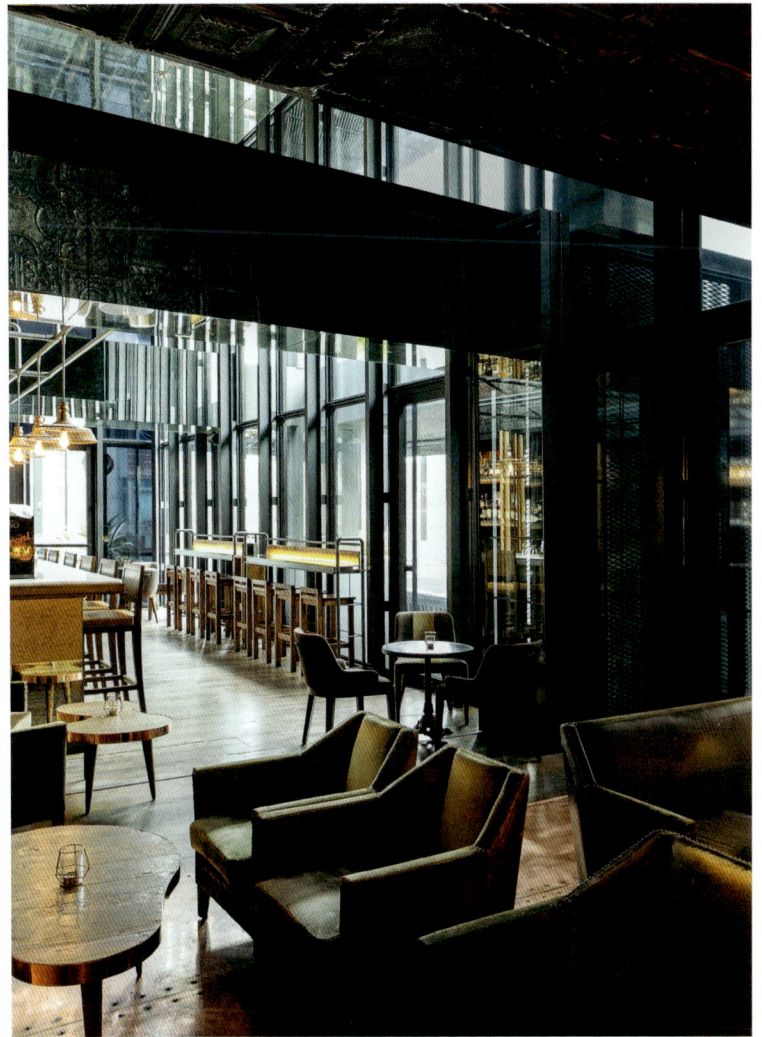

Hotel Proverbs Taipei

John Chen's Hotel Proverbs Taipei adheres to a brand philosophy that encourages guests to indulge themselves. Ray Chen's minimalist design, inspired by the surreal scenes of Goya's *Proverbios,* uses a material palette of copper, wood, leather, and stone, alongside delicate fabrics in the guest rooms for an overall sense of warmth and luxury. The hotel's imposing tower is split dramatically into two parts—the upper guest rooms and the lower hotel amenities—fronted by a delicate black steel-mesh façade. A touch of hedonism is encouraged, and the hotel's cocktail bar, East End, and the highly regarded L'Idiot Restaurant feed this with premium fare and a range of fine wines and champagnes beneath opulent lighting.

Zentis Osaka

Situated in Dojimahama, the top nightlife district in western Japan, Zentis Osaka provides a vital connection to, and refined escape from, the neighborhood bustle. The hotel features raw materials with a tonal color palette, exposed brick, and timber beams. Tara Bernerd executed the 16-story building's interior design, commissioning local Japanese artists and furnishings to pair with the hotel's sleek structure and abundant natural light. Guest rooms feature warm hues, muted tones, and touches of color—mustard, sea green—to brighten the spaces. The top-floor hospitality center, UPSTAIRZ Lounge, Bar, Restaurant, features a towering ceiling illuminated by a lightweight, modern chandelier, and large windows. The kitchen draws on premium seasonal ingredients to deliver an inventive Japanese take on French cuisine.

Destination
Slovenia

Destination
Greece

Location
Ljubljana

Location
Athens

Rooms
20

Rooms
51

Themes
Art & Culture, City, Offbeat

Themes
City, Sustainable

Vander Urbani Resort

Amanda and **Aleksander Vujandinovic's** Baroque-era hotel is set in Slovenia's charming, picturesque capital. In contrast to its storied exterior, the building's interior is colorful and filled with contemporary art and furniture. Steel, concrete, and chrome combine inside, with lavender-hued rooms punctuated by padded walls and leather seating. On the roof, a perforated shade invites shifting sunlight patterns, and an infinity pool looks out across the rooftops. A champagne bar and two Michelin Plate restaurants complete the sparkling, luxe atmosphere.

Semiramis

Semiramis is a hotel alive with neon fittings and a pop of art sensibility. Art collector **Dakis Joannou** commissioned architect and designer Karim Rashid for the project, producing an explosion of color, texture, technology, and art. Once through the radiant lobby, guests encounter curved corners, bright carpets, epoxy floors, railings made of pink glass, and a multicolored figure-eight pool. With every aspect of its impressive design carefully considered—from the uniforms to the stationery and shampoos—this hotel is inarguably a work of art.

Destination
United States

Location
Chattanooga, TN

Rooms
16

Themes
City, Offbeat

The Dwell Hotel

The Dwell Hotel brings vintage style to Southern hospitality in downtown Chattanooga. Housed in a 1909 brick-and-limestone building, the boutique property was reimagined by designer **Seija Ojanpera** as a vibrant blend of midcentury modern and retro glamour. Each room is uniquely styled with bold colors, vintage furniture, exposed brick, and whimsical patterned wallpaper alongside equally bold pieces of contemporary art. By completely reimagining the hotel bar and creating entirely new lounge areas, the design team has created multiple spaces that not only invite guests to experience hospitality Chattanooga-style, but serve as a gathering place for locals who come to enjoy the buzzing scene now created by the hotel. Set in the heart of Chattanooga's walkable city center, The Dwell is steps away from the art district, thriving cafes, and the Tennessee River, making it a perfect base for experiencing the city's creative energy.

Destination
Austria

Location
Graz

Rooms
57

Themes
Art & Culture, City

Destination
Germany

Location
Munich

Rooms
75

Themes
City

Augarten Art Hotel

Located in Graz, Augarten Art Hotel stands as a manifesto from the late architect Günther Domenig. Owned by **Dr. Helmut Marko,** this glass and metal structure is a dialogue between art and architecture. Domenig's reflective surfaces and exterior staircases play with light and structure. Interiors feature work by over 200 contemporary artists, and iconic, monochromatic midcentury furnishings are present throughout. Across 57 rooms, the hotel unites art, design, and comfort, while its courtyard, terrace, and pool provide space for rest and relaxation.

Cortiina Hotel

Munich's Cortiina Hotel, helmed by **Rudi Kull** and **Albert Weinzierl,** offers a modern retreat informed by feng shui and regional craftsmanship. Architect and co-owner Weinzierl's minimalist design incorporates local elements (e.g. bronze, aromatic stone pine) to unify the hotel's sites. Oak, limestone, and cotton sheets lend its 75 rooms a tranquil elegance, while bespoke furniture and custom wallpaper give the apartment wing character. Grapes Weinbar rounds out the experience with rare vintages, reflecting Cortiina's inimitable taste and soul.

Destination	Location	Rooms	Themes
France	Paris	40	Art & Culture, City

Le Pigalle

Designed by FESTEN Architecture's Charlotte de Tonnac and Hugo Sauzay, Le Pigalle is a love letter to the bohemian spirit of its namesake area. Located in the historic Nouvelle Athènes district, the hotel is a living, breathing tribute to Pigalle's creative soul. The hotel unites neoclassical architectural heritage with an irreverent mix of vintage and contemporary design. Each room is a unique composition, featuring works by local artists, curated music from DJs, and vintage postcards and posters that reflect the area's rich and hedonistic cultural tapestry. The ground floor buzzes with energy, housing a cafe, bar, restaurant, vinyl library, and book kiosk. From the delectable baked goods sourced from a nearby bakery to the photographs adorning the walls, every element celebrates the vibrant, eclectic spirit of South Pigalle—a neighborhood that continues to redefine Parisian creativity and culture.

The Whitby Hotel, Firmdale Hotels

In Midtown Manhattan, The Whitby is an enclave of artful sophistication. High-end boutiques, galleries, and restaurants surround the hotel, whose limestone façade by Stonehill & Taylor was designed in line with the surrounding cityscape. Steel-framed windows offer a glimpse of the hubbub within, where **Kit Kemp's** inimitable interiors provide a suitably inspiring backdrop for meetings and meet-ups. A masterclass in mixing prints and patterns, a whimsical interplay of textures and hues, defines every uniquely conceived room; elegant rugs, carefully curated ceramics, and artworks ensure the warmest of welcomes. Embellishments and embroidery enrich custom oversized headboards and fabric-lined walls. The top floor houses the spectacular two-bedroom Whitby Penthouse, while the The Whitby Bar & Restaurant, drawing room, orangery, and state-of-the-art cinema attract Manhattanites from dawn until long after dusk.

Nobis Hotel Stockholm

Nobis Hotel Stockholm by **Alessandro Catenacci** occupies two striking historical buildings on the iconic Norrmalmstorg square, bringing contemporary Scandinavian chic to traditional architecture. Designed by Claesson Koivisto Rune, the hotel's grand 19th-century architecture features a chateau-esque lounge with soaring 28-meter-high ceilings and two glass domes, creating a vast 800-square-meter public space. Rooms are designed with materials like native woods, zinc, and rusted iron that develop a beautiful patina over time. This uniquely Swedish aesthetic whispers luxury, with the design and service striking a fine balance between high-end style and low-key comfort.

There are two exceptional restaurants: NOI, known for its vibrant atmosphere and seasonal menu, and Bistro Nobis (Bino), a relaxed, elegant dining space. The Guldbaren (Gold Bar) offers a dazzling cocktail experience, its mirrored golden walls and ceilings providing a delightful counterpoint to the signature Strawberry Basil Smash.

Destination
Netherlands

Location
Eindhoven

Rooms
8

Themes
Art & Culture, City, History

Destination
China

Location
Hong Kong

Rooms
89

Themes
City, Sustainable

Kazerne

Annemoon Geurts and **Koen Rijnbeek's** Kazerne provides a home to international design lovers. Here, Van Helmond Architecten and Moon and Co. have united six buildings using industrial materials (i.e. glass, brick, steel). Since opening as a hotel/design exhibition space in 2009, many designers that have shown at the hotel have achieved global recognition. Moon and Co.'s interior includes monochromatic guest rooms, variously featuring eye-catching lofted ceilings and striking designer accents. Classic French cuisine is served against a backdrop of cutting-edge design pieces pieces.

Mira Moon

Inspired by a Shang dynasty-era lunar fairytale, Wanders & Yoo's designers adopted a Romantic, Chinoiserie style for their hotel. Featuring glazed ceramics, custom carpets, glass, crystal, and a rich color scheme, the interiors also boast intricate wood carvings and Chinese porcelain depicting scenes from regional mythology. Surrounded by markets and dining options, the hotel was opened by **Dr Martin Lee** in order to stimulate a new nexus of culture and lifestyle into its energetic Causeway Bay neighborhood— which is exactly what it's achieved.

The Shelborne by Proper

On Miami Beach's Collins Avenue, this 1941 art deco icon has been reimagined by ADC Atelier as The Shelborne by Proper. Honoring the area's storied past and local character, works by Latin American artists and lush greenery ground the bright and airy 251 guest rooms and suites. Natural light, tropical tones, blond wood, and vintage glass complement coastal views and scenes of city life. Located by the ocean and 18th Street, one of the city's most storied junctures, the hotel offers easy access to Miami Beach's myriad attractions, from museums to fine dining. Anchoring the hotel is the iconic Deco-era swimming pool with its retro diving board surrounded by shaded cabanas. Nearby is the Shelborne Beach Club's private sun lounge area. Dining is helmed by Michelin-starred chef Abram Bissell and beverage visionary Christopher Lowder, bringing vibrant Latin American and Caribbean flavors to life with Miami's fresh, electric energy. A world-class fitness studio, private spa treatments, complimentary bikes, and thoughtfully curated events complete the experience at this reenvisioned beachside landmark.

Hotel Spedition Thun

In the picture-book Swiss town of Thun, Hotel Spedition transforms a one-time cheese and leather trading house into a sophisticated 15-room retreat. Co-owner **Daniel Mani,** the driving force behind the project, preserved the building's character while entrusting Stylt Trampoli AB to reimagine its design. One-hundred-and-twenty-year-old exposed beams are juxtaposed with midcentury modern furnishings, putting the building's trading history in conversation with contemporary luxury. Forestal motifs and natural textiles—including cotton and linen—echo the natural landscape encircling the town. In the wine cellar where cheese once ripened, guests now gather around a table for tastings and cooking courses. The restaurant showcases Swiss-international cuisine prepared in the open kitchen, with house-matured meats as specialties. And with steps from winding 15th-century lanes leading to a flower-speckled 300-year-old wooden bridge, the hotel is the perfect starting point for exploring the city's riverside and the magical medieval castle that crowns this Alpine locale.

Destination	Location	Rooms	Themes
Italy	Rome	10	Art & Culture, City, History

G-Rough

In the center of Rome, a 17th-century palazzo houses G-Rough, where baroque origins come into contact with contemporary Italian design. Founder **Gabriele Salini** transformed his family's former residence into this design-forward retreat, collaborating with architect Giorgia Cerulli to preserve the structure's soul. The façade retains its original Latin inscription, promising security within its walls. Inside, time-worn wooden ceilings, patinated surfaces, and winding corridors evoke Roman residences of days gone by. Rather than using a conventional lobby, guests check in at the atmospheric Gallery Bar, resplendent with its brushed-brass counter, vintage leather chairs, and reflective tiled backdrop. Salini's personal art collection builds a narrative alongside modern pieces created by iconic Italian designers such as Ico Parisi and Gio Ponti. Two-tone cast-iron tubs in the bathrooms beckon guests home from the cinematic bustle of nearby Piazza Navona.

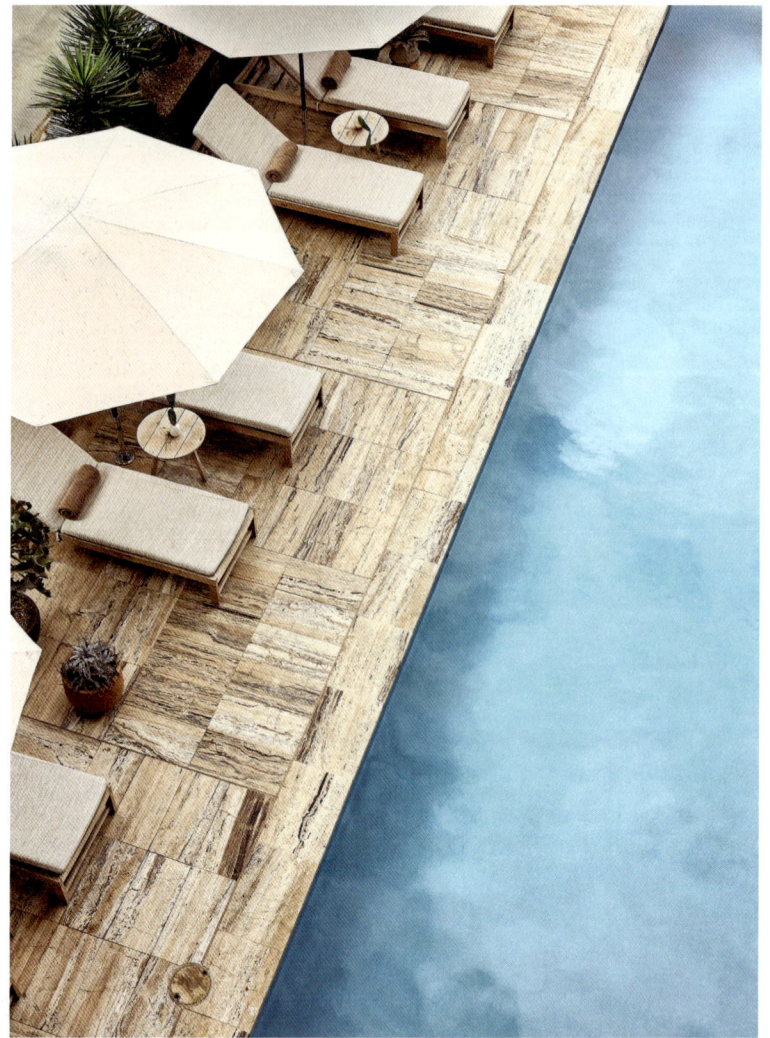

Destination	Location	Rooms	Themes
United States	Austin, TX	238	Art & Culture, City, Sustainable

Austin Proper Hotel

Sweeping views of Lady Bird Lake and Texas Hill Country, local art, and charming furnishings characterize this downtown Austin hotel. The soaring 32-story building sits among high-rises, a stone's throw from the 2nd Street district's vibrant mix of bustling shops and restaurants. Owners **Brad Korzen, Brian De Lowe,** and **Kelly Wearstler** brought Handel Architects onboard to define the precast-concrete-and-glass structure of the project, while Wearstler managed the interior design. Layering rich, textural materials such as vintage rugs, striking designer furniture, and playful ceramics from local artist Rick Van Dyke, Wearstler's design entices a community of global creative nomads to the hotel. Surprises appear around each corner, from the Catalan-style vaulted ceiling of the hotel's Mexican restaurant, La Piscina, to unexpected patterned ceilings and stairs, stained glass, and decorative wallpapers. Unique artisanal touches run across hundreds of rooms in the form of floral arrangements, sculptural furnishings, or ceramic displays that pay homage to the city's eclectic craftsmanship.

Destination
Mexico

Location
Mexico City

Rooms
25

Themes
Art & Culture, City

Círculo Mexicano

Set in an early 20th-century Mexican *vecindad*—a specific vernacular of building where individual apartments surround a central patio—Círculo Mexicano reimagines this historic setting with elegantly stripped-back rooms and luxury amenities. **Carlos Couturier** and **Moisés Micha** ensure local surroundings and traditions feature in every project, while atelier Ambrosi Etchegaray drew inspiration from the exterior façade's timber window frames and doors to determine the interior's nude color palette. Shaker-style furniture by Mexican atelier La Metropolitana is inventively arranged against soft white walls, alongside Oaxacan textiles and weaved palm. The design embraces the structure's original features, including vaulted ceilings, brick walls, and timber beams. Set in the heart of the city's historic district—just off the largest plaza in Latin America—the hotel provides ample opportunities for guests to explore the city's landmarks. On the rooftop, a pool provides respite from the heat alongside Mexican cuisine made with hyperlocal ingredients.

Elizabeth Country House

Just 20 minutes from Bologna, Elizabeth Country House is a stately, early 1900s residence transformed into a tranquil retreat. Restored under designer Fabrizio Cocchi, the property preserves original architectural details across three distinct villas. Eleven rooms—including four junior suites and a family suite—are designed to restore the senses. Hand-painted Provençal-style walls, exposed wooden beams, and 19th-century Thai and French antiques (many from the former resident's collection) create a warm, old-world atmosphere. Surrounded by manicured grounds and near the imposing 14th-century Rocca Isolani, the estate sits amid a cluster of historic buildings that echo Italy's glorious past. A swimming pool, yoga and meditation sessions, massages, a daily personal trainer, and cooking classes offer space to slow down between visits to the UNESCO World Heritage Site of Argenta or strolls through the Roman streets of Minerbio. Ideally located in the heart of Emilia-Romagna's food valley—and just 45 minutes from the famed Motor Valley—Elizabeth Country House invites guests to experience Italy at its most soulful.

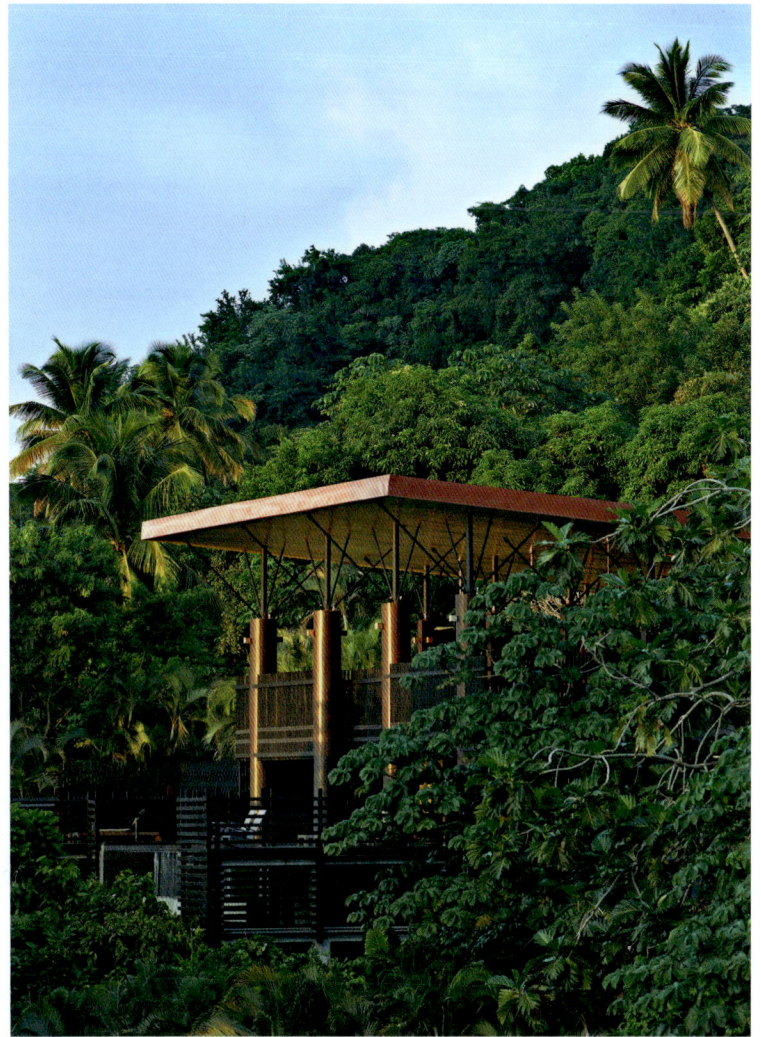

Destination	Location	Rooms	Themes
St. Lucia	Soufrière	25	Adults Only, Beach, Honeymoon, Offbeat, Sustainable

Rabot Hotel From Hotel Chocolat

Tropical seclusion and world-class chocolate meet in a breathtaking St. Lucian setting. British founders of Hotel Chocolat, **Peter Harris** and **Angus Thirlwell,** transformed the island's oldest cacao farm, Rabot Estate, into a lush, dreamlike retreat. The Rabot Restaurant gazes out over the volcanic peak of Petit Piton, serving cacao-laced dishes made from estate-grown ingredients. Guests can relax at the Beauté de Cacao Spa, where cocoa-infused therapies soothe body and soul. The 25 eco-conscious lodges—crafted by local stonemasons, carpenters, and painters—feature pitched wooden roofs, slatted shutters, and open-air rainforest showers. A black-quartz infinity pool and breezy bar complete the experience. Anchored by the restored Rabot Estate House, the property sits on the edge of a UNESCO World Heritage Site. The Island Growers Program supports 75 local cacao farmers, while rainwater harvesting and organic practices reflect a deep-rooted commitment to sustainability.

Destination	Location	Rooms	Themes
United Kingdom	London	99	Art & Culture, City, Gastronomy, Interior Design

The Soho Hotel, Firmdale Hotels

Colorful, eclectic fabrics contrast with traditional British furniture design in this idiosyncratic **Kit Kemp** hotel. Set in a red-brick warehouse in Soho, large industrial windows and high ceilings are among the outstanding features of this reimagined building, which once served as a car park. Kemp conceives of hotel design as a living thing, and that interiors are transitory and subject to passion—an ethos which she leans into with a display of art that reflects her personal taste and curation. The hotel features a Fernando Botero cat (a sister sculpture also appears in the Crosby Street Hotel in New York City), and a Breon O'Casey sculpture of Aphrodite, alongside a commissioned mural by Alexander Hollweg (who also completed the mural for Kemp's nearby Charlotte Street Hotel). Refuel Bar & Restaurant is nestled between Dean Street and Wardour Street, and serves British and European brasserie classics like côte de boeuf and roast pumpkin soup with Cornish Kern scone. In homage to the building's history, classic cars inspire the bar's list of cocktails.

Destination
France

Location
Paris

Rooms
57

Themes
City, Interior Design

La Maison
Champs Élysées

Set in Paris's coveted Golden Triangle, La Maison Champs-Élysées artfully fuses historic Haussmann architecture with bold, avant-garde design. The 17 Couture Collection suites weave optical illusions and surreal touches into a palette of minimalist elegance, seamlessly bridging heritage and modernity. The preservation of the classic façade sets the stage for interiors alive with trompe-l'œil murals and carpets that playfully invert perspectives. By day, Frivole's shaded terrace provides a tranquil retreat for leisurely lunches; by night, it pulses with dimmed lights, swelling music, and convivial laughter. Meanwhile, the Salon Louis XIII cigar lounge offers an intimate refuge for savoring rare spirits. Exclusive to guests, the Unlimited Club—a 370-square-meter wellness haven—boasts a pool, gym, sauna, and treatment rooms, where private coaching and group sessions cultivate balance and mastery. La Maison Champs Élysées stands as a contemporary Parisian sanctuary, rich with surprises and stories yet to be told.

Destination	Location	Rooms	Themes
Malaysia	George Town, Penang	8	City, Gastronomy, History

Macalister Mansion

Macalister Mansion is a quirky yet sophisticated reinvention of a 100-year-old heritage building in George Town, Penang. Honoring its namesake—Colonel Norman Macalister, one of the island's early British governors—the hotel blends rural charm with contemporary design. As the first Malaysian member of Design Hotels, it stands apart with just eight spacious rooms, each curated with colorful marble finishes, bespoke furnishings, and commissioned works by local artists. Originally restored in 2012 by Colin Seah of Ministry of Design, the interiors nod to art deco elegance while celebrating Penang's vibrant creative spirit. Set amid lush gardens, the property features a cafe, bar, and pool with a swim-up counter, along with Restaurant Blanc—awarded Michelin Selected 2025—where refined French-Asian cuisine is served in a stylish, intimate setting. Steps away from UNESCO World Heritage sites and beloved local eateries, Macalister Mansion offers a stylish, intimate base from which to explore Penang's cultural richness.

Destination
Mexico

Location
Mérida

Rooms
17

Themes
City, History, Well-Being

Destination
Spain

Location
Barcelona

Rooms
79

Themes
Art & Culture, City, Sustainable

Rosas & Xocolate

For this sublime, bright-pink hotel, owner **Carol Kolozs** used every element to inspire romance. Designed by Reyes Ríos and Larraín Arquitectos, it combines two historic mansions, bringing together custom floors and upholstery, restored antiques, and commissioned artworks. Rooms variously boast four-meter-high ceilings, luxe cotton linens, large double-glazed windows, four-poster beds, and open-sky bathtubs. Chef David Segovia leads the hotel's award-winning restaurant, with a focus on contemporary gastronomy, for a lush and intimate dining experience.

Sir Victor Hotel

With its striking façade and angular windows, **Liran Wizman's** Sir Victor is a modernist landmark. Here, Baranowitz + Kronenberg renovated the hotel in unmistakable Catalonian style. Inside, suspended lighting, marble surfaces, and oak floors create a playful atmosphere. Rooms are flooded with natural light and adorned with local art, while the rooftop terrace offers breathtaking views. Guests can relax at the Spa by Serena or mingle at MR PORTER, the hotel's signature restaurant. A stylish bar, library, and gym round out this contemporary retreat.

Miss Clara by Nobis

On Stockholm's bustling Sveavägen boulevard, **Alessandro Catenacci** presents Miss Clara, a chic hotel with heritage at its heart. Architect Gert Wingårdh has masterfully reinvented one of the city's beloved art nouveau edifices, originally designed by Hagström & Ekman in 1910, for an abstract, modern take on turn-of-the-century style. High ceilings, expansive windows, and grand proportions are preserved, while subtle, feminine touches—delicate floral arrangements, cut glass, and photographs of ballerinas—hint at the property's past as a girls' school. Swedish materials dominate: limestone, oak, natural leather, and parquet flooring make for a sophisticated palette beneath light-flooding arched windows. In the elegant restaurant, cut-glass pendant lamps, leather banquettes, and mirrors complement floor-to-ceiling views of the boulevard. A lively bar draws locals as well as guests, while a rejuvenating sauna provides a soul-enriching time-out.

Destination
France

Location
Cannes

Rooms
45

Themes
Beach, Sustainable

Destination
Greece

Location
Athens

Rooms
21

Themes
City, Gastronomy

Five Seas Cannes

Five Seas Cannes, nestled in the city center, is a refined escape minutes from the French Riviera's renowned beaches, boutiques, and the iconic Croisette. Designed by Pascal Allaman and Studio MHNA, this hotel embodies epicurean art de vivre. Guests can relax in the roof-top infinity pool, indulge at the Spa by Sothys, or savor shared small plates at Le Roof with panoramic views. Warm-toned interiors, glass-walled bathrooms, and luxurious amenities complete the experience. Private access to La Plage du Festival offers sun loungers and beachside service.

AthensWas

Sited close to the Acropolis, AthensWas offers a fresh take on luxury. Created by **Stavros Papayannis,** the 21-room hotel combines classicism and modernism. Street-level glass walls display a marble and walnut-lined lobby lit by fixtures from Konstantin Grcic. Throughout, furniture by Le Corbusier, Eileen Gray, and Grcic punctuate the restrained palette. Guestrooms feature spacious balconies and nods to antiquity. Sense Restaurant crowns the rooftop, while the ground-floor lounge, featuring Mediterranean and Asian flavors, is spoken of across town.

Destination	Location	Rooms	Themes
Japan	Tokyo	15	Adults Only, Art & Culture, City

TRUNK (HOTEL)
Cat Street

Shibuya local **Yoshitaka Nojiri** founded TRUNK (HOTEL) Cat Street for an audience of lifestyle connoisseurs. Nojiri's vision was simple yet ingenious: a hotel where service adapts to each visitor rather than a one-size-fits-all approach. He also hoped to reignite the creative members of Shibuya, the scene-setting neighborhood where he was raised and which formed the backdrop to his teens. Following this logic, the hotelier included a store in the hotel that sells a curated selection of boutique, local goods aimed at customers looking for something unique—including local honey and beer, Japanese art, and organic food and clothing. Mount Fuji Architects Studio designed the hotel, a mix of geometric forms, greenery, and a stone façade. Public spaces feature artworks by Ido Yoshimoto, Maru Michinori, David Horvitz, and Nigel Peake, alongside upcycled, Japanese-made furniture. The rooms and suites feel like personalized, high-end apartments, with a selection of hand-picked books, artworks, and sleek furnishings. The Trunk (Kushi) stand serves Shibuya soul food, while The Trunk Kitchen serves Japanese-Western fusion cuisine for lively meet-ups reminiscent of scenes from Sofia Coppola's *Lost in Translation.*

The Warehouse Hotel

Situated along Singapore's historic river, The Warehouse Hotel transforms a 19th-century warehouse into a 37-room boutique escape. Reimagined by Zarch Collaboratives and Asylum, this 1895 landmark imbues industrial design with local Singaporean soul. The design captures the hotel's rich history: once a storage site for spices and commodities brought by traders, the area later gained a colorful reputation for secret societies, illicit liquor distilleries, and vice dens. A triple-pitched roof creates uniquely angled spaces, while preserved elements like original trusses refinished in black nod to a bygone era. Rooms balance industrial aesthetics with warmth, from copper wall units to lighting merging natural and electric light. Heritage shines through every detail, from room keys featuring "welcome" carved in English, Chinese, Malay, and Tamil, honoring the multicultural migrant communities who built the city, to curated local neighborhood experiences. A rooftop infinity pool and spacious lobby hung with historic pulleys offer perfect spots for gathering and relaxing.

Destination	Location	Rooms	Themes
Malaysia	Kota Kinabalu, Sabah	115	City, Gastronomy

The Luma Hotel

In Kota Kinabalu, **Alan Wong, Dato' Steven Chin, Kelvin Hiew,** and **Jennifer Wang** channel a reverence for Sabah's culture and natural surroundings into The Luma Hotel—a design-forward property rooted in local spirit. Working with Seshan Design, the team transformed a former office building into a tactile, community-focused hub where every detail reflects Borneo's layered landscape. A soaring spiral staircase of local timber and marble anchors the double-height lobby, echoing the rainforest canopy, while polished concrete floors reference Mount Kinabalu. Rose gold details on the western façade catch the warmth of Sabah's signature sunsets. Throughout, locally crafted furniture and curated art underscore a deep connection to place. Meaning "home" in the Bajau language, Luma is both retreat and gathering space, with jewel-toned lounges, playlists by Sabahan artists, and guestrooms in earthy hues with Sarsi wood, travertine, and brass accents. Dining takes center stage at JoJo's modern Asian gastrobar and Flow Coffee's cafe by Crack Inc., uniting locals and travelers in a shared celebration of Sabah's evolving creative energy.

Destination	Location	Rooms	Themes
France	Dijon	42	City, History, Interior Design, Offbeat

Vertigo Hotel

This 1880s Haussmann-style building has been a hotel for more than a century, over the years attracting an array of famous guests ranging from Joan Baez to Jean Reno. Yvon Carminati carefully restored the hotel for brothers Bruno and Christophe Massucco, retaining the original, decorative ceilings from its belle epoque beginnings. Ludivine De Brito used black and white as the hotel's re-strained interior palette and employed a contrasting mix of antique frames, chandeliers, and modern furniture to gild the rooms. Each chamber contains small surprises, including suspended beds and mirrors doubling as media-entertainment systems. Carefully selected pieces, such as Hervé Langlais lights, Maria Jeglinska coffee tables, and Ligne Roset furniture, build the rooms' quirky, yet restful atmosphere. In Embassy Bar, futuristic blue backlighting offsets a liquor cabinet, making a lively contrast with surrounding gold-framed art. Here, guests can enjoy vintage Burgundy wine, champagne, and cocktails, or head to the hotel's vaults to relax in the spa, indoor pool, sauna, and Turkish bath.

Destination	Location	Rooms	Themes
United Kingdom	London	58	Art & Culture, City, Interior Design

Covent Garden Hotel, Firmdale Hotels

In the heart of London's theater district, this refined retreat on cobbled Monmouth Street reimagines a once-neglected 1890s French hospital into a dramatic sanctuary. A sweeping stone staircase leads to sumptuous rooms arrayed in quintessential English style, from wood-panelling and delicate wallpapers to rich fabrics. The hotel welcomes guests with grand curtains at reception—a fitting entrance to a property surrounded by over 20 theaters. Inside, abstract upholstery patterns adorn canopy beds and headboards, while curated artworks and antiques combine to make a distinctively eclectic atmosphere. Brasserie Max has become a favorite pre- and post-theater destination for locals and visitors alike, offering a lively contrast to the hotel's restful and cocooning accommodations. The property's stage-set interiors, complete with magical rural scenes on wallpapered walls, are the vision of owner–interior designer **Kit Kemp,** whose renowned personal style gives the hotel its elegant charm.

Destination
United Kingdom

Location
London

Rooms
42

Themes
Art & Culture, City, Interior Design

Number Sixteen

Utilizing custom textiles and curated art, **Kit Kemp** has devised a true-to-form uplifting and comfort-filled hotel steeped in modern British design. Situated in a row of white stucco mid-Victorian townhouses, complete with an orangery and a garden in the heart of South Kensington, Number Sixteen boasts wrought-iron balustrades, column-supported porticoes, and two drawing rooms with full-height windows overlooking Sumner Place. Pieces of antique and contemporary furniture sit alongside bold patterns and colorful bursts of art, upholstery, rugs, and wallpaper in individually designed rooms. As per Kemp's trademark style, contemporary art lines the public spaces. In the library, Scottish artist Jack Milroy's striking mixed media work depicts sea life on pages of books, while in one of the drawing rooms, Australian artist Allyson Reynolds's multicolored moth painting hangs above a plush sofa with similar hues. Just moments from London's major museums, the hotel is a perfect gateway to the city for art lovers.

Dorset Square Hotel, Firmdale Hotels

Set within the walls of two adjoining Regency townhouses is Dorset Square Hotel. **Kit Kemp** celebrates the property's Georgian heritage with bold, art-infused style, embracing eclectic fabrics from her own collection with textile expert Christopher Farr alongside hand-woven carpets from Argentina. The hotel sits on a quiet corner of Marylebone's Dorset Square, the site of Thomas Lord's original cricket ground; Kemp honors this history with cricket bats on the hotel's entrance plaque and selected memorabilia throughout. In summer, many of the rooms overlook the verdant private garden, while in winter, the hotel embraces cozy open fireplaces and mood lighting. With its tranquil location just a stone's throw from the shops and restaurants of Marylebone High Street, guests feel close to the action from a secluded vantage.

Destination	Location	Rooms	Themes
United States	New York, NY	86	Art & Culture, City, Interior Design, Sustainable

Crosby Street Hotel, Firmdale Hotels

Set in a quiet cobblestone street, Crosby Street Hotel's warehouse façade and sizable steel-framed windows nod to the industrial past of its SoHo locale. The hotel follows **Kit Kemp's** characteristically vivacious and art-focused style. The designer is renowned for her ability to layer eye-catching art and tasteful decor with dashes of vibrant color and bold patterns, resulting in wholly captivating, homely atmospheres. Here, she draws on English country and modernist styles, centering a work by Scottish artist Jack Milroy in the hotel lobby. Statement pieces from her own collection feature throughout the building, including a landmark-worthy Botero cat sculpture, an Anselm Kiefer painting, and joyful sculptures of dogs by Justine Smith. Following the design's art-led direction, the hotel also provides art walks through neighboring Tribeca and Chelsea with artist Lyora Pissarro.

Destination	Location	Rooms	Themes
United Kingdom	London	55	Art & Culture, City, Gastronomy, Interior Design

Haymarket Hotel

Kit Kemp's Haymarket Hotel is the epitome of eclectic luxury. John Nash, the master architect behind much of Regency London, was the architect of this historic Georgian gem, and Kemp draws on the hotel's history to infuse classical references with her signature modern English style. The designer's bold design choices and unique flair are evident from the moment guests step into the hotel's public spaces, where art lines the walls and halls—from a Tony Cragg stainless steel sculpture, to a Sue Lawty stone installation, and a John Virtue painting. Meanwhile, vibrantly colored and patterned upholstery on plush furniture clashes joyfully with a variety of multicolored wallpapers, textures, and decor. A grand underground swimming pool featuring a multihued Martin Richman light installation is an unexpected jewel in the hotel's crown. The establishment also boasts a collection of eclectic meeting and event spaces—each infused with the same bold character and creative spirit that defines Haymarket itself.

Destination
United Kingdom

Location
London

Rooms
44

Themes
Art & Culture, City, Interior Design

Knightsbridge Hotel, Firmdale Hotels

Originally a trio of Victorian townhouses, **Kit Kemp** draws on the historic fabric of Knightsbridge Hotel and pairs it with her modern English style. Set in the heart of the upscale Knightsbridge neighborhood, its premises are a stone's throw from Harrods, the international designer stores of Sloane Street, Hyde Park, the Serpentine Galleries, and the public museums of South Kensington. The lobby, drawing room, and library overlook elegant, tree-lined Beaufort Gardens through floor-to-ceiling windows. Following her signature aesthetic, Kemp integrates bright, contrasting patterns in wallpaper and upholstery with significant British artworks. A striking Graham Fransella painting greets guests on arrival while, in the plush, inviting library, a John Illsley abstract hangs above the stone mantlepiece near Peter Clarke's whimsical depictions of dogs. Each of the guestrooms feature cozy cushions with bright colors that carefully mix country style with modernity. Guests can enjoy afternoon tea and champagne served in the library.

Destination
Germany

Location
Munich

Rooms
72

Themes
City, Gastronomy, History,
Interior Design, Sustainable

Destination
United States

Location
Palm Springs, CA

Rooms
72

Themes
City

Louis Hotel

Louis Hotel is a chic gateway in the Bavarian
capital. Hild & K Architekten refurbished
the 100-year-old building, capitalizing
on its high ceilings, French balconies, and
baroque-style stucco windows. In the communal areas, warm-toned furnishings and
abundant timber exist alongside fireplaces,
making for welcoming spaces. The guestrooms are opulent, with walnut bed frames,
Sembella mattresses, bronze fittings, and
oak floors. The Grillroom provides indul-
gent seasonal, organic cuisine—including
a cauliflower T-bone steak—alongside a
sparkling wine bar.

Avalon Hotel &
Bungalows Palm Springs

Brad Korzen, Brian De Lowe, and **Kelly
Wearstler** bring Spanish-style architecture
and Hollywood Regency interiors to this
Palm Springs hotel. Composed of 72 lodg-
ings (including studios and private villas),
the hotel's exterior features palm trees
and manicured lawns, while the interior
boasts white-stucco walls and fireplaces.
Hemmed by hedges, the outdoor pool
allows guests to retreat from the surrounding desert. Back inside, the hotel also
features two Jacuzzis, a steam room, sauna,
24-hour gym, and yoga and meditation
classes—a veritable oasis.

Destination
Denmark

Location
Copenhagen

Rooms
75

Themes
Art & Culture, City, History,
Interior Design, Sustainable

Nobis Hotel
Copenhagen

In downtown Copenhagen, the Nobis Hotel Copenhagen inhabits an imposing 1903 landmark that once housed the Royal Danish Conservatory of Music. **Alessandro Catenacci's** signature perfectionism shaped the vision for this historic structure's transformation, executed by Gert Wingårdh's team. Located steps away from Copenhagen Central Station and the renowned Strøget shopping street, Wingårdh's thoughtful restoration preserves elaborate detailing while introducing high-quality natural materials, unified by a subtle color palette that is distinctly Scandinavian. The concrete reception desk offers a modern contrast to the heritage features, part of a bold

countervailing aesthetic inspired by Le Corbusier's modernist monastery (and final building), Sainte Marie de La Tourette. Guest rooms feature wooden parquet floors, high, white-painted windows, and spacious four-poster beds. A refined bar, restaurant serving Nordic cuisine, gym, and sauna draw a discerning local crowd alongside in-the-know travelers.

In a world of overstimulation, these hotels invite you to slow down. Immersed in nature and designed with sensory care, they offer quiet rhythms, tactile beauty, and space to breathe. Presence here is not a luxury—it's the point.

Natural Resonance

Why True
Hotels

Nicola Leigh Stewart

Speak to the
Senses

For the Paris-based British journalist Nicola Leigh Stewart, the most memorable hotels master the art of subtle sensory engagement, transforming spaces into profound wellsprings of emotion.

Even surrounded by the thrum of the French metropolis, I can still sense the exquisite sounds of the last two hotels I stayed in. One was a mountain retreat filled not with silence exactly, but with the sound of being in the mountains—almost alone—quietness, and the familiar crunch of snow underfoot. Another was a rural escape, which was practically the opposite. Here, I was engulfed in a constant soundtrack of twittering birds punctuated by braying donkeys.

It's impossible for me to say which I preferred. They both had their charms and they both sounded—and smelled and felt—exactly as they should. Their appeal was sensual. I still remember, for instance, the natural woody scent as I opened the door to my mountain retreat. Here, even the bathtub was crafted from a hollowed-out log, and at the pottery class I attended, taught by a local craftswoman from the nearby village,

I can clearly recall the coolness and dampness of the clay we used. Every surface, scent, texture, and sound felt luxuriant. Conversely, when I visited the rural escape, it wasn't my suite's scent that first struck me, but the warmth of spices cooking in the open kitchen —and later in the day, particularly the smell of cumin.

Creating multi-sensory experiences is the latest way hotels are trying to elevate guest experiences beyond visually appealing aesthetics—although some are more successful than others. Bigger brands often incorporate this in ways that frequently feel artificial, like a foreign scent carelessly sprayed in a hotel room or elevator muzak featuring the sounds of wildlife. Nevertheless, guests have come to expect such sensual pleasures from hotels. And to achieve this successfully, hospitality designers need to stay true to the space's surroundings.

It's no use, for instance, imbuing your hotel with an alpine olfactory element when it is located by the Mediterranean. Similarly, a packed, bustling layout might not be what guests would want at a remote wellness retreat. This might sound obvious, but it's surprising how many establishments fumble this element. Often,

Nicola Leigh Stewart

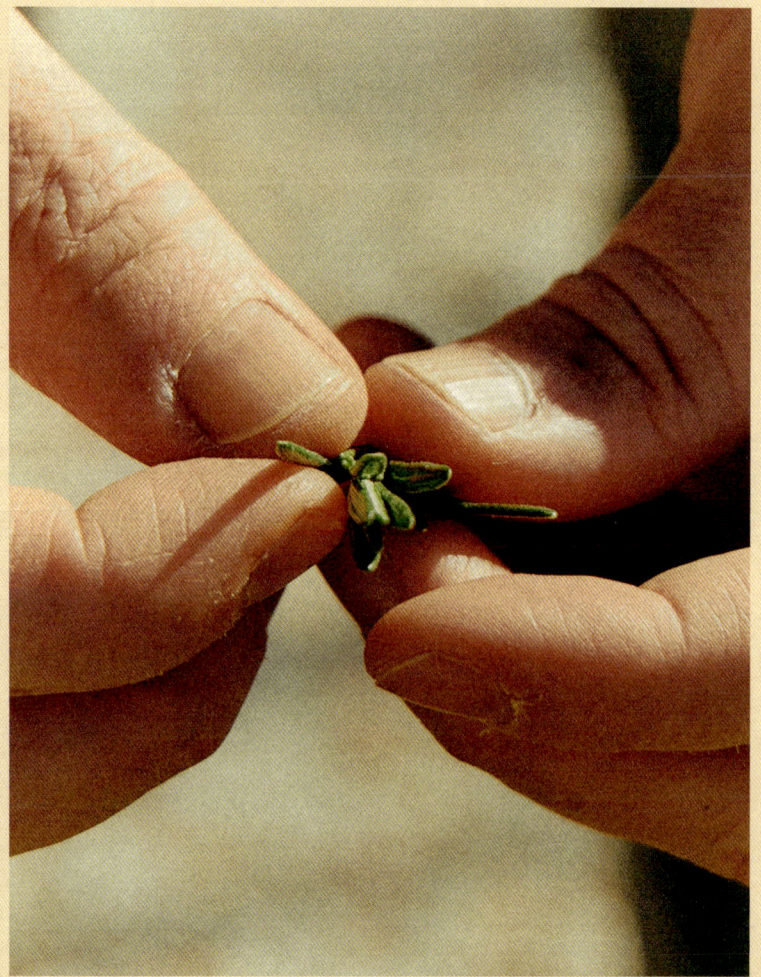

it seems, it's the smaller hotels that succeed in this regard. In my experience, they frequently feel not only like extensions of their locales but like homes away from home, as though one has traveled to stay with a friend. Tapping into the senses is thus a genuine way to welcome guests and immerse them in your hospitality experience.

At the mountain retreat I visited, for instance, the scent wasn't created through an overpowering room spray but via the subtly aroma of the nearby forest, a mix of pine wood and resin. Of course, if the hotel's concept store had sold this scent by the bottle—which it didn't—visitors might have been able to recreate this scene at home. But it wouldn't be the same, because the location would be different, and the connection to the surrounding world would be lost. The memories I have of that stay are specific to it, and restaging one element wouldn't bring them back.

In this respect, we often talk about the benefits of travel, from the most basic, such as a week of sleep and relaxation that eludes us at home, to how it opens our minds and our worlds. Yet, what travel always brings—although we don't always realize it at the time—is more than just a break; it's a sense of nostalgia that will hopefully endure long after it has ended. Appealing to the senses doesn't just enhance travel; it creates a sense of *time travel,* a place to continually return to via sensual memory.

Paris-based **Nicola Leigh Stewart,** a leading voice in luxury travel and design writing, brings a uniquely insightful perspective to her dispatches from global destinations. Her work, spanning *Wallpaper, Lonely Planet,* and *The Independent,* dives deep into the sensory worlds of hotels and cuisine, delivering fresh, immersive stories that champion sophisticated travel.

Destination	Location
Italy	Parrano

Rooms	Themes
17	Adults Only, Countryside, Offbeat, Sustainable, Well-Being

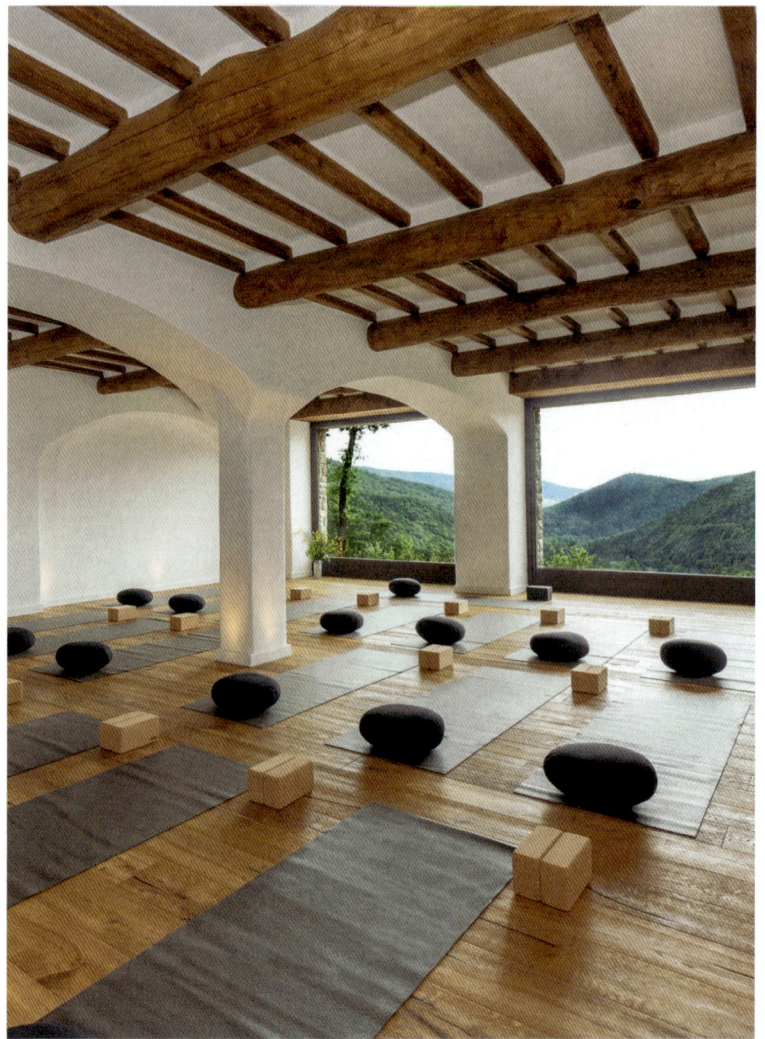

Eremito

Eremito (meaning 'hermit') is Italy's first digital detox hotel and encourages guests to meaningfully slow down and unwind. With its design inspired by Umbrian monasteries and Franciscan minimalism, the hotel welcomes solo travelers and larger groups looking to disconnect and find spiritual stillness. Guests participate in silent communal dinners and sleep on single beds, and the space is free of phones, televisions, and electronic appliances. Situated in a 13th-century house, this wellness-centered hotel is fittingly located beside a UNESCO Biosphere Reserve. Owner **Marcello Murzilli** appointed architect Nino Nenna to lead the reconstruction of the property using historic Italian masonry techniques. For all its antique, monastic appearance, the hotel is technologically and sustainably advanced, using solar panels for energy. The property's rich and geologically storied natural surroundings offer tranquil focus for stillness-seeking visitors.

Destination	Location	Rooms	Themes
Mexico	Loma Bonita, Guerrero	26	Beach, Gastronomy, Honeymoon, Offbeat, Sustainable

Hotelito at MUSA

Situated on the Pacific Ocean and near the peaks of the Sierra Madre, Hotelito at MUSA (Modern Utopian Society of Adventurers) is the creation of **Andrés Saavedra** and **Tara Medina.** This 26-room sanctuary transcends traditional hospitality, embodying a holistic vision of wellness, creativity, and sustainable living. Characterized by sleek design and a wabi-sabi—or a less is morecrustic—sensibility, here contemporary architecture merges with the beauty of the coastal landscape. Designed for the subtropical climate, Hotelito at MUSA features open-air spaces, lush rooftop gardens, and unobstructed ocean views. Each room is a testament to Mexican craftsmanship, incorporating handmade terrazzo tiles, Parota wood, and polished concrete, honoring local traditions while embracing a tropical modernist aesthetic. Much more than a hotel, it's part of a dynamic community that celebrates art, innovation, and philanthropy. With beachfront work-spaces, artist studios, and restaurants serving local dishes, Hotelito at MUSA offers a community-based approach to travel that honors a connection to place.

Destination	**Location**
Mexico	Tulum
Rooms	**Themes**
12	Beach, Well-being

XELA Tulum

Drawing inspiration from Middle Eastern divan rooms, interior designer Alex Heyde Ballengee set the tone for this Yucatán retreat with a cozy conversation pit in XELA's limewashed, thatched-roof lobby. The 12 sea-facing suites continue the same design language, with a palette of natural, warm tones, woven fibers, and stone finishes. Once a private beachfront home owned by a European family, the property was thoughtfully reimagined as a boutique hideaway through a collaboration between Heyde Ballengee and visionary hotelier **Yves Naman.** While preserving the building's original character, the transformation introduced new communal spaces, including a bar, spa, and gym—all designed with understated elegance. Rooted in a deep respect for Tulum's natural surroundings, XELA operates in alignment with a sustainability manifesto that prioritizes local biodiversity. Eco-conscious practices are woven into the guest experience, from reef-safe sunscreen to ingredients thoughtfully sourced from Mestiza de Indias, a regenerative, pesticide-free farm in the Yucatán.

Destination	Location
Mexico	Tulum

Rooms	Themes
53	Beach, Honeymoon, Sustainable, Well-Being

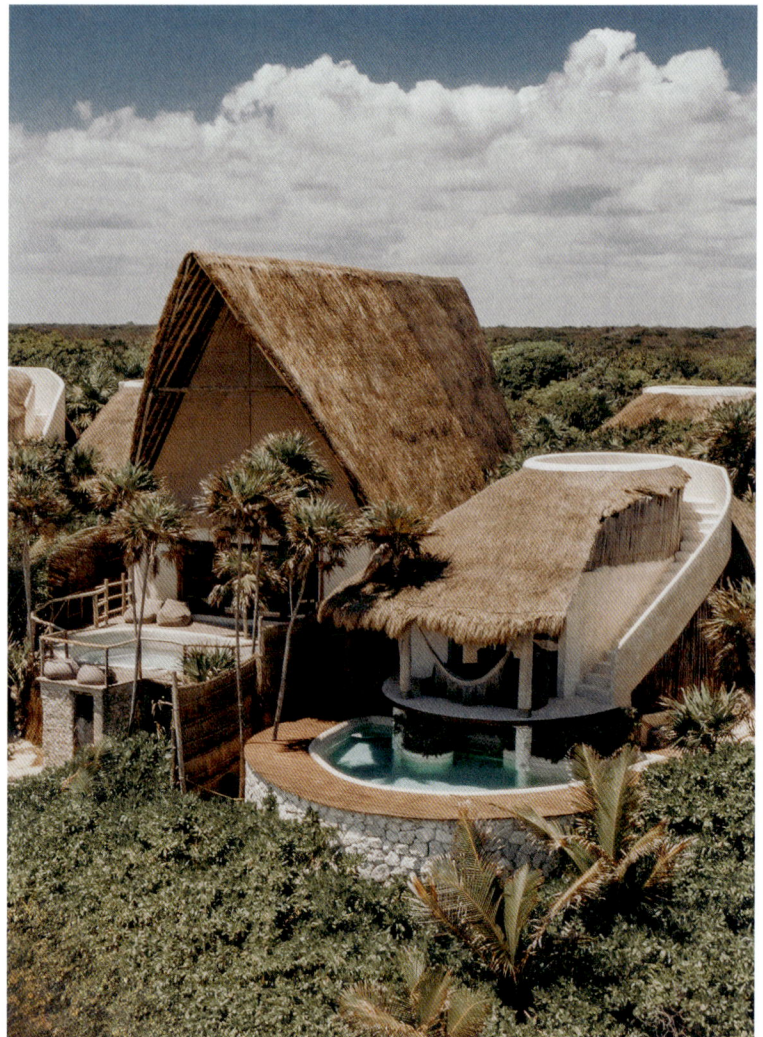

Papaya Playa Project

This communal hotel in the jungle located on a pristine stretch of the Caribbean coast was conceived of and designed by **Emilio Heredia.** Simplicity, relaxation, and respect for the landscape are the hotel's guiding principles. To encourage relaxation, Papaya Playa Project offers a range of holistic treatments, including massage treatments, guided yoga, tai chi, and meditation, as well as plunge pools and a temazcal (a traditional Mesoamerican steam bath, often used for purification and healing rituals). Local materials are abundant in the different accommodations—some of them up in the trees—with bamboo, palapa-thatched roofs, and lush greenery all around. Rustic luxury rules inside the pared-back rooms, where cream stone, natural wood, and an absence of electric outlets encourage guests to unplug. Set on the Mayan Riviera, the hotel's location gives guests ample opportunity to visit the only Mayan ruins on the sea. Daytimes can be spent whiling away the hours in hammocks or taking a dip in the beachside pool; evenings are made lively with sets by world-class musicians beneath swaying palms.

Destination	Location	Rooms	Themes
Maldives	Baa Atoll	125	Beach, Family-Friendly, Gastronomy, Honeymoon, Sustainable, Well-Being

Finolhu, A Seaside Collection Resort

Pristine white sand and aquamarine waters, combined with outdoor adventures and culinary delights, provide guests with the ultimate beachside holiday at Finolhu, A Seaside Collection Resort. Located in a UNESCO-protected biosphere, the island property has its own dedicated marine biologist to ensure the longevity and enjoyment of the local flora and fauna. Kulor Group architects designed the villas—which sit directly on the beach or on stilts above the lagoon, many with their own pools—with Maldivian influences, such as thatched roofs and white or green-painted exteriors that harmonize beautifully with the local topography. Muza Lab designers drew on the kaleidoscopic rhythm of refracted waves, pairing custom furniture, natural materials, and neutral tones to create a layered, nature-driven aesthetic.

Destination	Location	Rooms	Themes
Greece	Crete	20	Beach, Gastronomy, Honeymoon, Well-Being

Tella Thera

Nestled deep amongst the olive groves of Kissamos, Tella Thera is a nature-inspired boutique hotel shaped by a deep commitment to sustainability and soulful hospitality. Helmed by husband-and-wife duo **Loukas Tourkomanis** and **Chevon Low,** the retreat is thoughtfully integrated into its surroundings through bioclimatic architecture designed to minimize environmental impact. Its 20 earth-toned suites are carved into the hillside and topped with planted rooftops that echo the native terrain. The signature three-bedroom villa offers a more private escape, complete with its own infinity pool and outdoor dining terrace. Mornings begin with guided yoga at sunrise, followed by nourishing,

seasonal fare at Anemoia—a plant-forward, zero-waste restaurant rooted in local tradition. Guests can unwind with organic, restorative treatments at Thaleria Spa or meander the winding paths around the property. Wherever you go, the views of the Mediterranean offer a constant invitation to pause, breathe, and reconnect.

Destination
Ukraine

Location
Kyiv

Rooms
50

Themes
City

Destination
Bolivia

Location
La Paz

Rooms
53

Themes
Art & Culture, City, Gastronomy

11 Mirrors Design Hotel by FACE the Service

Set behind a granite façade blending 19th-century design with modern touches, Doctor **Wladimir Klitschko's** hotel embodies cosmopolitan Kyiv. Collaborating with Ukrainian designers Anatoliy Kirik and Maryna Leo, its interiors boast a rich, sophisticated color scheme and gleaming mirrored surfaces for timeless elegance. Common areas cater to every need: a rooftop offers sweeping city views, and a low-lit bar provides expertly crafted cocktails. The plush lobby combines natural materials and warm dark tones with deep purple accents, enhancing enduring luxury.

Atix Hotel

Atix is a celebration of Bolivian art and design. Set in La Paz, the **Rodríguez Calvo** siblings' hotel honors its geography with windows framing the landscape and artisanal touches. Jennifer Rusch commissioned works from Gastón Ugalde—the father of contemporary Bolivian art—that speak to the local culture. Stuart Narofsky designed the wood and stone-clad building to resemble the nearby mountains. Elsewhere, Proyecto Nativa restaurant celebrates Bolivian cuisine; and after the sauna and steam room guests can enjoy views of the valley from the indoor pool.

103

Destination	Location
Italy	Lana

Rooms	Themes
68	Countryside, Family-Friendly, Well-Being

Hotel Schwarzschmied

Scandinavian and Japanese design elements are combined in **Klaus** and **Moritz Dissertori's** relaxing spa escape in Italy's South Tyrol. Designer Christina Biasi-von Berg employed rich, regional materials such as larch, spruce, marble from the Vinschgau Valley, and porphyry tiles from the Sarntal Valley to build the peaceful and light-filled rooms. The aesthetic is Scandinavian-coded and profoundly homely, with light timber floors, wooden beams, natural materials, and white walls creating a feeling of softness and warmth. Large windows boast impressive views, including vineyards and orchards that extend towards the mountain-hemmed town of Lana. The hotel maintains a relaxed, unhurried atmosphere, encouraging guests to slow down and breathe deeply. On site is a sizable spa with views of the surrounding mountains, daily yoga classes, retreats, heated pools, saunas, and a library. Slow, regional food and drinks are accordingly prioritized at the restaurant La Fucina and Bar Luce.

Destination	Location	Rooms	Themes
Greece	Mykonos	27	Beach, Gastronomy, Sustainable, Well-Being

Rocabella Mykonos Hotel

On Mykonos, this boutique hotel—redesigned in 2025 by Eleftherios Design Studio—perches serenely above the cerulean Aegean Sea in Agios Stefanos, a five-minute drive from Chora. Here, **Roy Kalfopoulou** has created an inviting world of wellness within sun-kissed white walls, where guests and staff are treated like family, and new connections are forged along the infinity pool that spans the heart of the property. Neutral shades and minimalist design define the rooms, where simple lines, earthy tones, and curated details create a classic Cycladic vibe. Elements like sisal and basketry, alongside stones, reeds, and cacti, draw inspiration from the surrounding landscape. Signature scents and a lavender turn-down service enhance a sense of calm. World-class yoga instructors and a passion for botanicals set a healthy tone. The Rocabella Spa nurtures mind, body, and skin, while Reeza restaurant—a local favorite—offers creative Greek cuisine that reimagines local flavors in a beautiful natural setting. Guests can cook traditional dishes with the chef for intimate pergola dinners overlooking the sea, while a sommelier and Coravin wine list ensure perfect pairings.

Amyth of Nicosia

Eraclis Papachristou Architects and interior designer Maria Neophytou blend heritage with timeless elegance in Amyth of Nicosia, a 125-year-old villa in the center of Cyprus's historic capital. The team stripped the space back and made architectural interventions that would simultaneously allow its history to shine while also making room for new life. The materials and colors used—such as bronze, stone, and silk in neutral tones—align with original features like wood-carved ceilings, shutters, and a painted entranceway floor. For siblings and co-owners **Thanos, Anna,** and **Natasha Michaelides,** the hotel is a celebration of the island's storied history. Located in Old Nicosia, the property is neighbors with Byzantine churches and an ethnological museum housed in a grand 18th-century building, and guests can enjoy tours of the city with local archaeologist and art historian Anna Marangou. In the restaurant, chef David Goodridge celebrates the island's culinary heritage with refined dining made from locally sourced ingredients.

Destination
Spain

Location
Palma de Mallorca

Rooms
33

Themes
Adults Only, City, Well-Being

Destination
Spain

Location
Salamanca

Rooms
51

Themes
City, History, Honeymoon,
Offbeat, Sustainable

El Llorenç Parc de la Mar

With patterned floors echoing Arabic and Venetian design, El Llorenç Parc de la Mar expertly mixes heritage and contemporary sophistication. Alongside curated art and décor combining bold hues, walnut, oak, and chrome textures, guests can also enjoy the city's longest infinity pool, a traditional spa, and a menu filled with local cuisine. The rooftop offers panoramic views of the sea, while an 11th-century Arabic oven grounds the space in centuries of history. Here, designer Magnus Ehrland has created a modern tribute to Palma's past.

Hospes Palacio de San Esteban

This renovated Dominican convent and adjoining midcentury building comes courtesy of Fernando Población Iscar and Grupo Veintidós. Across the hotel, outward-facing rooms feature exposed beams and lighting that enhances the honeyed warmth of Villamayor stone. Guests can enjoy pristine amenities and fine dining featuring local cuisine at El Monje in the convent's original kitchen. Evenings end with refreshing cocktails on the terrace overlooking the Old City's cathedrals—a place of rest and refinement in one of Spain's most culturally significant cities.

Olea All Suite Hotel

Elevated on the northeastern coast of Zakynthos, Olea All Suite Hotel reimagines Greek hospitality through a tropical-modernist lens. Owned by **Christos Xenos** and **Venia Xenou,** the 89-suite property appears to float above a 4,000-square-meter lake-like pool, blending architectural innovation with the island's rugged splendor. Here, water is the defining element: streams meander between clusters of cubic structures that boast breathtaking views of both sea and countryside. Thatched roofs, oak wood, and bamboo soften geometrics forms, while earth-toned interiors and ambient lighting invite repose. Terraces and hidden gardens feature hanging seating and nest eggs that connect guests to the landscape. Beyond its architectural beauty, Olea offers guests a holistic experience, including a hammam and yoga pavilion alongside wellness treatments inspired by a range of international healing traditions. Mediterranean and modern Greek cuisine can be enjoyed in the hotel's restaurant, Flow Wine & Dine, while the vibrant Omikron buffet offers with global flavors and fine wines.

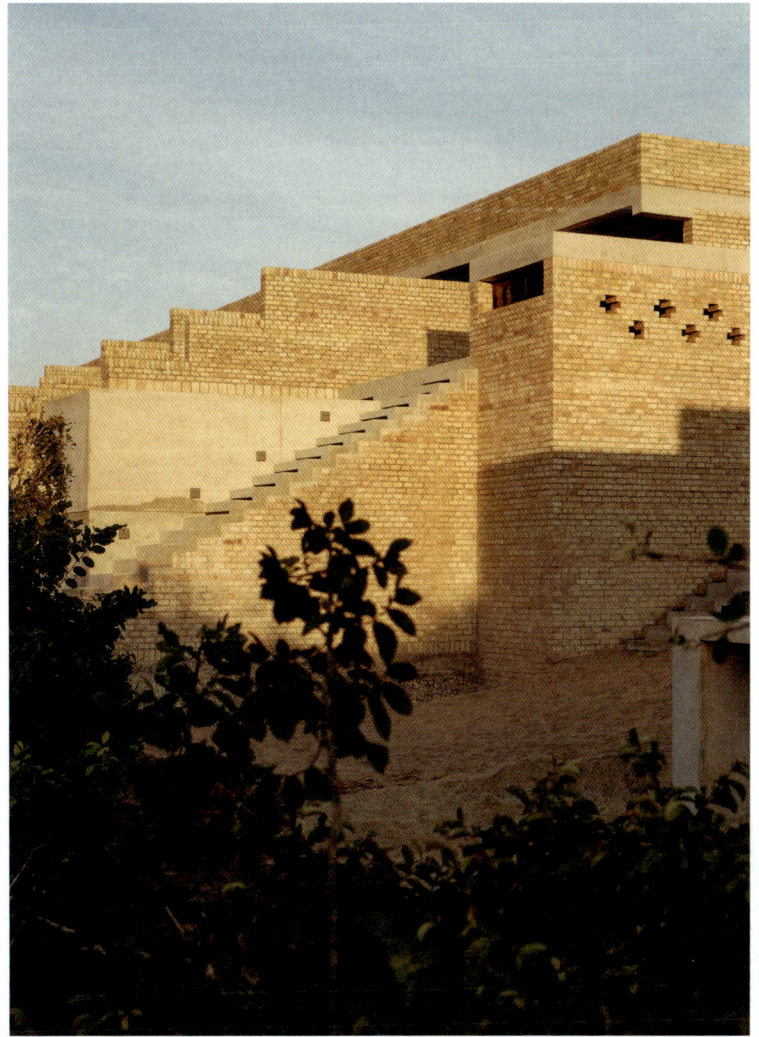

Destination	Location	Rooms	Themes
Mexico	Puerto Escondido	14	Adults Only, Beach, Countryside, Honeymoon, Well-Being

Hotel Terrestre

Carlos Couturier and **Moisés Micha** conceived of Hotel Terrestre as a space for eco-conscious nature lovers to connect with the outdoors. Nestled in a 20,000-square-meter ecological and regenerative development in Oaxaca, the hotel foregrounds a sustainable attitude to tourism. Powered by 100 percent solar energy, the hotel is reminiscent of a temple or a spaceship, surrounded by greenery and with views to the sea. To reduce energy consumption during the construction process, Alberto Kalach of Taller de Arquitectura X sourced local materials such as Mexican-made white mud bricks and employed local building techniques to execute the hotel's magical design. RB + K designed the interiors using an earthy palette of clay, wood, brick, and concrete, and integrated nature into each villa through timber-slatted doors, terraces, and outdoor showers. Each villa also features a private pool and furniture custom designed by Mexican architect Oscar Hagerman. The connection to the outdoors continues with a circular communal pool, a long swimming lane flanked by trees, and an open-air restaurant.

Destination
Switzerland

Location
Champfèr, St. Moritz

Rooms
77

Themes
Mountain, Well-Being

Destination
Switzerland

Location
Minusio-Locarno

Rooms
15

Themes
Countryside, Gastronomy,
Well-Being

Giardino Mountain

Giardino Mountain brings modern comfort to local traditions. Here, owners **Daniela** and **Philippe Frutiger** have turned seven buildings into a design-forward hideaway. Parchment-colored walls, engraved plasterwork, and natural woods meet velvets and sculptural lighting to create stylish interiors. Guests can unwind at Dipiù Spa, eat at Hide & Seek, or dine at the two-Michelin-starred Ecco St. Moritz. In winter, the hotels cozy corners invite rest and relaxation, while summer offers hikes and lake swims in the surrounding environs. Timeless and contemporary, every detail is Alpine.

Giardino Lago

This 15-room hideaway celebrates its verdant setting with expansive glass windows, a sinuous exterior staircase, and a 400 m² roof lounge offering panoramic views. Here, **Daniela** and **Philippe Frutiger** have crafted a tranquil luxury retreat. Inside, stone, wood, and vibrant accents define rooms decorated with Designers Guild fabrics and parquet. Once a chef, Philippe's gastronomic vision is showcased through lakeside dining, completing an experience where countryside beauty, culinary artistry, and personalized wellness unite under glorious sunshine.

Myconian O

Markos Daktylides grew up on Mykonos, with vivid memories of the days when the exceptionally accommodating locals would often give up their houses to visitors. This sense of hospitality is built on the principles of hard work, family values, and *meraki,* which describes undertaking your work or the task at hand with a sense of pride and passion; it is these ideals that underpin Myconian O., Daktylides's luxury beachfront resort. Architect George Stefanis and interior designer Antonis Kalogridis drew inspiration from the hotel's majestic location among the cluster of Aegean islands known as the Cyclades, resulting in highlights that include the infinity pool that overlooks the sparkling sea and the wellness space where guests can receive treatments in a grotto-like subterranean spa facility built into the rock. Here, contemporary Greek design is in active conversation with the simple luxuries of Mykonos life, with natural materials like bamboo, wicker, wood, and marble, combining with furniture crafted by local artisans to infuse the space with a uniquely local sensibility.

Destination	Location	Rooms	Themes
Greece	Sithonia Halkidiki	76	Beach, Family-Friendly, Sustainable

Ekies All Senses Resort

Tucked away in the tranquil bay of Vourvourou, on Halkidiki's Sithonia peninsula, Ekies All Senses Resort is the essence of laid-back luxury. Here, modern design meets Greek tradition in a setting framed by pine-covered hills, scattered islets, and crystal-clear waters—an invitation to slow down, breathe deeply, and reconnect with nature. Each of the 76 rooms and suites has its own character, inspired by the landscape and local customs. From sleek, minimalist spaces bathed in calming whites to rooms with mosaic floors and iconic design pieces, comfort meets creativity. Organic linens and handcrafted details reflect the resort's commitment to sustainability and thoughtful design. The philosophy behind Ekies blends Halkidiki and Macedonia's traditions with contemporary style, creating unique spaces that honor natural heritage. Handcrafted elements such as forged sinks and pebble mosaics sit alongside works by Greek artists and curated international design pieces, offering guests an authentic yet modern experience that celebrates tradition and innovation.

Destination
Portugal

Location
Ponta Do Sol, Madeira

Rooms
54

Themes
Beach, Offbeat

Destination
Taiwan

Location
Kenting

Rooms
65

Themes
Countryside, Offbeat, Sustainable

Estalagem da Ponta do Sol

Perched on high, Estalagem da Ponta do Sol is a minimalist marvel carved into the Madeiran cliffs. Architect Tiago Oliveira shaped it as a series of stark white geometric layers, which each one looking out onto the ocean. Inside, interior designer Carvalho Araújo added whitewashed walls, light wood, and stone floors softened by monochrome textiles. All 54 rooms feature balconies, while the infinity pool gives the illusion of merging with the Atlantic. A bridge connects the hotel to terraced gardens and hidden lookout points, bringing a new unique view at every turn.

Gloria Manor

Tucked away between mountain and sea in Kenting National Park, **John Chen's** Gloria Manor reimagines a 1958 building as a minimalist, eco-conscious retreat. Inside, bamboo ceiling art, geometric flooring, and minimal furnishings combine to create an atmosphere of refined comfort. Guests can enjoy a outdoor pool, yoga sessions, and seasonal cuisine at Mu Restaurant. Gloria Manor also partners with local ecological studios for immersive experiences in Taiwan's southernmost national park. With its deep respect for nature, the hotel is a model of sustainable luxury.

Kimamaya by Odin

Kimamaya by Odin is Nicolas Gontard's luxury mountain lodge in Niseko, Japan. The name, which translates to "be yourself," invites guests to do precisely that. The hotel draws on a range of European influences, from Scandinavian-Japanese design to Alpine cuisine in order to create its nourishing, Zen-like feel. Located in Niseko, a popular ski resort on Japan's northern island of Hokkaidō blessed each winter with famously powdery snow, the hotel provides ample access to snowboarding, hiking, and mountain biking opportunities, depending on the time of year. Atelier BNK's Koichi Ishiguro redesigned the structure while maintaining its original wooden framework and Swiss chalet-style roof. Materials are sustainable, renewable, and have been recycled wherever possible. Andrew Bell from Earth Home Limited designed the interiors, with minimal, luxurious spaces that enhance the original stucture's rich timbers with soft, warm colors, black granite, and plush down bedding. The Barn restaurant takes influence from Hokkaidō's traditional farm architecture and serves regional produce in a French style.

Villa Arnica

Among the green mountains of South Tyrol in Italy's northeast sits Villa Arnica—a luxury escape at the foot of the Dolomites. Hoteliers **Klaus** and **Moritz Dissertori** retained much of the 1925 building's unique history in their sensitive updates to its architecture and interior design. Large green shutters line the windows on the building's yellow and white façade, complementing the lush greenery all around. Inside, Studio Biquadra's interior design showcases a range of eras through antique market finds and Italian mid-century furniture. Paired with parquet floors and soft original colors, the rooms feel luxe and timeless. In the garden is a sun-dappled pool worthy of a Hockney painting. Beside it is the idyllic pool house, where hearty breakfasts and light fare are served from midday through to mid-evening. For further culinary delights, guests can walk to Villa Arnica's sister properties—Hotel Schwarzschmied and 1477 Reichhalter—where delicious dinners and a variety of spa and wellness offerings await.

Es Racó d'Artà

Once a traditional farmhouse, Es Racó d'Artà now hosts suites, cottages, and villas scattered across vineyards, olive groves, and orchards. The air is rich with the scents of nature, inviting guests to slow down and engage with the land. A holistic philosophy extends from the restored architecture to the farm-to-table dining experience, where ingredients are sourced directly from organic gardens and small local producers. Guests can take part in artisanal workshops or indulge in a session of Watsu, a Shiatsu-inspired warm-water hydrotherapy treatment designed to rejuvenate body and mind. Whether guests opt to stay in a private "casita" with a stone bathtub open to the sky, to relax by the infinity pool with mountain views and the monastery of San Salvador in the distance, or to enjoy the exclusive Sa Finqueta villa, every space at Es Racó d'Artà encourages a deepening of the mind-body connection.

Destination	Location
Italy	Castelrotto

Rooms	Themes
42	Countryside, Mountain, Well-Being

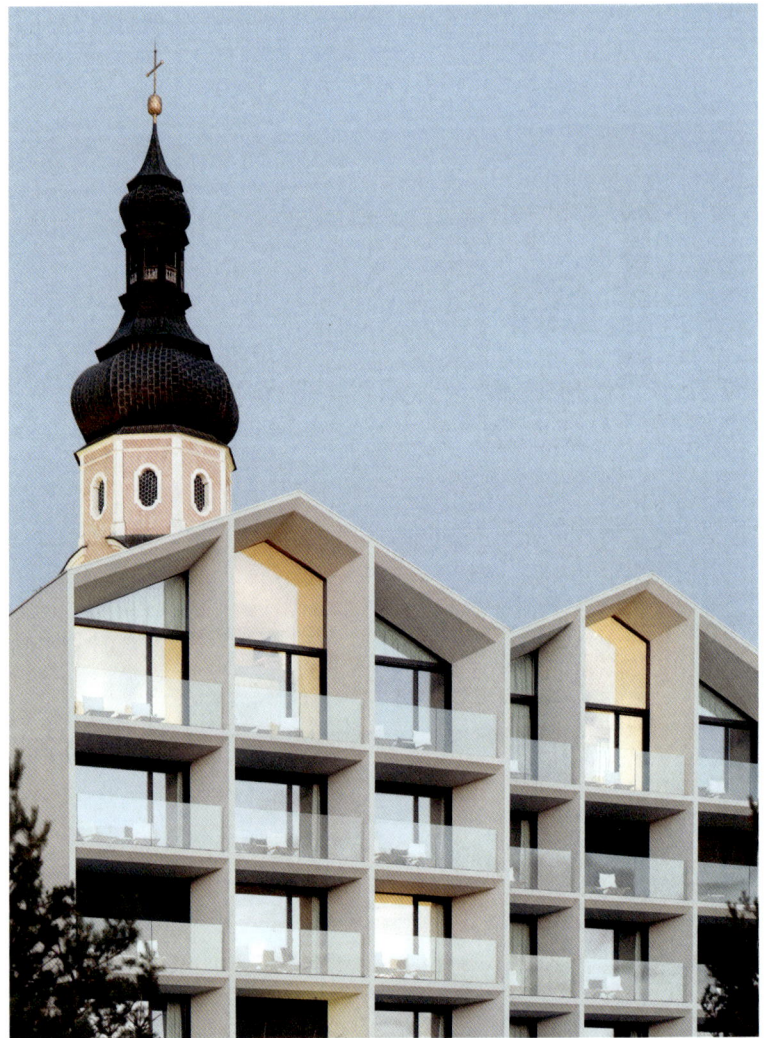

Schgaguler Hotel

The Schgaguler Hotel takes a bold architectural vision to Alpine hospitality. Owned by the **Schgaguler family** (Martin, Sandra, Tobias, and Peter) and designed by Peter Pichler Architecture, this thoroughly modern sanctuary is a sculptural vision in glass and white in view of the majestic Dolomites. A cubic, near-skeletal form echoes the snow-capped peaks in an ingenious reimagining of traditional Alpine design. Interiors embrace minimalist Scandinavian and Japanese aesthetics, with smooth resin floors, bespoke chestnut carpentry, and designer furnishings. Loden fabrics, Merino wool, and Martin Schgaguler's large-format spectral photographs of Alpine landscapes help to blur boundaries between the interior and surrounding natural mountains. Overlooking the Alpe di Siusi, the restaurant offers a sublime fusion of Alpine and Mediterranean experiences, while the world-class spa completes the Schgagulers' holistic conception.

Destination	Location	Rooms	Themes
Japan	Matsuyama	7	Countryside, Offbeat, Well-Being

Setouchi Retreat
by Onko Chishin

Where azure waters meet an infinite sky, Setouchi Retreat by Onko Chishin emerges as an exceptional fusion of architectural mastery and artistic expression. Conceived by legendary Japanese architect Tadao Ando, this seven-suite haven offers a living gallery experience, seamlessly intertwining contemporary art with minimalist luxury. Renowned artworks—from minimalist icon Frank Stella to rising local talents—create unique encounters throughout, each interpreting the philosophy of "surrendering to the blue sky and sea, finding stillness in calm." Luxurious spa treatments in two private suites overlook serene islands, complementing relaxation beside the iconic 30-meter infinity pool, a tranquil expanse merging harmoniously with Setouchi's lush treetops and distant coastline. The retreat's exquisite Japanese cuisine celebrates seasonal treasures from mountain and sea, further enriching the profound cultural sanctuary. Setouchi Retreat embodies refined hospitality, inviting discerning guests into an immersive artistic sanctuary designed for contemplation, renewal, and inspiration.

123

Destination	Location	Rooms	Themes
Switzerland	Zermatt	30	Mountain, Well-Being

The Omnia

The Omnia is a striking timber structure beneath Switzerland's preeminent four-thousander, the Matterhorn, with majestic views across the Visper Valley. Located above Zermatt among the clouds, the entrance to the hotel is dramatic and un-expected: guests approach on an electric trolley through a narrow tunnel in the side of the mountain. New York architect Ali Tayar designed the hotel in 2006, blending American modernism with European craftsmanship and local materials. Owner **Alexander Schärer** is also the founder of USM Haller, and custom furniture from the company lines the spaces. The layout encourages community, with several lounges featuring crackling fireplaces. In the restaurant, long tables allow guests to connect over comforting Alpine menus that the chefs develop seasonally. On top of world-class skiing and hiking, opportunities for recreation are available in the indoor/outdoor pool, Turkish bath caldarium, Finnish sauna, and outdoor whirlpool that looks out at the village and the striking planes of the Matterhorn.

Destination	Location	Rooms	Themes
France	Saint-Remy-de-Provence	9	Countryside, History, Offbeat

Hôtel de Tourrel

Margot Stängle and **Ralph Hüsgen's** Hôtel de Tourrel is housed in the impressive walls of a 17th-century private mansion in the Provence-Alpes-Côte d'Azur region. The couple undertook extensive historic restoration to redesign the nine rooms of this enchanting palais into nine spacious suites. While original features remain, such as stucco that the pair discovered and restored from under layers of paint, the duo instilled touches of midcentury and contemporary style into the residence. Interspersed throughout is furniture from the likes of Irish modernist designer Eileen Gray and contemporary German industrial designer Konstantin Grcic. The hotel's Michelin-starred Mediterranean Restaurant de Tourrel is also a highlight of any stay, with extensive rare and vintage wines and a fresh repertoire of regional produce. The hotel's pristine natural surroundings, including 34 nearby wine appellations and important historical sites, have a timeless appeal—as they were for Vincent van Gogh, who found healing as well as inspiration in the area's light and landscapes.

127

Destination	Location	Rooms	Themes
France	Montigny-la-Resle	10	Art & Culture, Countryside, Honeymoon, Sustainable

Château de la Resle

Château de la Resle is an ivy-clad 17th-century manor with the feel of a private home, situated in Burgundy's rolling countryside. Owner **Johan Bouman** transformed the château into a refined retreat with contemporary design touches, from neutral ceramics to sculptural furniture. Sweeping staircases, open fireplaces, and a striking tower complement chic, uncomplicated interiors adorned with works from Bouman's personal art collection. Guests can unwind in landscaped gardens, a heated outdoor pool, or the spa, complete with a sauna. The château is a short drive from wine villages like Chablis, but with its own vineyard and forest surroundings, there's little reason to leave. Set on five acres (two hectares), the château boasts glasshouses, orchards, and walking paths. Inside, modern furnishings highlight the building's original plasterwork and grand proportions. Every space feels curated yet welcoming, from the cozy library to the sun-drenched dining area. Whether relaxing by a fireplace or exploring the vineyards, guests experience both the culture and comforts of the countryside.

Destination
Italy

Location
Matera

Rooms
24

Themes
City, History, Offbeat

Sextantio Le Grotte della Civita

In Italy's south is Matera, a city famed for its UNESCO-listed network of limestone caves that have been occupied since the paleolithic era. A series of these long-abandoned dwellings, with their decaying stone walls and beautiful arches, have been reimagined as a hotel appealing to travelers enamored of history and authenticity. Local architects Sextantio carefully restored the series of hilltop stone caves into an elegant hotel that honors its multi-layered past, allowing guests to feel as if they have stepped back in time. The property's rooms are spacious and feature abundant light while still feeling secluded and snug. The designers employed local materials to create seating, beds, light fixtures, and bathtubs that blend into the architecture, for a stripped-back luxury based on the essentials. The result is a series of cozy, uniquely shaped, cavelike rooms that steep guests in the town's storied heritage.

Destination
Mexico

Location
San José del Cabo

Rooms
29

Themes
City, Well-Being

Destination
Italy

Location
Bolzano

Rooms
33

Themes
Art & Culture, City, Offbeat

Drift San Jose del Cabo

Drift invites guests to experience a design-forward boutique escape. Created by **Philip Bates** and designed by Rima, the 29-room property blends industrial minimalism with Mexican craftsmanship; think polished concrete with artisanal details. Preserving the original structure's character, its spaces feature sliding windows, scattered fruit trees, and built-in furniture. At Drift Kitchen + Mezcal Bar, guests can enjoy local fare, while weekly backyard gatherings foster a true sense of community. Here, visitors can connect to the region's spirit in style.

Hotel Greif

Hotel Greif balances tradition with modernity through Studio Boris Podrecca's 1993 renovation. The entrance—steel and glass framed by wood—introduces this centuries-old property, where **Franz Staffler's** vision comes to life. The 33 rooms feature Dolomite views and whirlpool baths. Antiques and restored items complement Italian textiles, Iranian carpets, and custom artworks. Wood floors and furnishings enhance the design. At Grifoncino Bar, guests can discover local wines and Bolzano's largest gin collection after exploring Italy's beautiful landscape.

Carlota

In the heart of UNESCO-listed Quito, the Carlota is a transformed 19th-century French-style residence and creative haven. Owners **Renato Solines** and **Veronica Reed** preserved the building's turn-of-the-century grandeur while infusing it with vibrant colors and rich patterns that nod to the city's diverse birdlife. As the country's first-ever LEED-certified hotel, the Carlota embraces sustainability through the use of solar energy, advanced water filtration, and natural ventilation. The interior courtyard functions as a lobby, connecting the entrance to the lush back patio, where a stone staircase rises against a Spanish-inspired wall garden. Guests can enjoy traditional Ecuadorian cuisine at the bistro or signature gin cocktails at the rooftop lounge alongside breathtaking views of the historic district. Steps from Independence Square and the Presidential Palace, this family-owned gem invites travelers to discover the treasures of one of Latin America's most enchanting locales.

Destination	Location	Rooms	Themes
Thailand	Phuket	185	Beach, Honeymoon, Sustainable, Well-Being

The Slate

Famed for its pristine beaches and balmy climate, the popular island of Phuket was once renowned for its tin mining industry. Paying homage to this lesser-known history, **Wichit Na-Ranong** and **Prakaikaew Na-Ranong's** The Slate embodies a Thai-style, industrial-chic aesthetic. Bill Bensley designed the hotel using recycled materials including reclaimed wood and aluminum, set in lush landscaped gardens. Suites feature polished timber floors and bursts of color in the form of handcrafted rugs, alongside luxe features like balcony bathtubs. A range of dining experiences is available, including all day dining at Tin Mine, Southern Thai cuisine at Black Ginger, and an open-fire grill and smokehouse at Rivet & Rebar. The on-site Thai cooking school and award-winning spa complete this total luxury experience.

Destination
United States

Location
Calistoga, CA

Rooms
50

Themes
City, Offbeat, Well-Being

Destination
Spain

Location
Las Palmas, San Bartolomé de Tirajana

Rooms
80

Themes
Adults Only, Beach, Sustainable, Well-Being

Dr. Wilkinson's Backyard Resort & Mineral Springs

Open since 1952, this northern Napa Valley classic has been reinvigorated by its owners, **Maki Nakamura Bara** and **Robert Kline,** and SB Architects, who sensitively updated the 50-room building. Featuring a neutral palette with pops of color, natural woods, and retro furniture, the hotel's spa and mineral-rich mud baths remain its beating heart. Outside, an emerald backyard with mountain views, swimming pool, and swings invites peacefulness, while custom picnic blankets and colorful Fermob chairs encourage guests to dine in the balmy Calistoga climate.

Bohemia Suites & Spa

In southern Gran Canaria, **Rembert Euling** envisioned this bohemian retreat above the Maspalomas dunes. Offering ocean-side luxury against a backdrop of volcanic peaks, its angular shutters mirror the dunes, filtering light into rooms featuring mahogany floors and olivewood furnishings. The hotel's communal spaces include a secluded wellness area with a vitality pool and multiple saunas, as well as the 360° Restaurant, where a futuristic, disc-like structure blurs the line between indoors and out. Jacuzzis and pools nestled in garden settings make for relaxed social spaces.

133

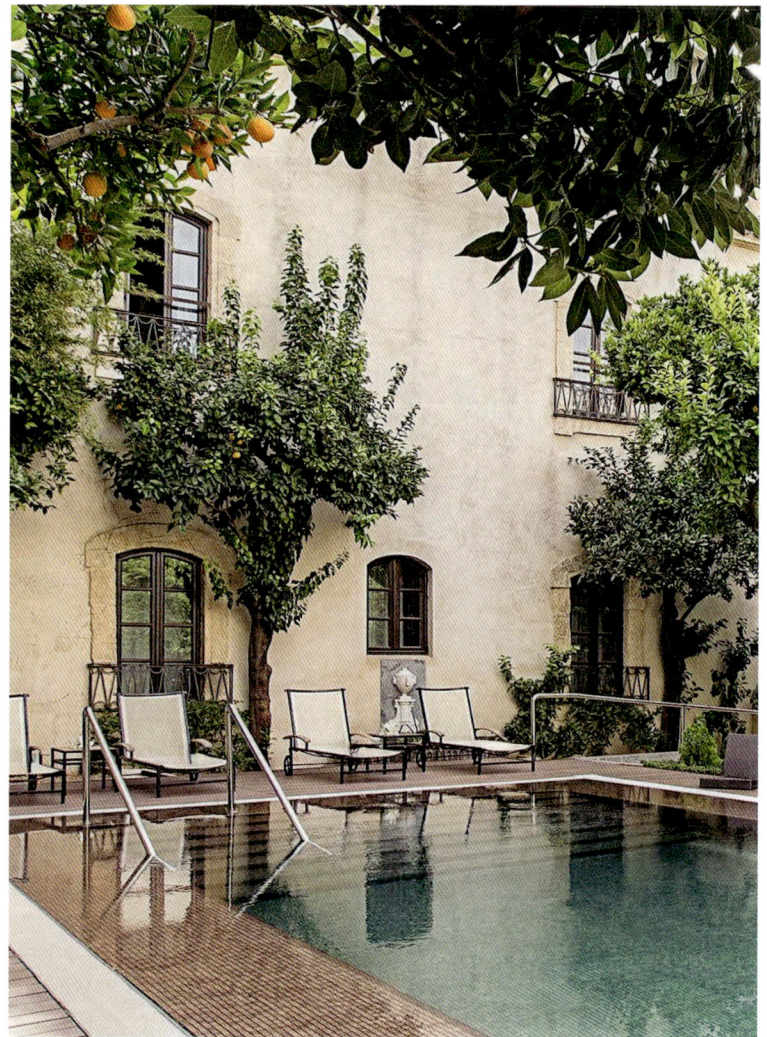

Destination
Switzerland

Location
Silvaplana, St. Moritz

Rooms
70

Themes
Gastronomy, Mountain

Destination
Spain

Location
Cordoba

Rooms
53

Themes
City, Gastronomy,
History, Sustainable

Nira Alpina

Nira Alpina was envisioned to appeal to independent travelers looking for an alternative Alpine experience. Its unique ski-in, ski-out accommodation provides quick and easy access to cable cars. Elsewhere, Hans Hirschi AG and Stricker Architekten designed the chic modern building with timber beams, polished glass, and local materials inside such as granite and animal-hide rugs. After the slopes, guests can visit Shanti Spa for holistic treatments, relax in light-filled rooms, and admire the landscape from spacious balconies and terraces.

Hospes Palacio del Bailío

Hospes Palacio del Bailío is a vision of modern luxury. Once a notable agrarian estate, the property fuses Roman, Moorish, and contemporary influences across a series of sites. A glass floor in the courtyard reveals ruins below, while restored frescos and a painted ceiling offer glimpses of the past. The Hospes Design Team, Barbara Chapartegui, and Tristán Domecq contrasts rich textures—champagne fabrics, dark walnut, and polished marble—with minimalist lines and floor-to-ceiling windows. The restaurant's fusion menu prepares traditional Andalusian flavors with global techniques.

Scribner's Catskill Lodge

Perched on a hillside in Hunter, New York, Scribner's Catskill Lodge is a reimagined mountain escape designed for all seasons. Originally a 1960s motor lodge, the property was brought back to life in 2016 by **Marc Chodock,** a former New York City resident seeking a deeper connection to nature. In collaboration with Post Company, the Lodge blends nostalgic charm with modern design, offering cozy guest rooms, communal spaces, and sweeping views of the Catskills. More recently, Scribner's expanded with The Rounds, twelve-sided cabins tucked just beyond the Lodge and nestled into the landscape. Designed for privacy and immersion, each Round features fireplaces, outdoor Japanese cedar soaking tubs, seasonal outdoor showers, and central skylights perfect for stargazing. Across both stays, guests can enjoy seasonal cuisine at Prospect, wind down fireside with s'mores, and explore nearby trails, all within a few miles of mountain peaks, ski slopes, and scenic outlooks.

Destination	Location	Rooms	Themes
Switzerland	Adelboden	72	Family-Friendly, Gastronomy, Mountain, Well-Being

The Cambrian

In the heart of Adelboden, The Cambrian redefines the Alpine escape—where modern design meets soaring peaks and cascading waterfalls. Rooted in the Welsh heritage of visionary **Grant Maunder,** the hotel brings a sense of warmth and understated ease to the Alps. Think natural textures, laid-back design, and a lobby lounge that spills out onto a sun-drenched terrace—fire pit included, where cocktails and fondue stretch long into the night. The spa opens out to a striking outdoor pool, heated for year-round swims and perfectly positioned for panoramic mountain views. Long soaks, slow afternoons, and something to sip—it's all part of the pace here. In the kitchen, chef patron Bryn Williams brings together Swiss produce and Welsh soul, creating seasonal dishes that are confident, considered, and deeply rooted in place. Whether it's powder days or wildflower hikes, The Cambrian delivers Alpine escape with style, soul, and a strong sense of place.

Destination	Location
Italy	Lezzeno, Lake Como

Rooms	Themes
34	Countryside, Gastronomy, Honeymoon, Well-Being

Filario Hotel & Residences

Rising from Lake Como's shoreline, Filario Hotel & Residences introduces contemporary Italian elegance to a landscape of timeless beauty. Owned by **Alessandro Sironi** and designed by Alessandro Agrati, this modern sanctuary transforms a former wire factory into a masterpiece of regional craftsmanship. Built with local Lombardy stone over five years, the structure harmonizes with its mountainside setting while offering unparalleled views from every private terrace. Inside, Agrati's vision celebrates Italian artisanship with furniture crafted by local makers from Cantù. Filario offers rarities along Lake Como's shores: a private beach with cabanas and a bar, an infinity pool, and a marina for water explorations. Culinary experiences at Restaurant Filo fuse Neapolitan flavors with regional influences, while Yeast Side serves gourmet pizza at the water's edge for a contemporary Italian experience in a picture-perfect setting.

Destination	Location	Rooms	Themes
Greece	Mykonos	160	Beach, Well-Being

Myconian Avaton

Rising from the rugged cliffs above Elia beach, Myconian Avaton strikes a harmonious balance between classic Cycladic architecture and contemporary style. Owned by the **Daktylides** family—irrepressible siblings **Vangelis, Panos, Markos,** and **Marios,** a veritable Mykonos hospitality clan—the 160-room property boasts breathtaking views over Mykonos's longest stretch of sand and the glittering Aegean Sea beyond. Inside, the design abounds with thoughtful contrasts: handcrafted wooden sinks meet sleek granite surfaces, while vintage pieces sit gracefully beside modern furnishings. Sunlit interiors, private pools, and Jacuzzis extend the invitation to rest and indulge, while the spa and open-air dining amplify the sense of escape. True to the vision of its owners, each element of the hotel feels both elevated and rooted in place. From its hillside perch, Myconian Avaton lulls guests into a magical and unmistakably Mykonian rhythm.

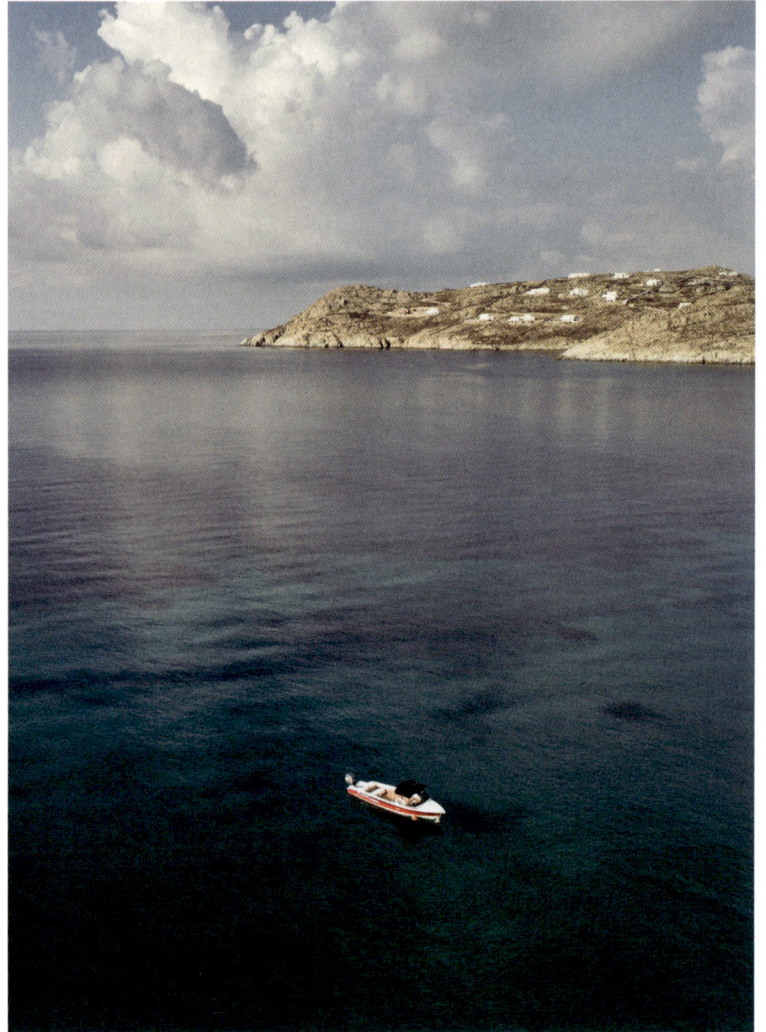

Destination	Location
Switzerland	Martigny

Rooms	Themes
50	City, Well-being

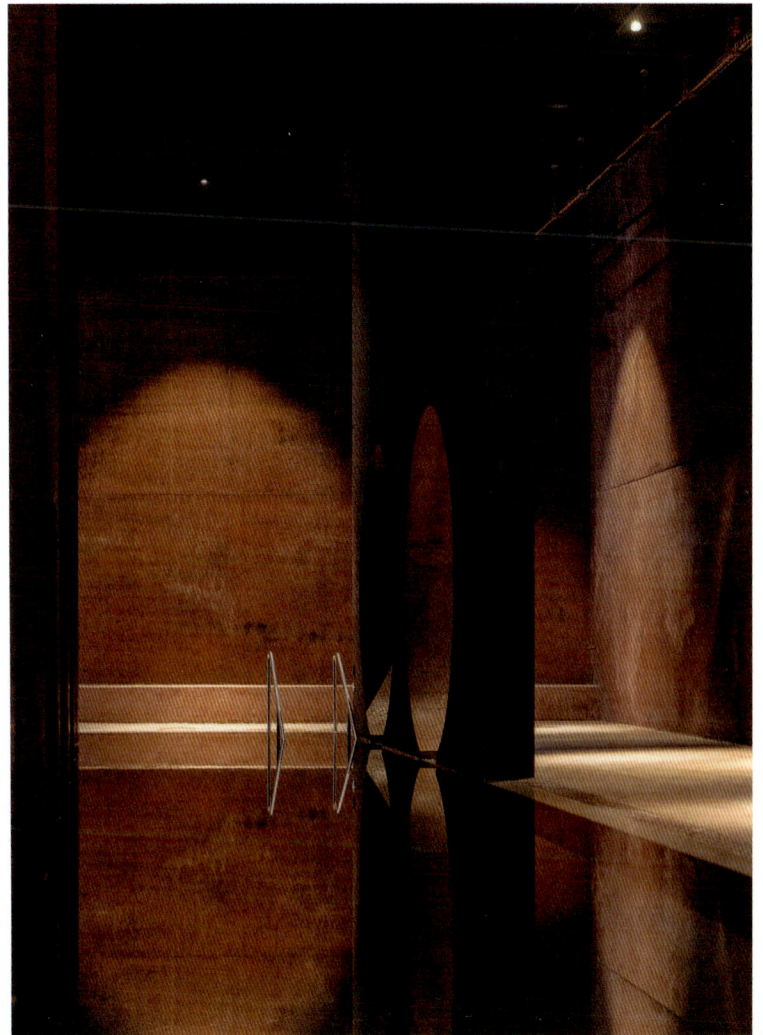

Hôtel Borsari

Industrial, midcentury modern, and Swiss and German influences inform the design of Hôtel Borsari. On the exterior, the hotel's Brutalist façade is composed of handmade deep red bricks. One side of the street façade is windowless apart from a half-moon opening, allowing the brickwork—sourced from British brick manufacturer York Handmade—to shine. The hotel is set in the historic town of Martigny in the southwest corner of Switzerland, which is home to several Gallo-Roman ruins, including three Roman bath houses. **John Cretton** employed a range of elements that nod to the history of the location, from rust-red brickwork referencing the wine caves that lie beneath the building to a cobblestone central courtyard evoking the region's Roman heritage. Hôtel Borsari's restaurant, 180, is named for the 180-kilometer radius from which the team sources its produce. The hotel is uniquely of its place, inviting guests to forge a deeper connection to the region.

Destination	Location
Georgia	Tbilisi

Rooms	Themes
62	City, History, Offbeat, Sustainable

Stamba Hotel

Lofty ceilings are met with towering bookshelves and sturdy brutalist beams in this former publishing house-turned-hotel. **Temur Ugulava** updated the expansive Soviet-era structure into a chic, book-laden space with the help of Collective Development. Now, it mirrors Tbilisi's thriving creative climate, drawing a dynamic, artistic crowd. The extensive library, which pays homage to the structure's history, softens the voluminous warehouse space, alongside slick timber floors, indoor greenery, and curated pieces of art and furniture. Collective Development's design repurposes original features, such as the former print-drying beam, which now supports foliage from the hotel's five-story-high atrium "jungle." Aligning with the hotel's industrial, inner-city aesthetic are a range of shops and eateries, including an artisanal chocolates and coffee store, Café Stamba, which offers farm-to-table dining with produce from its regenerative farm, Warehouse wine bar, and The Shop fashion store.

Destination	Location	Rooms	Themes
Indonesia	Lombok	20	Beach, Honeymoon, Offbeat, Well-Being

Somewhere Lombok

Cradled on Indonesia's Lombok Island, close to a beloved surf beach, Somewhere Lombok is a 20-room sanctuary where sustainable design meets barefoot luxury. Founders Claire and Valia Gontard have created a beach-chic retreat that celebrates local craftsmanship in harmony with the environment. The property's organic architecture boasts industrial materials alongside traditional Indonesian elements: geometric lines, wooden screens, and locally sourced materials define the spaces. Four rows of standalone villas appear to cascade down a steep landscape, each featuring a private plunge pool and open layout connecting them to the surrounding palms, mountains, and bay. The interiors, conceived by the Gontard sisters, showcase a thoughtfully curated collection of handmade design pieces: woven seagrass baskets, recycled textile rugs, and handcrafted pottery lamps alongside contemporary photography. Altogether, it provides a mindful, sustainable journey into Indonesian craft, culture, and landscape.

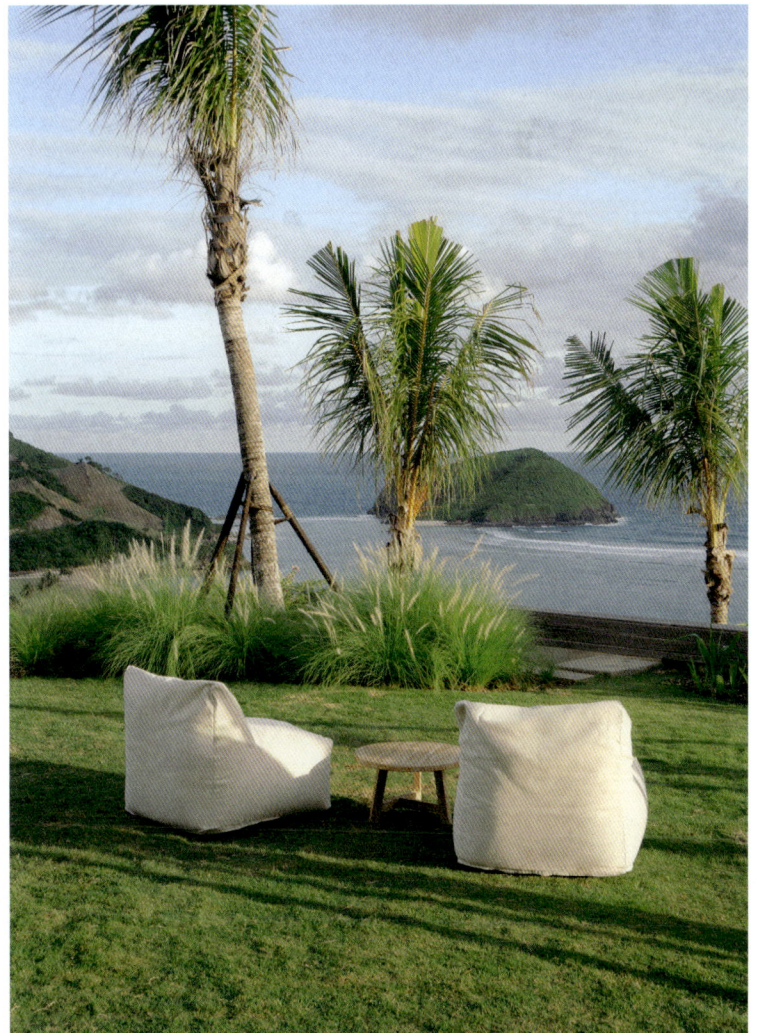

Esperanza Lake Resort

Nestled on the idyllic shores of Lake Ungurys Lake, Esperanza Lake Resort is a luxurious retreat amid the lush forests of Trakai, Lithuania. Originally built from 300-year-old Canadian cedar logs, this eco-conscious retreat has undergone major renovation to offer an authentic yet modern hotel experience. Each of the rooms and suites features natural materials, earthy tones, and expansive windows that frame captivating views of the lake or forest. Guests can indulge in the hotel's world-class spa, which includes an indoor pool, sauna, and steam room, as well as unique treatments like the horizontal shower and sand bed. Culinary delights await at the on-site restaurants, which serve fresh produce from the property's gardens. Just a 45-minute drive from Vilnius, Esperanza Lake Resort provides a restorative escape with tennis, fishing, and nature walks, appealing to both relaxation seekers and adventure enthusiasts alike.

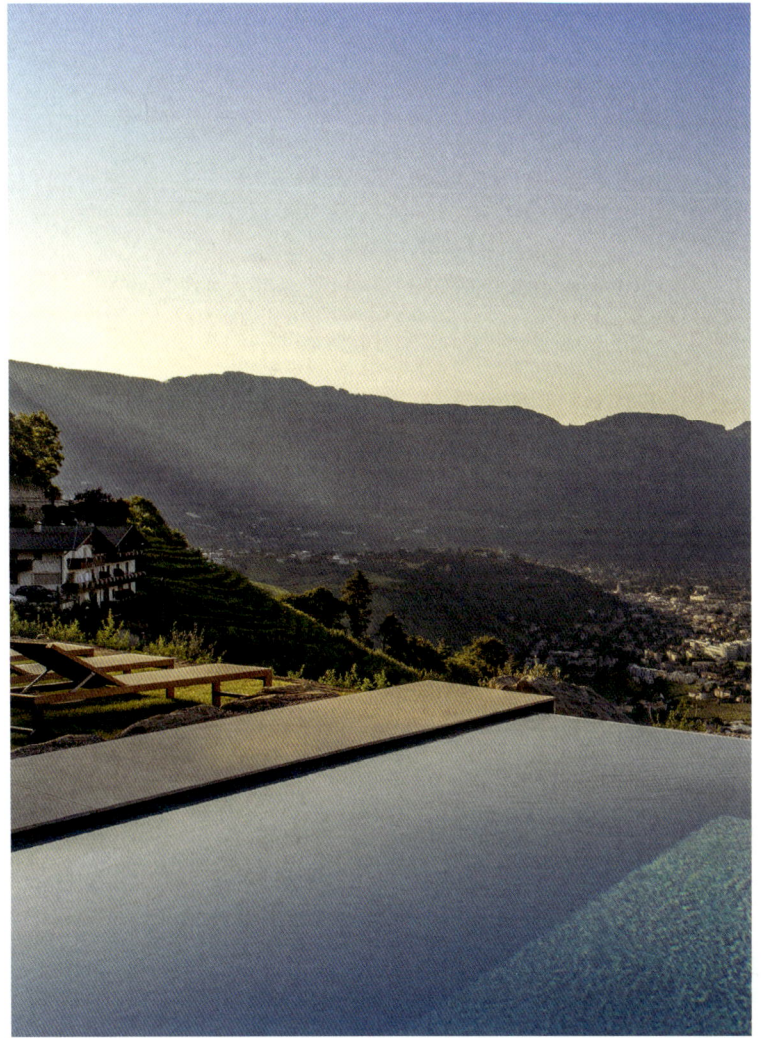

Destination
United States

Location
Encinitas, CA

Rooms
4

Themes
City, Sustainable, Well-Being

Destination
Italy

Location
Merano

Rooms
6

Themes
Countryside, Honeymoon,
Mountain, Well-Being

Twelve Senses Retreat

In 2019, owner **Anke Bodack** transformed her 1958 home into a hotel using sustainable materials. While the exterior is made from charred wood, the rooftop bar employs tiles made from ocean waste. Four guestrooms each follow a color scheme based on the four elements and feature Philippe Starck, Ethnicraft, and Lagos del Mundo design pieces. In terms of communal spaces, there's a library with Cappellini felt chairs and a Knoll marble table, while yoga, meditation, and reiki sessions taught inside bring guests together in this solar-powered hub.

Arua Private Spa Villas

While Arua Private Spa Villas's purpose may seem simple, its owners **Otto Mattivi** and **Johannes Gruss** have executed it with allure. Created by architect Wilfried Menz and designer Nicola Gallizia, the complex offers terraces overlooking the blissful Adige Valley. Culinary delights come courtesy of the hotel's on-site farm and its acclaimed Hidalgo and Aomi restaurants. The six spa villas are secluded, with heated pools, canopied terraces, and saunas. But the pièce de résistance is the infinity pool, which leaves guests floating in tranquillity.

Destination	Location	Rooms	Themes
Switzerland	Crans-Montana	19	Mountain, Sustainable

Chetzeron

Located 2,112 meters in the clouds at the world-renowned resort of Crans-Montana is an Alpine sanctuary offering an exclusive ski-in, ski-out experience. Owner **Sami Lamaa** collaborated with Actescollectifs Architects to create Chetzeron: a one-time gondola station transformed into a striking retreat that both integrates and boldly contrasts with its Alpine surroundings. Rooms and suites boast panoramic views stretching from the Matterhorn to Mont Blanc. The interior juxtaposes rough stone walls and concrete porticos with plush furnishings that embody modern Alpine luxury. Three terraced levels dotted with loungers encourage relaxation, while the restaurant serves refined mountain cuisine paired with Valais wines selected by Françoise Lamaa from the hotel's cellar. The wellness facilities provide post-slopes rejuvenation with an outdoor heated pool, steam room, and sauna. Therapist Szilvi—trained at the Centre for Ma-uri Healing Arts—offers massage treatments that complete this mountain sanctuary experience in one of Switzerland's best-loved ski spots.

Habita Monterrey

In northern Mexico, cofounders **Carlos Couturier** and **Moisés Micha** have crafted a sanctuary of minimal, midcentury charm. Their bold, curvilinear vision contrasts with Monterrey's colonial-style hotels, offering 39 rooms in a stark monochrome palette with subtle, vintage touches, and black-and-white photographs to match the overall cool-minimal aesthetic. Parisian designer Joseph Dirand's fittingly spare interiors put the focus on dining and lounging at the Lobby restaurant, where chef Gustavo Fernandez oversees culinary excellence amid magical city views. The rooftop terrace features dual infinity pools and sweeping 360-degree views of the Sierra Madre mountains. Here, global nomads can work and rest in serene tranquility. Beyond the hotel's walls, the bustling streets of Monterrey invite exploration of the city's rich history and vibrant culture.

Sextantio
Albergo Diffuso

Architects Sextantio provide guests with an authentic rural experience in this Abruzzo countryside hotel. Set within a medieval hilltop village across several historic buildings, the hotel references a bygone era with stripped-back luxury in beautiful, sparsely appointed spaces. Careful decisions ensure the hotel stays true to its past, while offering modern amenities—Sextantio painstakingly removed the stone floors to install under-floor heating, before carefully returning each stone to its original location. Rooms feature aged stone walls, wooden ceilings, fireplaces, carefully reproduced regional furniture, and freestanding curvilinear bathtubs. The dining room is similarly, gloriously rustic. Warmed by a fireplace beneath original arches, diners are treated to timeless regional cuisine. Guests can also enjoy massages, indoor and outdoor meditation, yoga, and pilates classes.

Destination	Location	Rooms	Themes
Iceland	Reykjavik	18	City, Gastronomy

ION City Hotel

Overlooking Reykjavik's charming rooftops and its ice-blue harbor, this modern showpiece reflects Ion Hotels founder Halldór Hafsteinsson's urban vision. The 18-room sibling to their award-winning countryside retreat carries the same spirit of adventure and clean Nordic design within a carefully renovated building. Minarc led the thoughtful renovation, preserving the structure's architectural character while introducing gunmetal grays and grained woods that shape organic spaces with crisp lines and local art. National references subtly surface in the design, including a custom "bird's nest" light suspended above reception. Sümac restaurant, among the country's most popular, reimagines Icelandic ingredients with bold influences from North Africa and the Levant. Reykjavik's compact center brims with culture, from first-class museums to smaller art galleries and a thriving live music scene, while day trips invite guests to explore lunar lava fields or venture out to sea for whale watching.

149

Destination	Location	Rooms	Themes
Spain	Port de Sóller, Mallorca	114	Adults Only, Beach, Countryside, Gastronomy, Interior Design, Well-Being

Bikini Island & Mountain Hotel Port de Sóller

Paradise awaits at the Bikini Island & Mountain Hotel Port de Sóller, an idyllic escape that captures the idiosyncratic essence of Mallorca. Revitalized from a 1970s Bauhaus-style hotel by Design Studio Dreimeta, in collaboration with Bikini visionary **Christian Zenka** and the original founders of 25hours Hotels, this gem channels laid-back elegance and the island's innate bohemian spirit. Handcrafted textiles, wooden tables, and vibrant rugs create an inviting atmosphere, welcoming guests to unwind in style. Neni Mallorca Port de Sóller offers delightful culinary experiences where eastern-Mediterranean flavors come alive, while the Pikkini and Donkey bars serve up refreshing drinks as day shifts to night. By day, the picturesque Port de Sóller beach boasts crystal-clear waters and hidden coves for swimming and snorkeling. For those seeking rejuvenation, the Santaverde Spa and outdoor yoga sessions with breathtaking bay views promise profound relaxation. A tranquil blend of comfort and charisma define this enchanting, dream-like retreat.

Destination	Location
Morocco	Marrakech

Rooms	Themes
5	City, History, Honeymoon

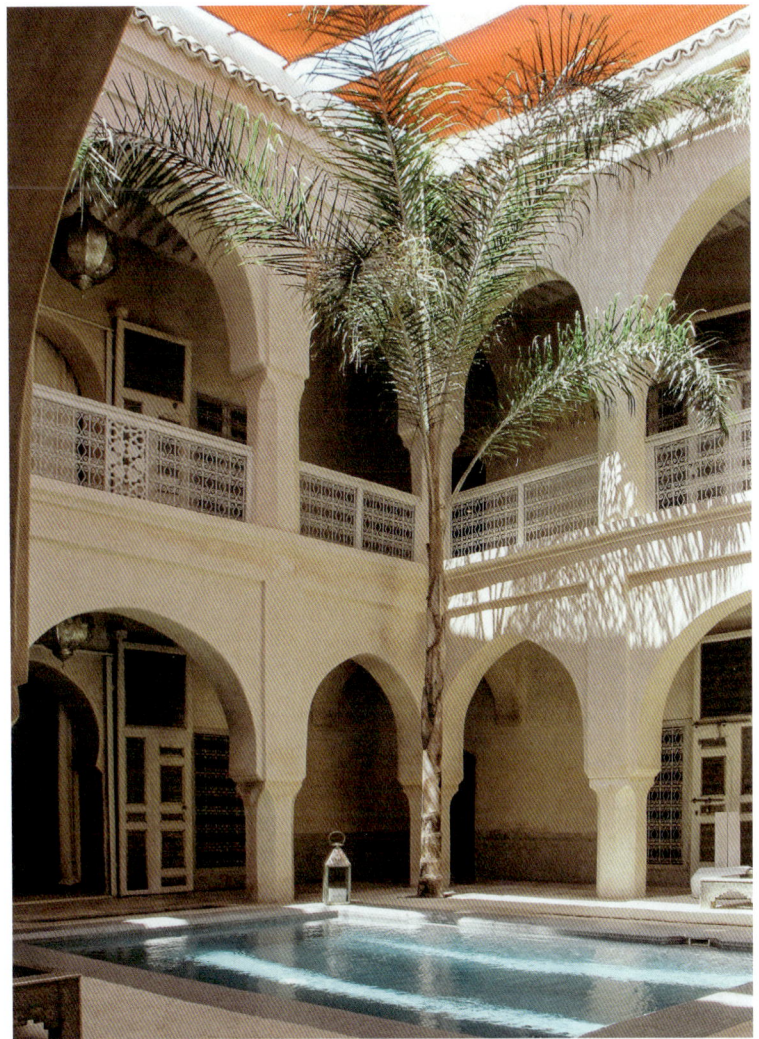

AnaYela

When German Original **Andrea Bury** found this 300-year-old former palace hidden among the lively hubbub of Marrakech's medina, her initial plan was to create a think tank for innovators. In 2008, she opened it as a hotel with her ex-husband Bernd Kolb instead, but the design and clientele continue to reflect Bury's original brief. Kolb executed the architectural plans, transforming it into an opulent hotel with the help of 100 local artisans. During construction, a handwritten manuscript was discovered in a hidden room that opened with the words "I am Yela," giving the hotel its name. A renowned Moroccan calligrapher chiseled the tale onto doors throughout the house, like the pages of a fantastical book. The hotel has just three rooms and two suites, providing a tailored experience for its lucky guests. A lush indoor courtyard provides respite from the flurry of the medina with the added luxury of a heated limestone pool. Alternatively, guests can relax on the rooftop terrace and enjoy views over the town, while on-site chef Kahdija prepares three-course meals from scratch each day.

Destination	Location	Rooms	Themes
Maldives	North Malé Atoll	110	Beach, Family-Friendly, Honeymoon, Sustainable, Well-Being

Patina Maldives, Fari Islands

Designed by **Marcio Kogan's** Studio MK27, Patina Maldives is a restful sanctuary that immerses guests in nature. Located in the Fari Islands, the resort is a testament to sustainable luxury, decorated with 16,800 transplanted trees and underpinned by a commitment to eliminating single-use plastics, including during construction. The design incorporates natural materials—wood, rattan, and stone—with works of visual art including a mesmerizing James Turrell *Skyspace* installation. Twelve unique dining concepts showcase culinary innovation, from the plant-based Roots to the Japanese-Nordic fusion at Kōen, each celebrating local and global flavors with organic ingredients. Beyond accommodation, Patina offers a holistic "Flow" wellness philosophy: the spa integrates therapeutic technologies with natural healing, offering experiences like couples' hammam beds, Watsu practice rooms, and contrast hydrotherapy. Here, every element, from architecture to cuisine to wellness, is crafted to amplify guests' connection to the natural world.

153

Destination	Location	Rooms	Themes
Greece	Crete	204	Beach, Family-Friendly, Gastronomy, Sustainable

Phāea Cretan Malia

An expansive pool hemmed by shaded sun loungers and potted plants is the centerpiece of Phāea Cretan Malia, a luxury hotel with extensive outdoor spaces that capitalize on the abundant Cretan sun. Greek architect Antonis Stylianides—who once worked with Bauhaus founder Walter Gropius—constructed the modernist buildings in 1980. In 2018, local sisters **Agapi** and **Costantza Sbokou** commissioned architect Vana Pernari Architecture Studio to entirely renovate the property. Their goal was to offer an authentic experience for guests and families that would provide a luxury, sustainable experience removed from commercial mass tourism. Pernari's design draws on an assortment of colors, materials, and stylistic eras, creating accommodation that stays true to its Cretan identity while still feeling like a home away from home. Surrounded by an ample garden featuring swaying palms, Indian figs, and banana trees, the hotel is awash with local delights; the four restaurants encourage an immersion into local life through food grown in the property's organic garden.

Zuri Zanzibar

Along Zanzibar's pristine coastline, Zuri reimagines tropical hospitality with a village-inspired retreat designed by Jestico + Whiles. Owned by **Vaclav Dejcmar,** Zuri's 56 bungalows embrace ecological sensitivity with an African-chic aesthetic along 300 meters of private beachfront. Inspired by the design and layout of traditional villages, the accommodations unfold across a lush garden. Thatched roofs, palm trees, and thoughtfully placed bungalows create intimate spaces cooled by incoming sea breezes. Natural materials celebrate local craftsmanship: polished woods, 1960s-inspired furniture, and artifacts from local markets weave together past and present, local and international. Culinary experiences reflect this approach, with a kaleidoscope of European, African, Arabic, and Indian flavors that transform each meal into a journey. Sustainability is at the heart of Zuri's ethos, with initiatives supporting environmental conservation and community development.

Rooms Kazbegi

Large windows look across lush green forest and soaring mountains in **Temur Ugulava's** Rooms Kazbegi. Fashioned from steel, glass, and timber, the hotel's building is a striking, geometric punctuation in the landscape. The interiors reflect a modern rustic sensibility, drawing on the country's Asian and European heritage. Warm, natural textures and colors soften the rooms. Communal spaces feature an abundance of timber furniture and raw wood floors, indigenous rugs, books, and comfortable sofas, creating spaces that invite guests to relax anywhere. Local inspiration continues into the hotel's restaurant. Here, the mountain setting informs a menu that balances traditional Georgian recipes with European fare. There is plenty to enjoy, whether on-site in the heated indoor pool or on tours with a local guide through the rolling hills, either on horseback, or following in the footsteps of spiritual pilgrims.

Destination
Thailand

Location
Phuket

Rooms
95

Themes
Beach, Honeymoon, Offbeat,
Sustainable, Well-Being

Destination
Spain

Location
Maspalomas, Gran Canaria

Rooms
328

Themes
Beach, Family-Friendly, Sustainable

The Naka Phuket

Duangrit Bunnag, Sompong Dowpiset,
and **Thaveesakdi Phucharoen** created
The Naka Phuket with nature and sustainability at the fore. The hotel is a tropical escape with panoramic views of the
sparkling Andaman Sea. Visitors are
welcomed by a pagoda-style reception,
soon becoming entranced by the building's combination of glass, greenery,
timber, and concrete. Eschewing traditional bungalows or high-rise architecture,
Bunnag instead opted for a cantilevered
village of stone-and-glass villas featuring
rich timber floors, impressive views, and
private pools.

Seaside Palm Beach

Seaside Palm Beach, owned by **Theo
Gerlach,** is a grand building inspired
by Miami. Parisian architect and designer
Alberto Pinto took a retro approach to
the hotel aesthetic, using bright colors
to enliven the property. Hence, the white
lobby vies with Mies van der Rohe's
iconic Barcelona chairs and red vinyl
ottomans. In the guestrooms, the beige,
brown, and apricot palette takes its origin
from the 1970s. Add in the delectable
Esencia restaurant, pools, a tennis court,
a salt cave, a sauna, a golf course, and
a gym, and the end product is inimitable.

Destination
Mexico

Location
Oaxaca

Rooms
16

Themes
City, Gastronomy, Well-Being

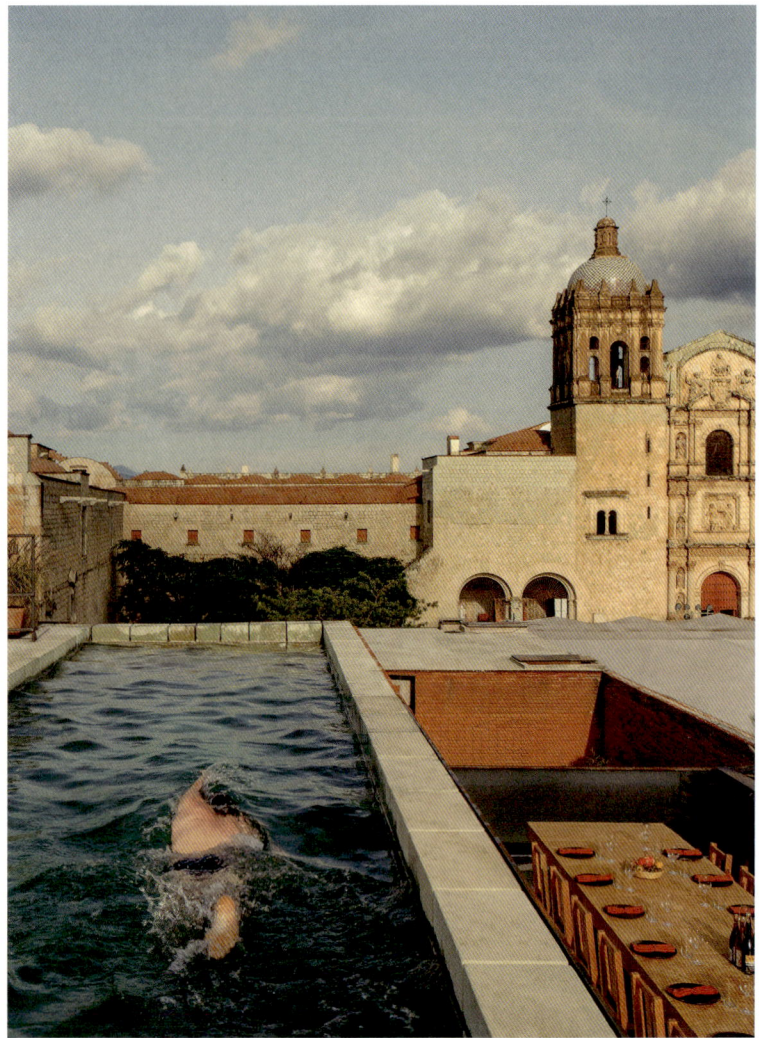

Otro Oaxaca

Oaxacan hospitality, cuisine, and craft-manship come to the fore at Otro Oaxaca. Celebrated local creative João Boto Caeiro of RootStudio designed the building for **Carlos Couturier** and **Moisés Micha,** hewing to the duo's eternal prioritization of local culture. The floorplan of the nearby UNESCO World Heritage Site of Mitla inspired Boto Caeiro's design, which centers around a cross-shaped walkway. Reclaimed wood and board-formed concrete with a distinctly wooden grain pattern complement the building's brickwork walls and limestone rooftop. A sleek 20-foot pool and comfortable lounges sit atop the building, boasting sweeping views of the centuries-old Santo Domingo Church. The hotel aims to embed guests in the authentic local landscape of Oaxaca, while also providing a luxurious experience through amenities such as the subterranean spa, traditional slow cuisine underneath shady trees at Otro restaurant, and a ground level hybrid co-working and cultural event space.

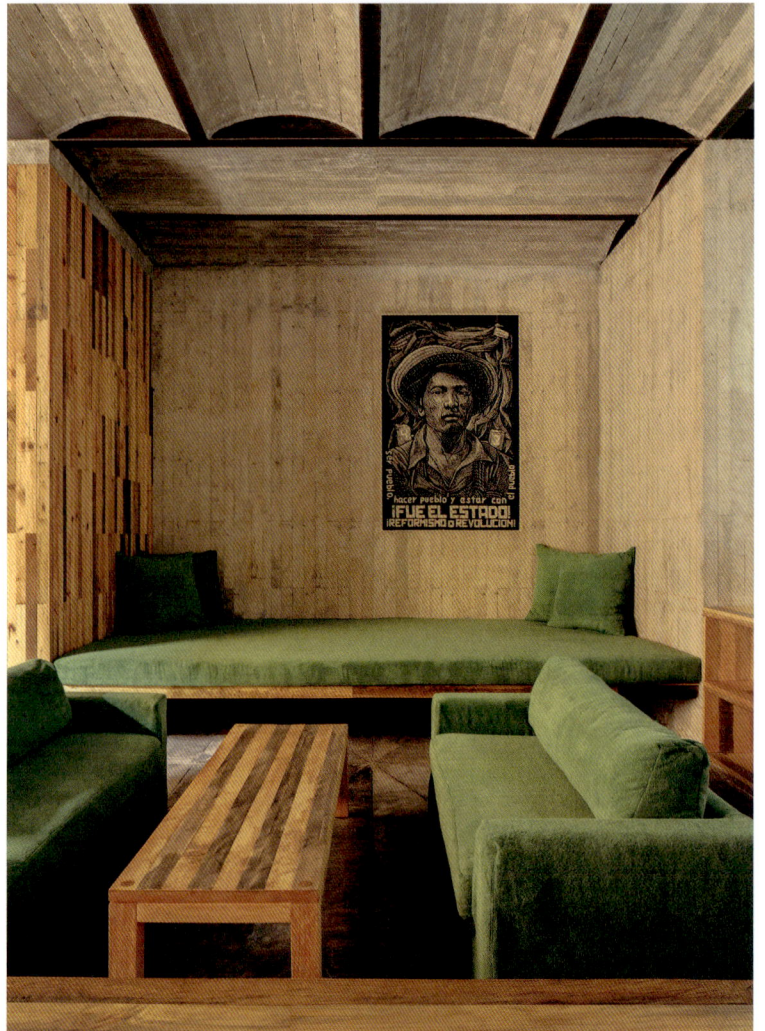

Destination
Mexico

Location
La Paz, Baja California Sur

Rooms
32

Themes
Beach, History

Baja Club

This classic Mexican mission-style hacienda is a breezy gateway to Malecón, the historic seafront promenade of La Paz. **Carlos Couturier** and **Moises Micha** commissioned Max von Werz Arquitectos and Jaune Architecture to update the traditional 1910 villa with a modern five-story extension. The resulting waterfront oasis, punctuated with patios and gardens, sees retro charm infused with contemporary luxury amenities. The hotel takes material inspiration from the house of renowned architect Luis Barragán in Mexico City, known for its use of light, natural materials, and bold colors. In communal spaces, lofty ceilings impart a sense of expansive openness, while glossy wine-red tiles, terrazzo, timber furniture, and ornamental iron accents create a welcoming atmosphere in colonial-era style. The red and green palette is reminiscent of Mexican earthenware, while modern touches are apparent everywhere, notably the museum-worthy spiral staircase that winds up from pool level. At once historic yet polished, Baja Club is a tranquil haven at the heart of buzzing La Paz.

Destination	Location	Rooms	Themes
Austria	Bad Gastein	70	Family-Friendly, Interior Design, Mountain, Sustainable, Well-Being

the cōmodo

Perched in the sleepy village of Bad Gastein, elevated at 1,000 meters, is the cōmodo by **Barbara Elwardt** and **Piotr Wisniewski.** This midcentury-modern inspired retreat, reborn from a historic 1881 clinic, strikes the ideal balance between artistic expression and natural beauty in a destination increasingly dubbed "the next Berlin." Its design evokes the 1960s with rich wine and bottle-green hues alongside terrazzo floors, while panoramic windows frame Alpine vistas. Custom furniture, wood flooring, and organic textiles honor both the region's heritage and its contemporary renaissance. Culinary offerings showcase farm-to-table Austrian cuisine under the guidance of chef Max Jensen, while the bar serves classic drinks and Winzersekt from small-batch vineyards. The wellness center harnesses the legendary healing properties of Gastein's thermal waters with two saunas, an indoor pool, and treatments that continue the area's long tradition as a haven for travelers seeking nature's restorative power.

Destination	Location	Rooms	Themes
Thailand	Phang Nag	34	Beach, Well-Being

Casa de La Flora

Along a pristine white sand beach, Casa de la Flora's geometric villas mix Brutalist architecture with tropical tranquility. The angular white structures by VaSLab Architecture, framed by lush topiary, invoke Le Corbusier. Each villa features its own pool, patio, or balcony, with oversized windows creating a sense of flow between interior and exterior. The concrete façades are softened by minimalist interiors warmed by teak wood accents and monochromatic lighting. At Spa La Casa, treatments harness the healing powers of the local mineral-rich water, combining aromatic oils and marine ingredients with holistic techniques. Nearby, La Aranya restaurant serves international cuisine with Thai influences. Offering sublime privacy, this architectural gem nonetheless sits just five minutes from Khao Lak's center. **Sompong Dowpiset's** vision delivers rest and relaxation amid cutting-edge design that pays homage to modernist principles and Thailand's natural beauty.

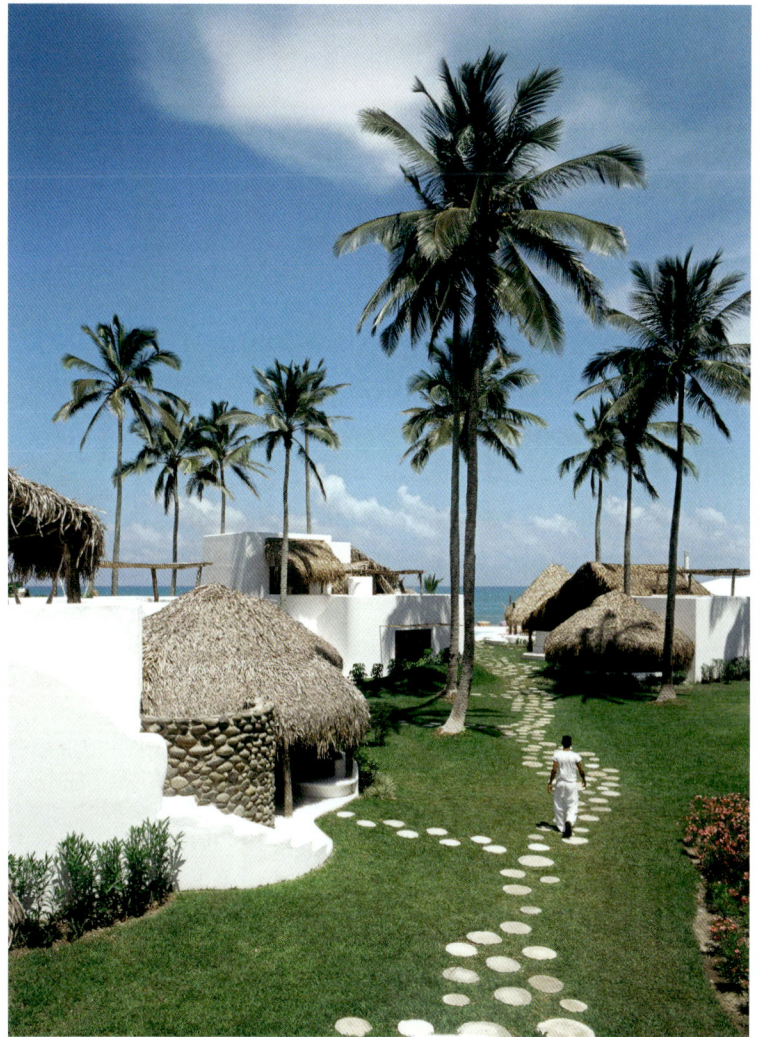

Destination
Spain

Location
Pollença, Mallorca

Rooms
35

Themes
Adults Only, Beach, Well-Being

Destination
Mexico

Location
Monte Gordo

Rooms
20

Themes
Adults Only, Beach, Honeymoon, Well-Being

El Vicenç de la Mar

An intimate hideaway, El Vicenç de la Mar invites guests to unwind with pools, a rooftop bar, a spa, an award-winning menu, and a movie theater. Designed by Rafael Balaguer, the building blends modern angles with natural textures. Inside, owner and designer Magnus Ehrland has created a soothing space with earth tones and soft textiles. Spacious rooms—some with private pools—have terraces, and the penthouse suite offers panoramic views and privacy. All of this is located in a part of Mallorca known for its crystal-clear waters, hiking trails, and majestic mountains.

Azúcar

Azúcar, meaning "sugar" in Spanish, is a seaside retreat built from wood reclaimed by **Carlos Couturier** after a flood as well as stone. Along with **Moisés Micha,** Couturier paired the timber with a light palette to create eco-minded, relaxing guest rooms. Palapa-style thatched roofs and a palm-lined stone pathway forge an idyllic ambience at this Emerald Coast haven. Taller de Arquitectura's tropical and ranch-style architecture features minimal, quirky elements such as curved, in-built furniture that enhance the hotel's organic, ecological focus.

163

Immerso Hotel

Nestled in the surfing paradise of Ericeira, Immerso Hotel is the area's first world-class accommodation. The vision of owner **Alexandra Almeida d'Eça,** this remarkable retreat harmonizes with its natural surroundings while offering sophisticated luxury just a short journey from Lisbon. The property features thoughtfully designed rooms where custom furniture, local artwork, and handcrafted textiles are arranged beneath wave-inspired vaulted ceilings. Each room draws the eye toward camera-shaped windows that frame the breathtaking coastal landscape. The Emme restaurant celebrates regional flavors with fresh, straightforward cuisine utilizing organic local ingredients, while the spacious bar offers signature cocktails with panoramic valley and sea views. The grounds include walking paths, a sculpture park, two pools, a yoga deck overlooking the ocean, and an outdoor fire pit. The fully equipped spa and gym complete this tranquil coastal sanctuary, which embodies the spirit of Portugal's top surfing destination while remaining blissfully sheltered from the outside world.

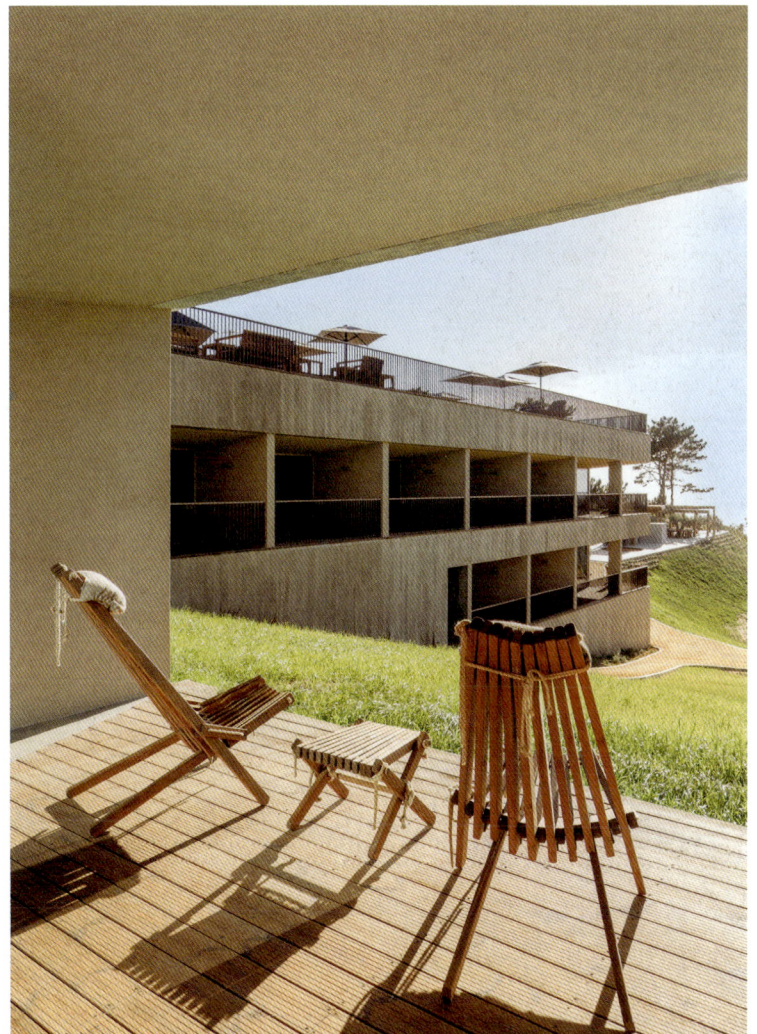

From Arrival to Departure:

Alexis Dornier

The Hotel as Cinematic Gesamt-kunstwerk

Inspired by the sets of classic films, the German-born architect Alexis Dornier choreographs immersive hospitality environments built to orchestrate emotion, etch lasting memories, and evoke deeper levels of meaning.

My architectural education began with the diagram, a tool I acquired during my time at the Office for Metropolitan Architecture. Diagrams allow for the translation of complex ideas into precise spatial forms. They offer clarity, but they also imply narrative. In parallel, my early emotional engagement with space came through cinema. I was captivated by the work of Ken Adam, whose expressive set designs for the James Bond films demonstrated how architecture could carry atmosphere, intention, and drama. These two forces— rigorous conceptual thinking and a cinematic approach to storytelling—continue to shape my design approach today.

This is where the idea of the Gesamt-kunstwerk, a German term translated as "total work of art", becomes, for me, a powerful one, resulting in the synthesis of architecture, interiors, landscape, and furniture into a single, emotionally

cohesive expression. After all, in hospitality, architecture must be more than merely functional. It must play host to an experience. When every detail speaks the same language, a guest's stay becomes immersive, intuitive, and lasting. An example that I was involved in is Lost Lindenberg in Bali, a hotel we designed as a kind of vertical jungle. Its blackened timber towers emerge from the landscape, replete with elevated living spaces that float among the trees. From the curvature of the staircases to the tactile transitions underfoot, every choice contributes to a sense of spacial unity.

And that, fundamentally, is how I conceive of hospitality architecture. Since hotel guests inhabit a space only briefly, designing for temporality becomes critical. You have limited time to make an impression, and that impression must be choreographed. Light at a particular hour, the way a corridor opens into a communal area, or how materials shift from one zone to another are not only decorative gestures, they are emotional cues. At one property, for example, we created tight passageways before opening up to soaring spaces to heighten the contrast. Elsewhere, we modulated light

Alexis Dornier

levels to shift the mood. These transitions are not always consciously noticed, but they are felt and they do shape memory in subtle, lasting ways.

To put it succinctly, architecture is arguably a kind of storytelling process. It is a language of contrast and rhythm. Light and shadow are punctuation, materials are tone. A rough-cut stone wall may evoke images of volcanic terrain. A woven surface might echo a local craft. These references are not always literal, but they help a space resonate more deeply with guests. I often think about how a guest enters a building, not just physically but *psychologically*. For instance, in one project I worked on, the entry was a narrow garden path. This forced a deceleration, a moment of stillness and awareness, before guests arrived in the interior. That spatial sequence created a kind of prelude, an emotional cue that framed everything that followed.

These techniques create a narrative, and working in natural settings can enhance them. Nature has its own drama and rhythm. We don't try to compete with it or reduce it to a backdrop; we collaborate with it. At Lulu Villas in Bali, we worked with the rawness of the jungle, shaping breezeways to channel wind and light, using water to reflect and soften, and designing with materials that age and shift over time. The goal wasn't perfection but presence—a space that breathes, adapts, and invites deeper engagement with its environment.

Ultimately, architecture in hospitality is concerned with how buildings are experienced—how they guide, surprise, comfort, and linger. It's about creating spaces that feel alive and help others feel more alive within them.

Alexis Dornier is a German-born architect based in Bali whose work explores the intersection of nature, structure, and narrative. Trained in Berlin and shaped by his early experience at the world-famous Office for Metropolitan Architecture, his practice is defined by a cinematic approach to space, where architecture becomes a vehicle for storytelling. Known for his holistic vision and Gesamtkunstwerk philosophy, Dornier designs hotels, homes, and cultural spaces that offer not only shelter and comfort, but also a rich, immersive experience.

169

Rooms Batumi

Draped in leafy vines and punctuated by blue shutters, Rooms Batumi's striking white Soviet-era façade stands out among the historic masonry and cobblestone streets of the coastal city's Old Town. Quiet luxury shines in the hotel, harnessing inspiration from the building's past as a 19th-century hotel. Collective Development and Rooms Studio collaborated on the design, with the result of a 1970s-style fitout that takes cues from Japanese, European, and Californian influences. The palette combines natural wood with white, yellow, blue, and baby pink hues to cultivate a welcoming atmosphere. The grand building boasts an internal palm-filled courtyard, hemmed by timber and glass to create a relaxing oasis at the heart of the hotel. Next to a sun-kissed rooftop pool, The Kitchen restaurant serves up seafood and vegetarian dishes sourced from local producers, while the Rubber Duck eatery merges Georgian gastronomy with international influences.

Destination	Location	Rooms	Themes
Portugal	Manteigas	20	Honeymoon, Mountain, Offbeat, Well-Being

Casa de São Lourenço

Perched high among the Serra de Estrela Mountain range, with sweeping views of Portugal's largest natural park, is Casa de São Lourenço. Porto-born modernist architect Rogério de Azevedo designed the original granite, schist stone, and timber eaves hotel in the 1940s. Under the direction of owners **Isabel Costa** and **João Tomás,** architects Paulo Costa and Patrícia Marques redesigned and enlarged the construction, adding full-height windows, balconies, and a concrete extension to the south. The minimalist design underlines the hotel's exceptional views from its 1250-meter-high vantage point, providing a refined escape from cold winters, or a base for walking curated hikes in the mild summers. Regional references are paramount, such as locally produced sheep's wool textures and artwork and furniture by 20th-century Portuguese artist Maria Keil. The owners' interest in regional histories is exemplified by another project of theirs in the valley which aims to keep the traditional Burel wool-making process alive. In the hotel restaurant, Chef Manuel Figueira keeps to the local theme with reinterpreted regional recipes using seasonal produce.

173

La Maison Palmier

La Maison Palmier is a pioneering boutique hotel in Abidjan, located in the tranquil Les Deux Plateaux neighborhood. This tropical sanctuary reimagines contemporary design with a vintage feel, featuring nine low-slung structures embraced by 200 palm trees and lush greenery. The hotel blends sophisticated design—terrazzo floors, neutral linens, and carpets in earthy reds and greens—with local artistic influences. Each space tells a story of bygone elegance through modern design, from garden-view rooms with wood paneling to a sparkling green marble pool. Le Bistro Palmier, led by chef Matthieu Gasnier, offers a culinary journey through seasonal ingredients, while Le Bar has become an Abidjan hotspot, serving innovative cocktails and beckoning guests into its vibrant atmosphere. Beyond its design and dining, La Maison Palmier is a trailblazer in the Ivory Coast's emerging luxury hospitality scene, inviting travelers to experience the character of modern Abidjan.

Iniala Beach House

Along the unspoiled stretches of Natai Beach in Phang Nga, Iniala Beach House is a radical expression of design, privacy, and Thai culture. The vision of **Mark Weingard** and architect Graham Lamb, the property brings together ten world-renowned designers to create an extraordinary ensemble of four villas, a penthouse, and five one-bedroom suites. Each space is a singular work of art, from the Campana Brothers' jungle-inspired private cinema to Jaime Hayon's sculptural interiors and the Collector's Villa, a homage to Thai tradition crafted by four design legends. Locally sourced teak, rattan, and coconut skin form the textural foundation of this "living gallery," where custom furniture, artworks, and architectural accents spark curiosity. Gastronomy is equally visionary, with pop-up dinners by elite chefs and immersive Thai cooking experiences. Beyond a resort, Iniala Beach House is a rare intersection of design, culture, and hospitality, where each moment and detail is carefully considered.

Destination	Location	Rooms	Themes
Mauritius	Palmar Belle Mare	59	Adults Only, Beach, Interior Design, Sustainable, Well-Being

Salt of Palmar

The vivid colors of SALT of Palmar are perfectly aligned with those of Mauritius itself—turquoise waters, powdery white sand, rainbows of fruits and vegetables at the local markets, and cobalt blue skies. Passionate hotelier **Paul Jones** moved to Mauritius in 1975 to bring the hotel to life, with the goal of giving visitors a transformative experience outside of the daily routine. Originally built by Jean-François Adam, artist Camille Walala—famed for her irreverent use of color and geometry—re-designed the interiors. The result is a boutique hotel that brims with positivity. In the central courtyard, black-and-white striped columns mirror the monochrome-tiled pool to entrancing effect. Food is a focus of the hotel and staff take guests on visits to the markets to experience local produce and beverages. The hotel's restaurant, The Good Kitchen, embraces fresh seafood and local vegetables—stalwarts of Mauritian cuisine.

177

Destination	Location	Rooms	Themes
Greece	Tinos	3	Adults Only, Countryside, Gastronomy, Honeymoon, Well-Being

Pnoēs Tinos

Located on the enchanting Tinos Island in the Cyclades, just a short boat ride from Mykonos, Pnoēs is a three-villa sanctuary designed by celebrated Greek architect **Aristides Dallas.** This extraordinary retreat embodies a profound connection with the elements, soundtracked by nearby rippling water and rustling olive trees. The custom-crafted villas mix contemporary architecture with traditional Greek craftsmanship: minimal steel and wood details complement stone walls and lime-washed surfaces, forging spaces that breathe with the surrounding landscape. Private pools extend toward the horizon, softening architectural volumes and inviting tranquil contemplation beside organic gardens. Each villa features bespoke furnishings by local artisans, with warm neutrals, natural fabrics, and earthy wooden décor alongside sculptures and ceramics. En-suite bathrooms echo traditional hammam design, with smooth, continuous surfaces that envelop guests in a feeling of boundless luxury in tune with the hotel's oasis feel.

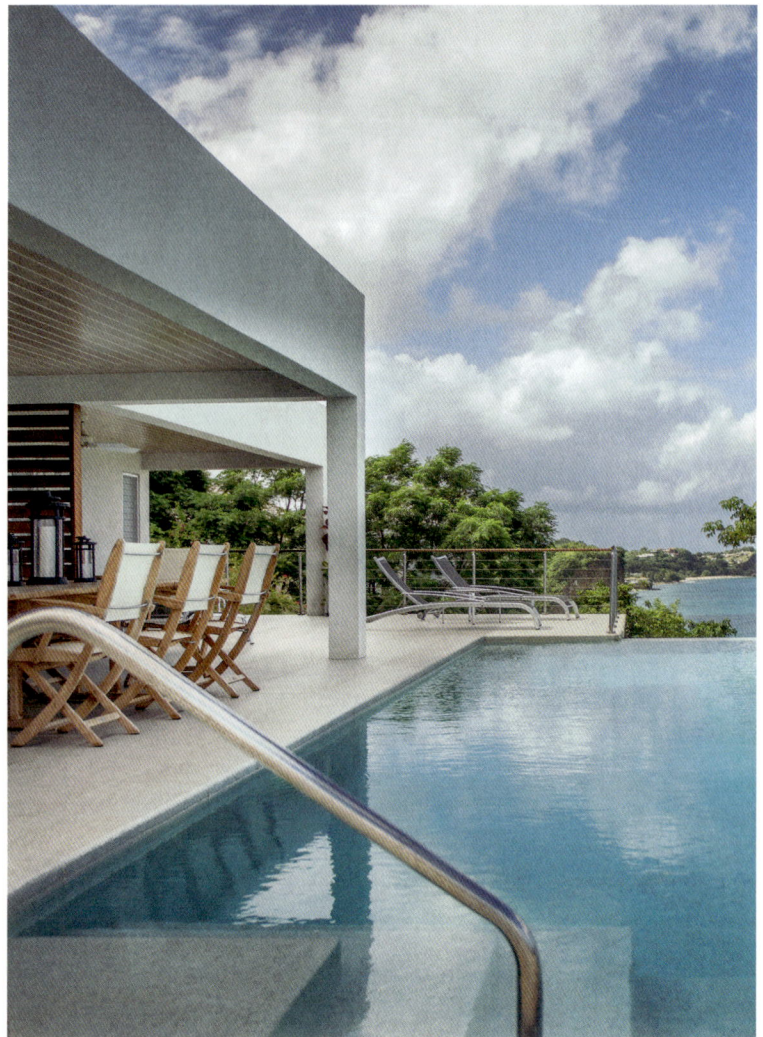

Destination
Portugal

Location
Sagres

Rooms
145

Themes
Beach, Sustainable

Destination
Grenada

Location
St. George's

Rooms
16

Themes
Adults Only, Beach,
Honeymoon, Well-Being

Memmo Baleeira

At Portugal's southwestern tip, **Rodrigo Machaz** has reimagined this 1960s seaside hotel into Memmo Baleeira, a minimalist retreat. Restored in 2007, the 145-room property features pared-back interiors in neutral tones and clean lines that let the Atlantic light in. Decorative elements are deliberately restrained; the view does the work. Machaz preserved structural elements, grounding the renovation in memory and place. A surf school, spa, and sunlit communal areas complete the experience, with the result being calm, contemporary, and invigorating.

LaLuna

Inspired by a Caribbean sailing trip, former fashion designer **Bernardo Bertucci** and his wife **Wendy** created a retreat in Grenada to celebrate their love of the island. Mixing elements of Caribbean, Balinese, and Italian design, interior designers Carmelina Santoro and Gabriella Giuntoli fashioned nautical villas and cottages with thatched roofs and four-poster beds. Sprinkled across a lush coastal hillside, the hotel features plunge pools, Italian and Caribbean cuisine and a deluxe pool overlooking the beach. Guests can also explore the LaLuna's Art Project, which features local exhibitions.

Destination	Location	Rooms	Themes
Cyprus	Paphos	187	Beach, Family-Friendly, Gastronomy, Sustainable, Well-Being

Almyra

The white walls of **Thanos Michaelides'** Almyra hotel are set within eight sprawling acres (3.2 hectares) of oceanfront garden on Cyprus's southwest coast. Inhabited since Neolithic times, Paphos is rich with ancient history, boasting several sites relating to the goddess Aphrodite. J + A Philippou Architects renovated the hotel's terraces, while Parisian designer Joelle Pléot took inspiration from the goddess of love and beauty to design interiors with natural materials, glass, and Carrara marble. Local, artisanal wooden, silk, and leather pieces abound in the standalone Kyma rooms, which sit seaside looking out to the azure horizon. Fresh seafood and Cypriot dishes take center stage at Ouzeri, while Asian-Mediterranean fusion is served at Notios. A spa, freshwater pool, and wine tours complete the experience.

Noūs Santorini

Part of **Dakis Jouannou's** impressive hotel portfolio, this gorgeous hotel, designed by Divercity Architects and MPlusMArchitects, feels like a private oasis on its own island. Yoga, a naturalist garden, and a convivial fire pit all put well-being at the heart of guests' stay. Noūs Santorini's standalone structures, unified by burnt timber cladding, organically follow the natural slope of the ground, inspired by local architectural techniques and the island's volcanic landscape. Guestrooms draw their color palette from the earthy, red, and gray hues of the island's famous beaches. The spa takes a holistic approach with five treatment rooms offering tailored mind-body experiences, while the Signature restaurant showcases the simplicity of Greek cuisine with fresh, local products alongside the Pool Restaurant and Vitamin Bar.

Destination	Location	Rooms	Themes
Iceland	Selfoss	66	Countryside, Honeymoon, Offbeat, Sustainable

ION Adventure Hotel

Once a workers' inn for a geothermal power plant, **Halldór Hafsteinsson** acquired the building of this Icelandic escape in 2011. With the assistance of American design studio Minarc, Hafsteinsson redesigned the space and added a prefabricated wing that exceeds environmentally safe building standards. Set in an isolated region an hour east of Reykjavik, the hotel's location provides ample opportunity for exploring the wilderness, whether trekking across an ancient glacier or fly-fishing in an icy river. ION Adventure Hotel uses Iceland's natural delights as its own star features; the extension is perched on stilts above a geothermally heated external pool, while the glass-enclosed Northern Lights bar is the perfect spot for viewing its namesake aurora borealis. Enhancing the hotel's eco-friendly position, designer Erla Dögg Ingjaldsdóttir incorporated salvaged driftwood and lava into the design, along- side organic linens, wooden flooring, and other sustainable, natural materials.

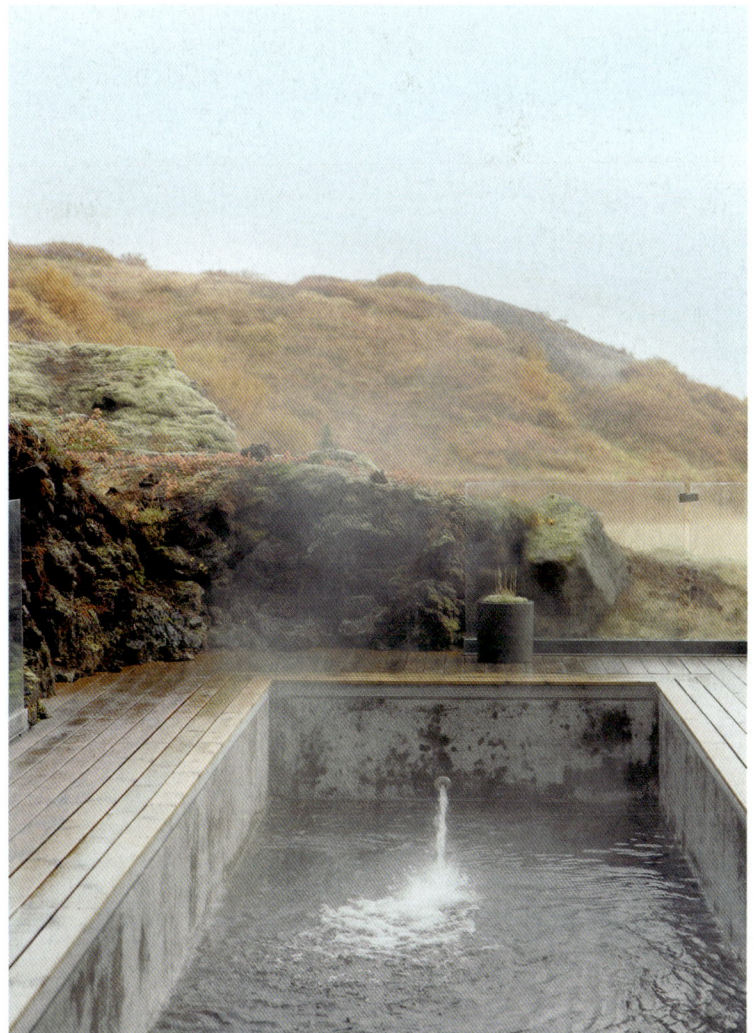

Parīlio

Colored concrete, terracotta floors and local marble contribute to this calm and light-filled hotel on the island of Paros. **Kalia** and **Antonis Eliopoulos** created Parīlio with the help of Interior Design Laboratorium as a celebration of the island's carefree, sun-kissed spirit. (The hotel's name is a portmanteau of Paros, and ilios, the Greek word for sun). The design team drew inspiration from traditional local houses and monasteries, using distinctive features of Cycladic architecture such as arches, concrete columns, and thick white walls. These provide a subtle backdrop for curated designer furniture, including bespoke IDLaboratorium pieces, Toscot lighting, and 101 Copenhagen bedside tables. Each of the suites has a tranquil atmosphere, with local natural fibers, ceramic objects, and graphic textile artworks, all set against a warm, neutral colorway. Sustainability is instilled into the hotel's core: partnerships with local nonprofits support educational and environmental initiatives, while Michelin-garlanded Chef Thanos Feskos serves Aegean produce with a commitment to zero waste.

186

Destination	Location
Switzerland	Zermatt

Rooms	Themes
54	Mountain, Sustainable, Well-Being

CERVO Mountain Resort

With 54 rooms across seven lodges, three restaurants, and extensive amenities, Cervo Mountain Resort nevertheless feels cohesive, welcoming, and warm. Owners **Seraina Lauber** and **Daniel Lauber** created the hotel as a gateway to Europe's finest ski slopes with community at its core. An extensive cultural program of concerts, workshops, and other events is designed to foster interactions between guests, employees, and locals, with sustainability, hyper-locality, and mindfulness prioritized. These principles are reflected in the hotel's three restaurants, which source all ingredients from within a 150-kilometer radius. At the lodge's center is Bazaar, a relaxed eatery serving mainly vegetarian dishes. Alternatively, Ferdinand serves local Valais cuisine using only Swiss products, including fondue and raclette for dairy lovers. For fans of Italian, Madre Nostra celebrates pasta and grilled food. The resort embodies traditional mountain style with a palette of native alpine colors and materials, predominantly timber and stone, and each chalet is equipped with its own spa and sauna.

Hotel Escondido

Immersed in nature and only footsteps from the sea, the rustic bungalows of Hotel Escondido offer a serene, private retreat. Hoteliers **Carlos Couturier** and **Moisés Micha** collaborated with architect Federico Rivera Río to design this series of bungalows in this Oaxacan village by the sea. The rooms are modern versions of traditional palapa beach huts—small, open-sided dwellings with thatched roofs made of dried palm leaves. The rooms feature private sundecks with pools, direct access to the beach, and views of the surrounding landscape; the combination of natural woods, concrete bathrooms, and bright touches creates a relaxed and inviting atmosphere inside. A 50-meter pool runs parallel to the coast, offering a tranquil, ocean-side dip. Through simple yet stylish design, the hotel elevates a beach vacation—with the option of spa massages, cocktails at the bar, surfing, fishing, and beach club socializing—to new heights.

Destination	Location	Rooms	Themes
Mexico	Puerto Escondido	45	Beach, Offbeat

Hotel Humano

Geometric brickwork, towering palms, and modern Mexican design combine in **Carlos Couturier** and **Moisés Micha's** Hotel Humano. The hotel embodies the duo's laid-back, coastal style and spirit of "barefoot luxury." Set moments from surfing hotspot Zicatela Beach, and boasting Pacific views, fire pits, and lush gardens, the hotel draws a relaxed, surf-loving crowd. Alongside the architecture studio Plantea Estudio, renowned architect Jorge Hernández de la Garza embraced Oaxacan artisanal design with bespoke textiles and handmade bathroom tiles complementing the building's concrete and clay. Angled bricks form part of the exterior walls' façade, a motif

which reappears in the reception desk, and Mexican artist Lucio Muniain's drawings can be appreciated throughout the hotel. With a spa and bistro, the overall atmosphere strikes the delicate balance between highly refined yet easygoing, for maximum repose.

Destination
Malaysia

Location
Kuala Lumpur

Rooms
49

Themes
History, Honeymoon, Sustainable

Destination
France

Location
Saint-Tropez

Rooms
37

Themes
Beach, Well-Being

Else

Else is a sanctuary for contemporary nomads searching for meaningful connections. Inhabiting a 1930s building, architects Studio Bikin honor its original Art Deco elements while introducing clean lines and regional influences. Conscious hospitality drives every choice, including workshops, sound baths, and DJ sets. Throughout the day, the hotel's communal space acts as a dining area where chef Yellow Fin Horse delivers drinks and local flavors. Else is a city escape reimagined through deliberate, soul-centered service—something else entirely.

Hôtel Sezz Saint-Tropez

Christophe Pillet and **Shahe Kaladjian's** luxurious establishment was born out of the ruins of a former hotel. Pillet spearheaded the design, adding modern amenities to Provencal style. The hotel is hemmed by a mimosa and palm garden, and centered around a swimming pool lined with Pillet-designed furniture. In the Michelin-star restaurant Colette, chef Philippe Colinet serves local and foraged produce alongside locally sourced and sustainable meats and seafoods. A complimentary shuttle takes guests to the town center and glamorous Pampelonne beach.

Destination
Mexico

Location
Merida

Rooms
21

Themes
City, Interior Design, Offbeat

Hotel Sevilla

In downtown Mérida, Hotel Sevilla is a masterfully restored 19th-century gem in which time periods gracefully overlap. Owners **Carlos Couturier** and **Moisés Micha** entrusted architecture firm Zeller & Moye to preserve the building's historic soul while bringing fresh perspectives into its rooms. The architects maintained the vintage façade and original walls, with generous communal spaces that include sheltered gardens and poolside gathering spots. Throughout, a palette of whites and grays provides a canvas against which lush greenery thrives. Original wood beams stretch overhead while wall tiles and preserved frescoes nod to bygone eras. Echoing the layouts of traditional houses in the Yucatan, heritage elements harmonize with modern comforts across this tranquil, welcoming escape.

Myconian Kyma

Set just above the town of Mykonos yet worlds away in atmosphere, **Marios** and **George Daktylides'** Myconian Kyma captures a rare balance between refined luxury and relaxed island living. Designed by the renowned architect Galal Mahmoud, the 74-room property is a contemporary homage to Cycladic tradition, where clean white forms, flowing marble, and natural textures merge gracefully with the hilltop landscape. The mood is one of understated elegance: a splash of 1960s-inspired design here, a thoughtfully placed artwork there, all framed by sweeping Aegean views. Guests can relax on private terraces, take a dip in an infinity pool or Jacuzzi, and enjoy local cuisine that celebrates the island's sun-soaked fare. The energy of Mykonos township is just minutes away; if so inclined, guests can party all night before returning to the serene seclusion of the hotel for fabulously luxurious Champagne breakfasts.

Destination	Location	Rooms	Themes
Greece	Mykonos	49	Beach, History

Mykonos Theoxenia

A national heritage property on a rugged coastline within sight of the island's iconic whitewashed windmills, Mykonos Theoxenia blends Cycladic architecture with 1960s-inspired flair. The original heritage-listed building, designed by architect Aris Konstantinidis, has been lovingly preserved, incorporating local stone and traditional elements. Owner **Marissa Loizou-Middleton** has honored its legacy with a modern update, merging clean lines and warm textures. Stone-clad rooms feature neutral tones and handcrafted details, while vintage pieces and artisanal finds from Greece and Cyprus lend subtle character. Soft hues complement the whitewashed walls and blue skies of the surrounding landscape. The spa at Mykonos Theoxenia offers a serene escape, fusing ancient and modern wellness rituals—ideal for unwinding. The pool is a tranquil haven, surrounded by the scents of fruit orchards, olive trees, and wild herbs. Drawing on fresh ingredients and regional flavors, the hotel's Apanemi restaurant celebrates local products, adding to an elevated Mykonos experience.

197

Destination	Location	Rooms	Themes
Indonesia	Sumba Island	64	Beach, Family-Friendly, Gastronomy, Honeymoon, Offbeat

Cap Karoso

Glistening turquoise water lies tantalizingly close to island hotel Cap Karoso. When French couple **Fabrice** and **Evguenia Ivara** first visited Sumba—known for its world-class surfing, distinctive textiles, and pristine limestone hills and ocean pools—they were quick to fall in love with it. Aiming to share the island's natural treasures with like-minded travelers, the Ivaras decided to open this eco-friendly hotel. The pair employed Jakarta-based Bitte Design Studio to lead on the interiors of their modernist- style resort, with a focus on elevating local references, art, and materials to create a culturally immersive experience for guests. Indonesian artists including Alexander Sebastianus Hartanto were commissioned to create art interpreting Sumbanese culture. The hotel is surrounded by organic farmland, which supplies its restaurants—including the casual Mediterranean-Indonesian Beach Club, the intimate 20-seat fine-dining restaurant Julang, and Apicine, an elegant Indonesian dining spot set beside the main pool.

Destination	**Location**	**Rooms**	**Themes**
Greece	Amaliada	44	Beach, History, Offbeat, Sustainable

Dexamenes Seaside Hotel

Shaped from an abandoned 1920s winery on the edge of the Ionian Sea, this concrete site has played an integral part in Greece's industrial and trading history. For **Nikos Karaflos,** the goal was to celebrate the raw history of the buildings while infusing their Brutalist frames with contemporary luxury. Originally built on the water so that the wine could be transported directly onto ships, guests now benefit from being steps from the shore. Designers K-Studio used steel, engineered glass, and timber to reinvigorate the former wine tanks, keeping their aged patina on guest room walls as a visceral reminder of the building's history. From the outset, Karaflos established the

hotel's eco-friendly foundations via adaptive reuse, merging aesthetics with conscious responsibility by using renewable energy, practising regenerative agriculture, and providing resource-conscious wellness activities like sound baths, exhibitions, and wine tastings.

Destination	Location	Rooms	Themes
Greece	Arcadia	32	Adults Only, Countryside, Offbeat

Manna

In Greece's fir forests, a 1929 sanatorium has been transformed into Manna, a neoclassical sanctuary 1,200 meters above sea level. Led by **Stratis Batagias,** K-Studio preserves original features through thoughtful restoration, blending contemporary luxury with copper fixtures and rattan ceilings. The 32 rooms mix airy linens with rich woods and wools in an earthy palette. Inspired by mountain living rooms, communal spaces invite connection—by the fireplace indoors or beside tranquil ponds outdoors. Award-winning chef Athinagoras Kostakos crafts Greek-inspired dishes from local ingredients, while the apothecary-style bar serves artisanal spirits. The Wellness & Spa offers a cave-like pool with skylights, indoor and outdoor saunas in the woods, couple's treatments, a jacuzzi, and a 24-hour forest-view gym. Unique experiences include truffle hunting with Lagotto dogs, river rafting, horse riding, and cooking sessions in the forest. Elli Pangalou's landscape design guides guests to the Lousios River and nearby villages like Dimitsana for an authentic Arcadian escape.

Destination	Location	Rooms	Themes
Portugal	Lisbon	42	Adults Only, City, Sustainable

Memmo Alfama

Lisbonite **Rodrigo Machaz** puts leisure and a slow pace front and center in Memmo hotels. At Alfama, this ethos is paramount, demonstrated through the use of long-lasting materials like wood and stone to create a soothing atmosphere. Madrid-based architect Samuel Torres de Carvalho reinvigorated the original 19th-century building, preserving the original façade and adding a red-riled rooftop pool and sun deck. The latter is a prime spot for locals as well as guests, providing stunning views of ships entering the River Tagus and nearby rooftops. Inside, contemporary minimalism reigns, with high-quality white linens and a white and taupe palette accented by cool grays and subtle pops of yellow. Guests can take a complimentary neighborhood walking tour around Alfama, the city's oldest and most character-filled neighborhood. A heated outdoor pool, wine bar, and appealing Portuguese cuisine make for a supremely stylish stay.

Cugó Gran Macina Malta

Set against the historic fortress walls of Senglea, Cugó Gran Macina Malta layers past and present within its 16th-century walls. Originally built in 1554, this iconic landmark was transformed by **Samuel Santos** into a chic retreat just minutes from Malta's capital, Valletta. Its 21 suites feature chalk-white walls alongside neutral materials like limestone, and slate, providing a tranquil contrast to the surrounding, dramatic fortifications. Architect Edwin Mintoff's masterfully streamlined design balances grandeur with contemporary elegance, preserving the structure's high-vaulted ceilings and vast communal spaces, while interiors by Daaa Haus incorporate tufted wool rugs, bespoke Italian furnishings, and materials like Carrara marble, lava stone, and Maltese hard stone. A breathtaking rooftop terrace and pool opens out to panoramic views of the harbor, marina, and skyline—a perfect spot for yoga, Pilates, and unhurried relaxation.

Hospes Maricel & Spa

At Hospes Maricel & Spa, grandeur meets tranquility atop a dramatic cliff, where sandstone archways and neoclassical pillars appear to be tumbling into the Mediterranean. Originally built in 1949, this palatial retreat has been reimagined by the Hospes Design Team and Tomás Alía with natural materials, soothing tones, and refined textures for a minimalist effect. Everything points to the sea, from an infinity pool that meets the horizon, to a private jetty welcoming sea-borne arrivals. A dramatic underground walkway connects the mansion to the sleek Natura annex and the outdoors Bodyna Spa, where stone, wood, and air combine for deeply restorative treatments. From sun-drenched terraces overlooking the coastline to softly lit interiors boasting deceptively simple, award-winning cuisine, every detail embraces island calm.

Destination	Location	Rooms	Themes
Japan	Minami-Uonuma	17	Adults Only, Gastronomy, Honeymoon, Mountain, Offbeat, Sustainable

Satoyama Jujo

Slow luxury defines Satoyama Jujo, a Michelin Key hotel situated amidst the tranquil forests and terraced rice fields of Japan's Niigata region. With just 15 rooms, the hotel provides a considered and curated experience to a limited number of guests. **Toru Iwasa** collaborated on the architecture with Kei Kaihoh and Musashino Art University, adding a modern extension with a hot spring spa onto the hotel's main, 150-year-old building. Cedar wood and tatami mats nod to the region's residential traditions, alongside Zelkova wood and pine. Shun Kawakami, Ryuichi Ohira, and Kanzo Shibata crafted the interiors, striking the balance between Japanese interiors and modern Western style. Arne Jacobsen, Isamu Noguchi, and Eames furniture feature against cream-colored walls and dark cedar floors. The hotel spotlights local gastronomy, with Michelin-starred chef Keiko Kuwakino creating Niigata- and Uonuma-inspired dishes from vegetables and wild mountain plants grown nearby.

Destination	Location
Greece	Apollonia, Sifnos

Rooms	Themes
20	Beach, Gastronomy Hotels, Honeymoon, Offbeat Destinations

Stamna Sifnos

Tucked away on the peaceful Greek island of Sifnos, Stamna offers a luxurious retreat amidst a rugged landscape. With just 20 rooms, each uniquely designed and offering gorgeous sea views, this intimate hotel exudes traditional charm while also offering modern luxuries. Guests can explore the extensive gardens and olive groves, relax by the pool, or enjoy the sweeping cliff views. Pilós, the hotel's restaurant, is open to the public and serves up elevated local cuisine, offering an authentic taste of the island with breakfast, lunch, and dinner menus using the finest locally sourced ingredients, including aromatic herbs and fresh vegetables harvested from the garden. The menu is curated by chef Gkikas Xenakis, whose culinary expertise brings a refined touch to traditional island flavors. With a yoga deck, meditation instructors, hiking trails, and pebble beaches nearby, the property invites guests to embrace both relaxation and adventure. Only two hours from Athens by ferry, Stamna Sifnos is a perfect getaway for travelers seeking tranquility and tradition.

Timber Cove Resort

Perched atop a rugged bluff, Timber Cove Resort is a soulful retreat where 1960s architecture meets cool, contemporary design. Originally designed by Frank Lloyd Wright devotee Richard Clements, Jr., the A-frame lodge nestles into the natural sandstone with Douglas fir and redwood details that honor its coastal setting. The resort's rooms feature forest or ocean views, and interiors by The Novogratz mix rustic-modern style with vintage California charm—including preppy plaids, worn leather, and heritage hues. Guests can socialize in the outdoor living room or dine on seasonal fare at Coast Kitchen surrounded by natural wood and Pacific vistas. Throughout the hotel, local artwork adds warmth and regional flavor, while an in-room vinyl collection reinforces the vintage vibe. A gateway to the Sonoma Coast's hiking trails, scenic drives, and nearby wineries, Timber Cove perfectly reflects the vision of co-owners **Michael Barry** and **Jens von Gierke** for a timeless escape anchored in nature.

Destination	Location	Rooms	Themes
Portugal	Monforte	19	Countryside, Gastronomy, Offbeat, Sustainable

Torre de Palma Wine Hotel

Paulo Barradas Rebelo and **Ana Isabel** Rebelo take a personal role in the running of their hotel in Portugal's historic Alentejo wine region. The pharmacists-turned-hoteliers are known to take their guests to the property's medieval tower at sunset for a personalized talk on the rich history of the region. It's this engagement with guests that underpins the pair's welcoming and comfortable hotel that celebrates the unique cultural value of its setting. With the help of architect João Mendes Ribeiro, they built the hotel from the remains of a house dating back to 1338. The restored and new buildings are centered around the property's centuries-old tower, and feature simple, whitewashed walls, set in spacious grounds that include an orchard, vineyard, and pool. Inside, designer Rosarinho Gabriel's mix of handpicked vintage furniture, woods, textiles, and curios gives a personal touch to spaces. Chef Miguel Laffan elevates Alentejo cuisine in the hotel's Palma Restaurant, pairing it with delicious, local artisanal wines.

Hotel Escondido Oaxaca

In Oaxaca's historic heart, Hotel Escondido Oaxaca is an intimate hideaway that balances heritage with contemporary Mexican design. Hoteliers **Carlos Couturier** and **Moisés Micha** teamed up with architect Alberto Kalach to preserve a 19th-century residence and introduce a Brutalist-inspired tower. Interior designers Lucía Corredor and Cecilia Tena layered warm ochres, handwoven textiles, and sabino wood furnishings crafted by local artisans to foster a refined sense of comfort. The original house, with its lush rooftop pool and bar, welcomes guests and locals alike, while the modern tower is a sanctuary inviting reflection and rest. The on-site restaurant celebrates Oaxaca's bold culinary heritage through fresh and organic ingredients. From recessed stone shelves to handmade robes and art by regional creatives, every detail in this homage to Oaxaca's craft and culture is considered, reflecting a commitment to authenticity and pared-back luxury.

Destination
Mexico

Location
San Rafael, Veracruz

Rooms
18

Themes
Countryside, Offbeat, Well-Being

Destination
Switzerland

Location
Ascona

Rooms
71

Themes
Countryside, Well-Being

Maison Couturier

Carlos Couturier and **Moisés Micha**
have transformed this former agricultural
estate into a paean to luxury. Sited a
few kilometers from the Gulf of Mexico,
the hotel is accessible by land, sea, and
air, allowing culture and nature to coexist.
Here, a reverence for the earth is reflected in sumptuous greenery and bright
interiors. Black-tile bathrooms, deep
bathtubs, antique lamps, and vintage
telephones decorate the rooms. Each of
these private spaces also opens to the
central pool and outdoor area, celebrating
the hotel's heritage and surroundings.

Giardino Ascona

Nestled by Lake Maggiore, Giardino
Ascona is a Tuscan-style retreat embodying dolce vita. Husband-and-wife
Daniela and **Philippe Frutiger** oversee
this casually elegant property, renovated
by Rolf Balmer, echoing Frank Lloyd
Wright's spirit. Interiors feature a subtly
Mediterranean aesthetic. Philippe's
culinary roots shine through in the two-
Michelin-star restaurant. Daniela's expertise defines the renowned dipiù Spa,
offering tailored treatments. This Swiss
boutique hotel converges nature, elegance, and culinary mastery for a legendary experience.

213

Destination	Location	Rooms	Themes
Spain	Begur, Sa Riera	38	Adults Only, Beach, Offbeat

Finca Victoria Hotel & Spa

Once a retreat for artists and free spirits, Finca Victoria Hotel & Spa has been reimagined as a soulful hideaway where well-being, creativity, and culinary excellence meet. Located in Begur, just steps from one of Costa Brava's most idyllic beaches—Sa Riera Beach—the hotel has undergone an extensive restoration that honors its 20th-century Mediterranean roots. Architecturally, the property nods to grand seaside homes with whitewashed walls, wood detailing that recalls traditional fishing boats, and earthy materials typical of masia farmhouses. Inside, rooms are simple yet refined, designed to soothe, inspire, and ground guests in the rhythms of the sea and land.

Wellness and food are central, with yoga and mindfulness sessions offered daily, while two restaurants—Finca Kitchen & Bar and Al Kostat del Mar by Jordi Vilà— guide the hotel's culinary spirit, helmed by the Michelin-starred chef. From relaxing poolside to taking in sweeping views of the Medes Islands, this is where Costa Brava's rugged beauty meets intentional living.

C-Hotel & Spa

Located in the undulating landscape surrounding Lake Como, C-Hotel & Spa is a family-run retreat created by **Andrea Colzani** in collaboration with lighting maestro Mario Nanni. The property showcases locally quarried limestone from the Berici Hills, which form a luminous overall canvas. The design philosophy eschews trends in favor of enduring elegance, with polished stone surfaces complementing teak furnishings, and Nanni's distinctive lighting concept bathing corridors in warm amber hues. Sustainability drives this bio-architectural marvel, with moveable walls and climate control systems creating a soothing sense of isolation. The C-Spa encourages relaxation with three thermal pools, a Turkish bath, waterfall, and personalized treatments. At Materia Prima restaurant, the chef selects every ingredient in line with a strict farm-to-table philosophy. Fresh bread and desserts are baked daily, complemented by rich local coffees in the lively enoteca for a truly authentic Italian experience.

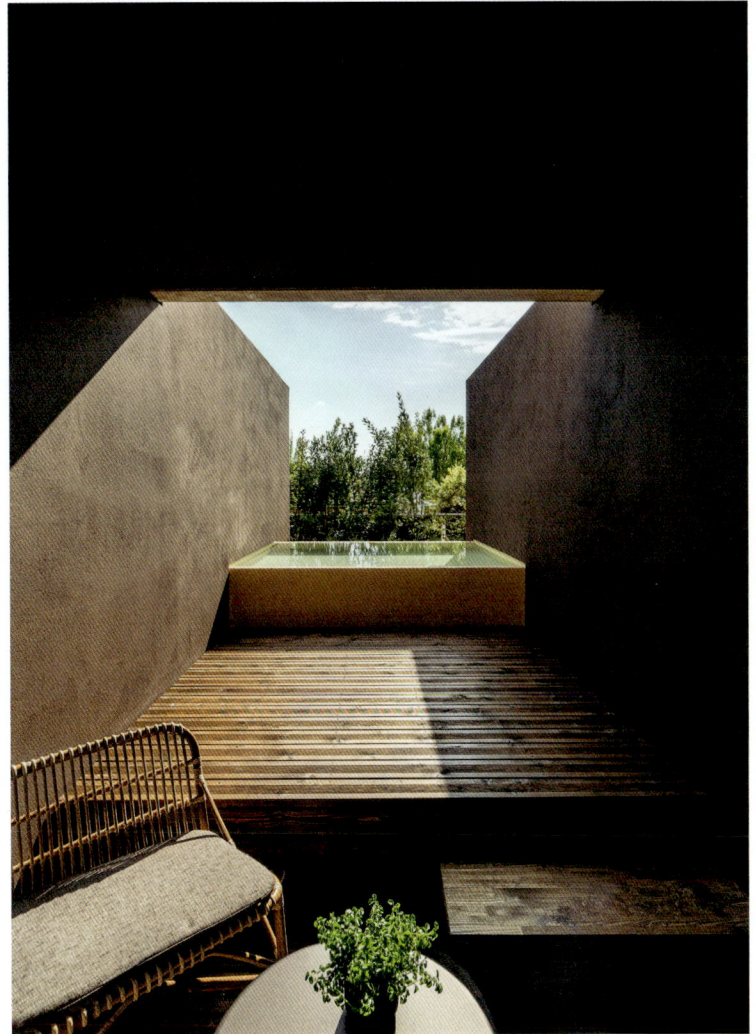

Destination	Location	Rooms	Themes
Germany	Gonnesweiler	97	Countryside, Gastronomy, Offbeat, Sustainable, Well-Being

Seezeitlodge Hotel & SPA

On the shores of Bostalsee lake in south-western Germany, Seezeitlodge Hotel & Spa is a magical mirror to the area's surrounding natural landscape. Owners **Kathrin** and **Christian Sersch** have created a restorative retreat prioritizing natural materials and breathtaking lake views. Made from charred larch, the hotel's slatted wooden façade reflects the immediate topography with a silvery-black luster, while Birgit Nicolay's interiors beckon the outdoors in through floor-to-ceiling windows: earth-toned colors, diaphanous fabrics, and Celtic knot designs abound. Some rooms even feature freestanding wooden bathtubs. A 5,000-square-meter wellness refuge includes an indoor–outdoor infinity pool, a natural swimming pond, and an outdoor sauna arranged according to earth-energies—alongside comprehensive treatments. The lake offers sailing, swimming, and paddling activities. At Restaurant Lumi, chef Daniel Schöfisch presents seasonal dishes enhanced with herbs handpicked from the garden. Bar Nox, with its convivial fireside lounge, serves signature cocktails and regional wines.

Destination
Switzerland

Location
Laax

Rooms
196

Themes
Family-Friendly, Mountain,
Sustainable, Well-Being

Destination
Switzerland

Location
Chandolin

Rooms
25

Themes
Mountain, Sustainable, Well-Being

Rocksresort

Reto Gurtner's Rocksresort offers guests
the chance to step from directly the stunning cubist property onto a ski slope
gondola. Designed with the environment—
both local and general—in mind, the
hotel has sustainability at its core. Thus,
Domenig & Domenig Architekten sourced
climate-friendly building materials, including a 40-million-year-old rough-
hewn quartzite stone for the façade. The
resort comprises 11 structures, including
varied guestrooms and apartments.
Come summer, it transforms into a serene
destination for hikers, climbers, and bikers.

Chandolin Boutique Hotel

Perched in the mountains, Chandolin
Boutique Hotel offers Alpine luxury.
Realized by Kittel SA architects, the hotel
reinterprets classic Swiss chalet style
with a contemporary, eco-conscious
approach. The façade showcases solar
panels with wooden slats and balconies,
while interiors feature stone and parquet
floors. Guests can enjoy locally sourced
food at the 14-point Gault & Millau restaurant; après-ski drinks at the Sunset Chalet
and the Wine Bar; and sauna, hammam,
and mountain-view treatments at the
Altitude Wellness Spa. A hidden gem
of elegance and sustainability.

217

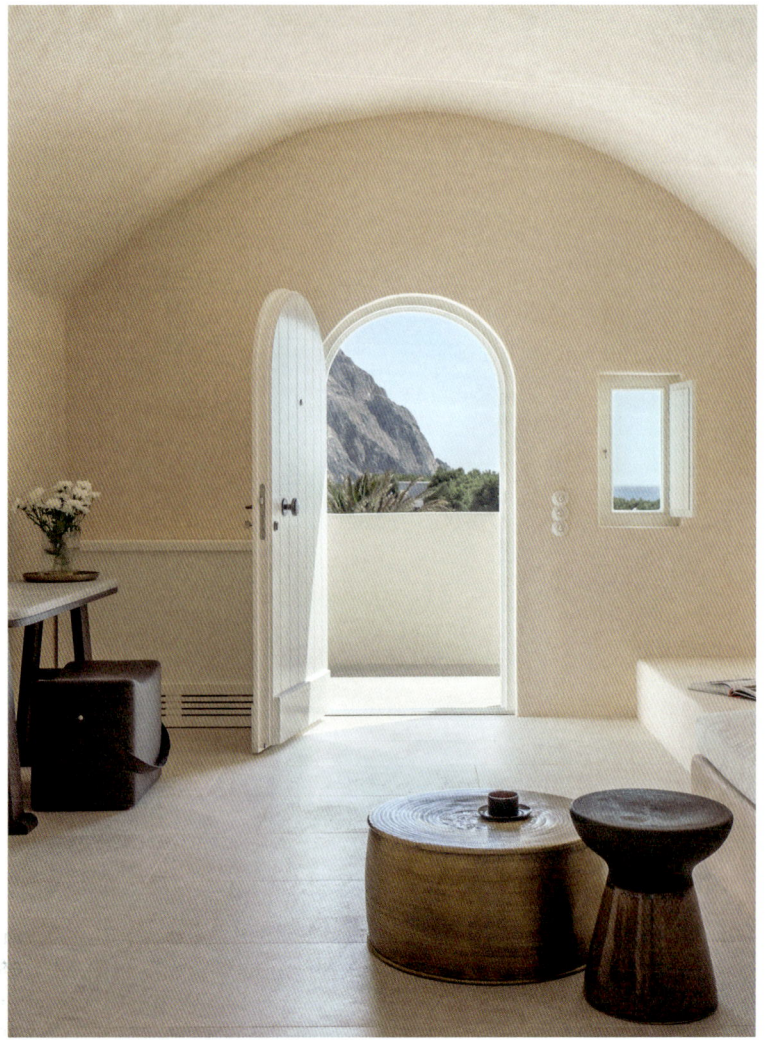

Destination	**Location**	**Rooms**	**Themes**
Greece	Santorini	12	Beach, Honeymoon, Offbeat, Well-Being

Istoria

Basking in the Cycladic sun on the famed dark volcanic sand of Santorini's Perivolos Beach is Istoria. With just 12 suites, the hotel provides a highly personalized experience allowing guests to escape the crowds from the comfort of a Santorini mansion. In the suites, limewashed walls with built-in couches create a sense of lived-in comfort, while arched doorways open out onto private white balconies with sweeping views of the pool or the Aegean Sea; most suites feature private pools or hot tubs. **Kalia** and **Antonis Eliopoulos** and Interior Design Laboratorium preserved wherever possible the estate's original wooden roofs and stone columns, sourcing a collection of local furniture, both old and new, to complement the terracotta, natural wood, and traditional materials of the hotel. Public spaces include a private beach club, a large pool encased within protective walls, and restaurant Mr. E, located on the black sand beach and serving seafood in line with Santorini's epicurean traditions.

The Surin Phuket

Nestled along the scenic Pansea Beach, The Surin Phuket is a tranquil retreat where nature meets refined simplicity. Designed by pioneering hotel architect **Ed Tuttle,** the resort's 109 hillside cottages and suites blend flawlessly into the lush tropical landscape. Inside, shuttered doors, granite floors, woven palm panels, and earth-toned fabrics invite the outdoors in. Private verandas and secluded sundecks provide calming spaces for relaxation, while jungle walkways connect and wind down to the beach. Guests can enjoy traditional Thai cuisine by the sea at the Beach Restaurant and sunset cocktails at the Beach Bar. A hexagonal black-tiled pool reflects the sky like polished stone, and handcrafted furnishings throughout the spaces nod to Tuttle's thoughtful, minimalistic vision. Combining local craftsmanship with pared-back elegance, The Surin offers a deeply peaceful, home-away-from-home experience that honors Phuket's natural beauty with deceptively easy grace.

Destination	Location	Rooms	Themes
United States	Nashville, TN	104	City, Interior Design, Well-Being

Drift Nashville

In Nashville's evolving East Bank, Drift reimagines a 1966 midcentury modern structure through the vision of **Philip Bates** and **Alexis Soler,** blending a coastal-California sensibility with local character. Bates brings his worldly perspective to this building's striking minimalist-modern design, preserving the building's clean lines and retro feel. White-painted exteriors contrast dramatically with the deep-sea green and blue accents that appear to dip the lower portion of the façade in a dark color. Inside, a thoughtful material dialogue unfolds—brick, terrazzo, concrete, terracotta, soft velvets, and leather create a harmony of textures with a Baja flair.

Artisanal touches bring depth, and include custom wooden door handles, plaster lighting sculptures, and handcrafted tiles. The outdoor pool deck and courtyard offer a laid-back vibe for sipping seasonal cocktails, with drinks and small plates available in The Sun Room. Mornings begin at Dawn Cafe, a bright and easygoing spot for locally roasted coffee and light fare. The Nashville community vibe resonates in every corner here, from the regional artwork to the warm, uncomplicated hospitality that underpins this distinctive retreat.

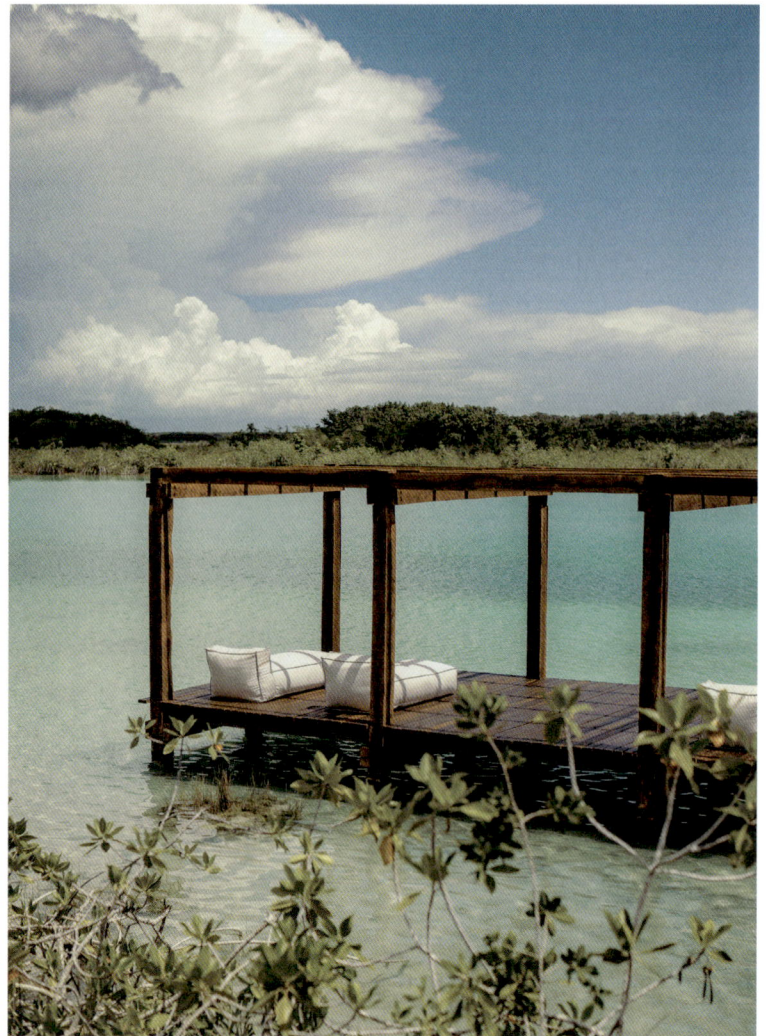

Destination	Location	Rooms	Themes
Mexico	Bacalar	22	Honeymoon, Offbeat, Well-Being

Boca de Agua

Amid the verdant jungle of Mexico's Mayan east coast, on the shores of Bacalar Lagoon, sits Boca de Agua, a treehouse resort prioritizing sustainability and mental wellbeing. First-time hotelier and co-designer **Rodrigo Juarez** wanted to create a space that would encourage guests to pause, breathe, read, write, and re-connect with themselves and nature. For Juarez, combining design and sustain-ability was a no-brainer, and he brought Mexico City architect Frida Escobedo on board to create spaces that would have positive impacts on guests' state of mind as well as the environment. The one- and two-bedroom interconnected tree-house-style villas are built from salvaged materials, using local construction tech-niques like latticework to provide both ventilation and shade, inviting the outside in. Ensuring Mexican culture is at the heart of the hotel, restaurant Flora focuses on contemporary Mexican cuisine.

Destination	Location
Italy	Lana

Rooms	Themes
8	Countryside, History, Mountain

1477 Reichhalter

Over five centuries, this historic structure has served its local community as a bakery, a sawmill, a barn, and a tavern. In 2018, after a decade of sitting empty, **Klaus** and **Moritz Dissertori** lovingly converted the building into a boutique guesthouse with eight rooms. Set in a small town in a valley in Northeast Italy, the building embodies the region's traditional architecture—sensitively, minimally restored by architect Zeno Bampi, who maintained the original blush façade and mint green shutters. Designer Christina Biasi-von Berg restored period features like the timber panelling, polished floors, and wall plastering to establish a balance between modern minimalism and historic character. While much of the antique furniture was already in the building, the Dissertori brothers added flea-market finds, midcentury pieces, and playful, atmospheric photographs by Jasmine Deporta. The resulting hotel celebrates the heritage of the surrounding village with a light touch, effortlessly warm hospitality, and delicious homemade food.

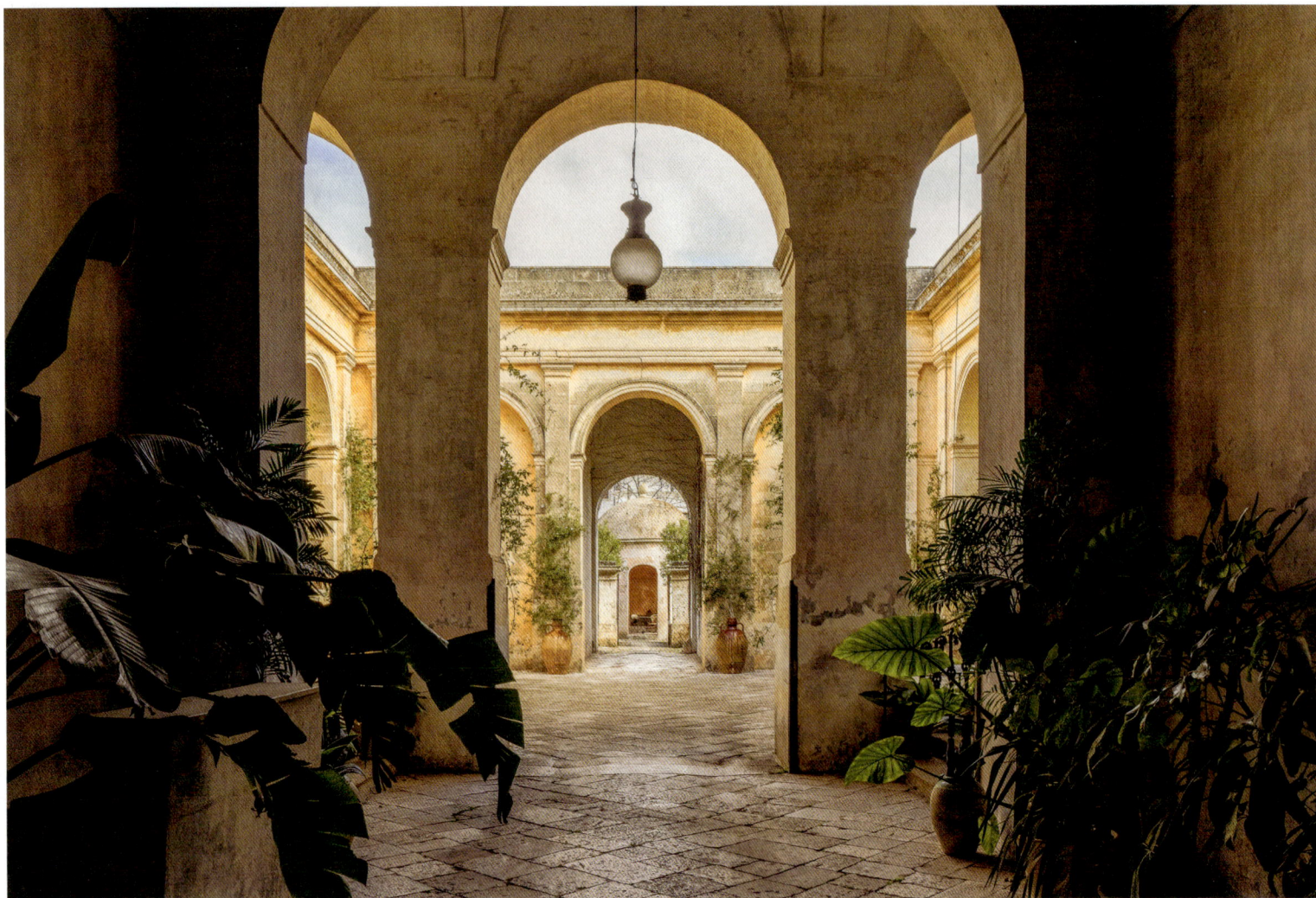

Destination	Location	Rooms	Themes
Italy	Gagliano del Capo, Puglia	17	Art & Culture, Countryside, Gastronomy, History, Honeymoon

Palazzo Daniele

Palazzo Daniele is where contemporary art, historic grandeur, and minimalist design converge in a uniquely atmospheric setting. **Gabriele Salini** and **Francesco Petrucci** worked with designers Ludovica and Roberto Palomba to create a hotel destined to draw art lovers and aficionados of authentic Italy. The team elected for sparse, monastic décor in order to enhance the scale and grandeur of the building. Petrucci chose site-specific works to punctuate the spaces: a Luigi Presicce lamp; Nicolas Party stools; Roberto Cuoghi sculpture; and Simon d'Exea light box. The minimal furnishings and site-specific artworks bring subtle contrasts to the ancient portraits, frescoed ceilings, and delicately patterned 19th-century floors. Four women with regional roots lead the hotel's kitchen team and the menu is seasonal and unfussy, deploying local ingredients to honor Salento and Apulian culinary traditions, served at tables arranged in a series of charming courtyards.

Destination	Location	Rooms	Themes
Italy	Lana	41	Countryside, Mountain, Offbeat, Sustainable, Well-Being

vigilius mountain resort

Accessible only by cable car, vigilius mountain resort offers panoramic views of the Dolomites from the quiet of a nature reserve. Designed by Matteo Thun with visionary hotelier **Ulrich Ladurner,** the resort reflects a philosophy of harmony with nature and is now run by his daughter, Ingrid. Built from natural materials like wood, glass, and stone, the resort blends effortlessly into its alpine surroundings. Inside, rooms are filled with warm mountain light, and thick-curtained windows frame sweeping views of larch forests. Sustainability is central to the resort's ethos. Its car-free location, geothermal heating, low-energy systems, and EarthCheck certification reflect deep environmental respect. A minimal building footprint preserves the landscape, while local sourcing and waste reduction practices minimize impact. Guests can enjoy regional cuisine at Restaurant 1500 or seasonal South Tyrolean dishes at Stube Ida, depending on the day. A rooftop prairie crowns the resort, while culture pulses through its halls: local musicians, winemakers, and producers are regularly invited for tastings and events that connect guests to the spirit of the mountain.

227

Destination
Spain

Location
Torroja del Priorat

Rooms
13

Themes
Adults Only, Countryside, Gastronomy, Honeymoon

ORA Hotel Priorat

Housed within the walls of an 18th-century abbey, ORA Hotel Priorat—an adults-only retreat—builds on its historic setting with modern fittings and timeless, comfortable design. Set in a traditional Catalonian village in the heart of Priorat wine country, the hotel is a hub for oenophiles to explore the region's exceptional viniculture, gastronomy, and ancient sites from a picturesque, cobblestone town. With just 13 rooms, the hotel is boutique, allowing for a refined and customized guest experience. Maria Vives designed the interiors, opting for a mix of contemporary and historic elements. In the dining space, traditional Catalan vaulted ceilings, large, arched windows, and tiled floors meet contemporary rattan furniture and clean lines. Guest rooms embrace old-world charm alongside modern amenities, providing the very best of both worlds. With a culinary philosophy underpinned by a mantra of "local, simple, and good," the restaurant serves traditional regional dishes and locally produced wine.

Destination
Portugal

Location
Porto

Rooms
62

Themes
City, Gastronomy,
History, Sustainable

Vila Foz Hotel & Spa

Facing the Atlantic in Porto's Foz do Douro
district, Vila Foz elegantly threads contemporary design through a fabulous Old
World manor. Architect Miguel Cardoso
preserved the 19th-century building's
grand turreted exterior, while Nini Andrade
Silva lightened the opulent interiors with
a mixture of stone, mirrors, and bronze.
Lofty spaces with high ceilings are balanced by warm colors, concept lighting,
and sculptural seating. Recently awarded
a MICHELIN Key for its distinctive character and exceptional service, Vila Foz is
home to the Michelin-starred restaurant
of the same name, where Chef Azevedo
presents coastal-inspired cuisine and
intimate chef's table experiences, alongside Flor de Lis' seasonal fare. Guests
can slow down in the light-kissed pool,
or in the sauna and Turkish bath—never
far from Porto's vibrant cultural center
and the sea on the horizon.

Destination	Location
Spain	Palma

Rooms	Themes
37	City, History

Nobis Hotel Palma

Among the walls of a former medieval-era Islamic palace is **Alessandro Catenacci's** Nobis Hotel Palma. The antique building was constructed in the 1100s and has been carefully restored to preserve its Old Town character. Jordi Herrero Arquitectos and Eduardo Garcia Acuna Arquitectos carefully peeled away layers of history to let the structure's original elements shine, revealing original stone, brick walls, and vaulted ceilings. The design team at Wingårdhs enhanced these features with natural and sustainable materials such as wool and leather, and a curated collection of custom furniture, textiles, and carpets. Guests can enjoy European cuisine with a Mediterranean twist in the share-style Noi Palma restaurant, or relax in an indoor pool and sauna reminiscent of ancient Roman baths in the hotel's vaults. A short stroll from many of Palma's famous sights, the hotel's distinctive and storied spaces embody the beauty of Mallorca's Old Town.

Destination	Location	Rooms	Themes
Japan	Nagasaki	12	Countryside, Offbeat, Well-Being

Iki Retreat
by Onko Chishin

Along the pristine coast of Japan's Iki Island, Iki Retreat by Onko Chishin offers a rare communion of nature, wellness, and understated luxury. This intimate 12-room sanctuary—celebrated as the island's only Michelin Guide–listed 5 Pavilions ryokan—overlooks Yunomoto Bay, with each suite featuring a private open-air hot spring bath fed by golden natural waters and panoramic sea views. Architecturally, the property embraces minimalism; natural wood tones, low furnishings, and traditional Japanese elements blend with subtle Western touches to create a calming, cocooning atmosphere. Floor-to-ceiling windows dissolve the boundary between indoors and out,

immersing guests in the stillness of the Genkai Sea. Dining is a heartfelt celebration of Iki's blessings, with seasonal seafood, Iki beef, and island vegetables sourced and prepared to showcase their pure flavors. Every dish reflects deep respect for nature and a commitment to authenticity. Guided by a vision of harmony between land, culture, and design, Iki Retreat invites guests into a meditative hideaway where stillness, connection, and genuine hospitality flourish.

Parkhotel Mondschein

Abundant vines cover the wall of this aptly named park hotel, their green leaves reflected in the green-tiled pool in the spacious garden. Set in a 14th-century building extended in 1890 in Belle Époque style, it features sweeping corridors, high ceilings, and stucco flourishes. The building's storied past blends styles from the Middle Ages with midcentury modernism, creating a multi-layered appeal. Under **Klaus** and **Moritz Dissertori's** direction, heritage features were retained, and Studio Biquadra reused materials to develop a terracotta, green, and timber palette—serving as a canvas for world-class artworks. Popular with locals and guests, Luna Restaurant serves an ample breakfast buffet with produce from their own fields and local farmers. At lunch and dinner, the elegant space becomes an Italian restaurant with Mediterranean specialties. The hotel also includes the new Alto Pizza, the nonchalant Luna Bar, a yoga studio that offers retreats, a gym, and a sauna.

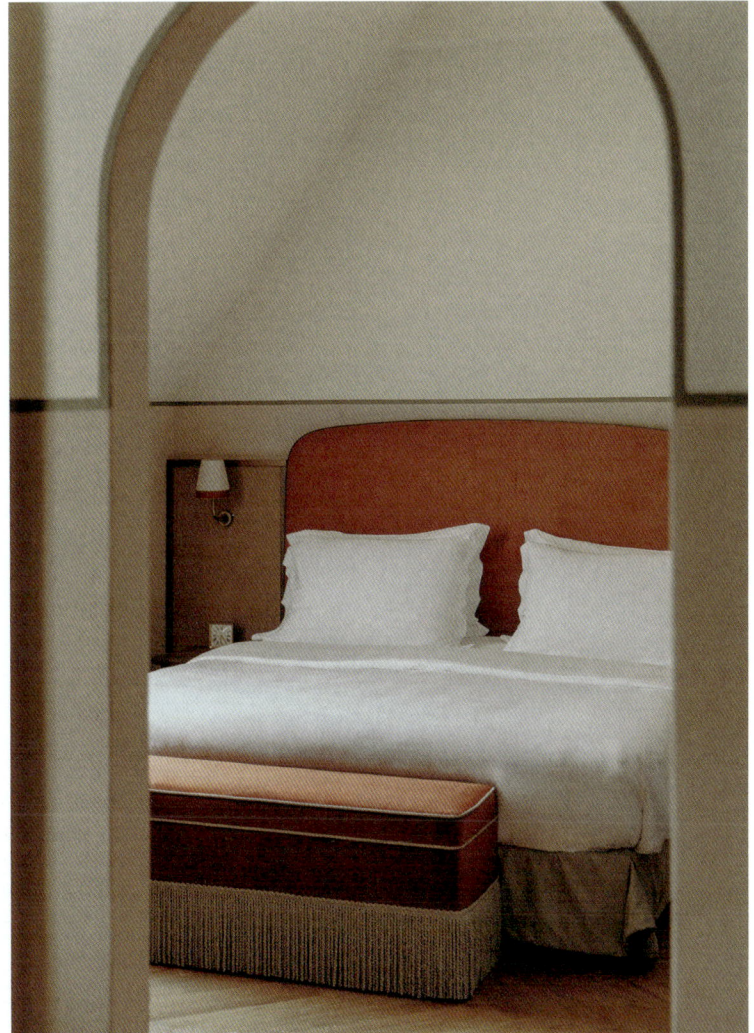

Some hotels don't just reflect their surroundings—they belong to them. These are places shaped by local culture, creative communities, and lived experience. Here, hospitality becomes a form of cultural grounding: warm, authentic, and deeply connected to the rhythms of the world around them.

Rooted in Place

In Spaces Shaped by Care,

Christina Ohly Evans

Culture Becomes Second Nature

It's through a heritage-sharpened lens and a life immersed in business that *Financial Times* journalist Christina Ohly Evans is able to cut straight to the heart of design issues. Here, she discusses how great hotels are dynamic cultural hubs that connect us to local life and express a universal sense of identity.

I grew up in the small town of Woodstock, Vermont, where the central inn—a white, grand-dame built in the 1960s by the Rockefeller family—served as a community hub. Set on the picturesque village green, this hotel was—and still is—special in many ways. From its manicured gardens in summer to an enormous roaring fireplace and holiday finery in the winter months; it shaped my ideas about hospitality, aesthetics, and my connection to local life, as well as what makes a visit truly memorable. While I was a local and never had to stay there as a child, the inn always served as our epicenter for meals, concerts, and special events, including, many years later, parts of my own wedding.

This childhood experience of the hotel-as-hub has informed my thinking wherever I go—and I have been fortunate enough to live abroad and travel extensively. While the Woodstock Inn was very Green Mountain chic, my sensibilities were shaped by my family, which included architects and artists. I was raised to revere the Harvard Five, Philip Johnson, midcentury modernism, and essentially anything with a somewhat discernibly Scandinavian or Japanese aesthetic. My love of hotels—and immersion in local cities, remote mountain villages, and islands in general—combines my respect for traditional hotel design with a passion for modern, minimalist architecture. For me, the best hotels celebrate both culture and heritage, and innovate and experiment when it makes sense to do so.

Thus, when people ask me where they should stay on their trips away, I often think of those locations around the world that, in my subjective experience, have set the bar. For me, one of the earliest and most revelatory hotel experiences was my first stay in Rome. It was 1984. I was 14, and the hotel was a lavish establishment frequented by travelers on their Grand Tours. It had opulent velvet draperies, heavy wooden shutters that were closed each night, and sumptuous bed linens. Its requisite American Bar blew me away,

Christina Ohly Evans

as did the warmth, kindness, and beaming pride of the hoteliers. This was my first experience with fine Italian cuisine, and I can still taste the cannelloni finished with warm bechamel all these years later. And while the gilding and formality of this five-star property wouldn't necessarily be my personal choice, it seemed to epitomize the glamour of Rome. Everything from its art collection to its gilded furnishings and the crisp white uniforms worn by its staff helped to set the Italian stage for me on this special trip.

On other occasions when people ask where the best hotels are, I often think about stays in smaller properties in Kyoto and New Zealand—a traditional *ryokan* inn and a lodge on a sheep station, respectively—where pared-down aesthetics led to warm, welcoming stays. These hotels were more in line with my architectural vernacular: local wood and stone, linen and wool, glass, and plenty of natural light. And while the hoteliers were dressed differently to those in Rome, they were no less proud of their respective products. From showcasing local delicacies to experiencing the surrounding natural beauty with insider guides, I came away from each stay with a clearer sense of

that country's tradition—all while being surrounded by luxury.

At heart, the best hotels I've experienced fuse a rich sense of history with warmth and creativity. The British are masters of this art; just visit a Grade II listed Georgian mansion-turned-hotel in the English countryside to revel in the authenticity of period art and furnishings, seamlessly blended with state-of-the-art spas, sumptuous rooms in neutral hues, and farm-to-table cuisine. This is the perfect hotel solution: old meets new, often with art and nature on offer, making every visit a revelation.

Christina Ohly Evans is a journalist and editor specializing in design, culture, and luxury travel. As the U.S. Correspondent for the *Financial Times*'s magazine *How to Spend It,* she brings a refined eye to the world's most compelling destinations. Her work blends cultural insight with a deep understanding of how places shape experience and identity.

239

Hotel Skeppsholmen

Alessandro Catenacci's hotel is set within the walls of two former Royal Marine barracks on Skeppsholmen island in the center of Stockholm. The buildings, which date back to 1699, are recognized historic landmarks, and Catenacci built the hotel and brand's personality to reflect this rich 300-year history. Stockholm-based interior architects Claesson Koivisto Rune designed a characteristically Nordic concept to overlook the water, mixed with bespoke Italian Tacchini furniture in reference to Catenacci's Italian heritage. Inspired by the hotel's maritime surroundings and weather patterns, the design's artistic theme is "fog," manifested in the peaceful color scheme and lightweight elements including translucent curtains and diffused lighting from teardrop-shaped downlights. Partnering with icons such as Swedish fashion label Acne Studios and the Swedish Museum of Modern Art, the hotel provides guests with the best of Sweden's modern features from its historic heart.

Hotel Hotel

A bold experiment in community and creativity, Hotel Hotel is a vibrant cultural hub in central Lisbon. Conceived by **Alexandre Martins** and designed by Pedrita Studio, the property inhabits a refurbished historical building transformed into a polyphonous space where art, wellness, and social connection come together. The interiors, marked by red-and-black marble, open-plan layouts, and nature-inspired hues, were shaped in collaboration with local designers and artists to reflect the rhythm and spirit of the city. A tribute to Lisbon's nearby Botanical Garden, the hotel garden flows into the communal spaces, where guests can mix over immersive dinners, live music, and meditation workshops. At Animal, the in-house restaurant, inventive flavors meet simple, plant-forward fare in an inviting, airy space. More than a place to stay, Hotel Hotel is a dynamic cultural platform—an invitation to feel Lisbon through its people, art, and ever-evolving energy.

Destination	Location	Rooms	Themes
Sweden	Stockholm	249	City, Gastronomy, Sustainable

Blique by Nobis

Blique by Nobis is a hub for creatives in Stockholm's colorful Vasastan neighborhood. Originally a 1930s warehouse, this Sigurd Lewerentz-designed architectural gem was revived by Gert Wingårdh and owner **Alessandro Catenacci** into a social space marrying 1930s functionalism with contemporary elegance. The design brings together raw materials like metal and concrete with warmer elements including leather, textiles, and wood. Spanning a historic warehouse and a modern rear house, the hotel boasts multiple gathering points, from a courtyard to several restaurants, and bars, and a rooftop terrace with panoramic city views. Located in the Stockholm Gallery District, Blique by Nobis is a gateway to the city's cultural scene, with sustainability quite literally at its core—the hotel has its own indoor farm, with produce cultivated in the courtyard and on the rooftop, too. Food offerings combine European and Asian influences using organic, home-grown ingredients. Hosting live music, exhibitions, and cultural events, the hotel is a meeting place and celebration of the local creative scene.

Destination	Location
United States	Baltimore, MD

Rooms	Themes
7	City, Interior Design

guesthouse by good neighbor

Perched above its namesake coffee shop in Baltimore, this seven-room sanctuary by **Shawn Chopra** and **Anne Morgan** reimagines hospitality as an intimate homecoming. Global design influences mix with hyperlocal craftsmanship for a retreat that feels both worldly and deeply rooted. Each room showcases Charm City's creative spirit through Maryland oak bed frames, reclaimed Douglas fir floors, and handcrafted concrete sinks by neighboring Luke Works. The design narrative weaves from Denmark to Japan, Egypt to India, and is especially evident in the calming lobby, where all of these influences converge. Distinguishing this design-led haven is its fully shoppable concept; every object enhancing a guest's stay can journey home with them, from Le Labo scents to vintage Braun record players. Beyond accommodation, guesthouse hosts creative events like Design Camp, where diverse artists collaborate in unexpected ways—a place where rest and inspiration coexist.

Destination	Location	Rooms	Themes
Italy	Pienza	12	Countryside, Gastronomy, History

La Bandita Townhouse

Located in the heart of Pienza, a UNESCO-listed renaissance gem in southern Tuscany, La Bandita Townhouse encapsulates history, comfort, and contemporary style. Once a convent, this 500-year-old, 12-room boutique retreat has been masterfully restored by architects Ernesto Bartolini and Arianna Pieri, in collaboration with owner **John Voigtmann,** to reveal original stone walls, vaulted brick corridors, and wood-beamed ceilings. Spacious guest rooms combine elements from past and present, with warm parquet floors, airy high ceilings, and sweeping views over the breathtaking Val d'Orcia. The intimate cafe, led by Glaswegian chef David Mangan, showcases the region's finest ingredients in mouthwatering dishes like hand-cut tagliatelle with lemon-rocket pesto. An invitation to slow down, savor, and be immersed in the rhythms of authentic Tuscan life, guests can use the hotel as a base for wandering through Pienza's medieval alleys or simply gazing across the distant vineyards in lush rolling countryside.

Harmon Guest House

In Healdsburg, California's sun-kissed culinary and wine center, Harmon Guest House is a sustainable, industrial-chic haven named for the town's 19th-century founder. The property embodies its namesake's social and community-minded spirit through thoughtful design by David Baker Architects. A striking redwood slatted façade—functioning as both a solar shield and textural artwork—introduces the guest house's "modern organic" aesthetic. Once inside, a transparent lobby flows into a sunlit stairwell showcasing a four-story hanging macramé sculpture. Guestrooms feature custom fire-glazed tiles, cast-concrete sinks, and quilted headboards, creating warm and inviting environments. Owners **Paolo Petrone** and **Circe Sher** enhance the experience through local partnerships, from private tours of nearby farm Noci Sonomato to Warnecke Ranch, where artist-winemaker Alice Sutro discusses parallels between art and viticulture, connecting guests to Sonoma's abundantly rich terroir.

Vora

Overlooking Santorini's submerged caldera, Vora is an architectural marvel carved into the island's dramatic cliffs. Conceived by local visionary **Yannis Bellonias** and brought to life by K-Studio, this stylish escape reimagines Cycladic hospitality by way of a living, gravity-defying sculpture in a steep cliffside that fully embraces its volcanic landscape. White cement and dark stone merge for a bold architectural statement that seems to float between sea and sky. The villas cascade down the cliffside in complete seclusion, each offering 100-percent privacy—a rare luxury on such a busy island. Each features a private pool and sun-drenched terrace that feels as if suspended above the Aegean. Minimalist interiors temper the dramatic exterior; custom furniture, Myrto Zirini ceramics, and Piet Boon fixtures in a soothing palette of white and stone make for intimate sanctuaries. Design details are carefully folded into the inviting rooms: marble from Gascoigne and Vassaltis, Ceppo di Gré stone, Piet Boon fixtures, and discreet Bang & Olufsen sound systems to soundtrack the exquisite tranquility.

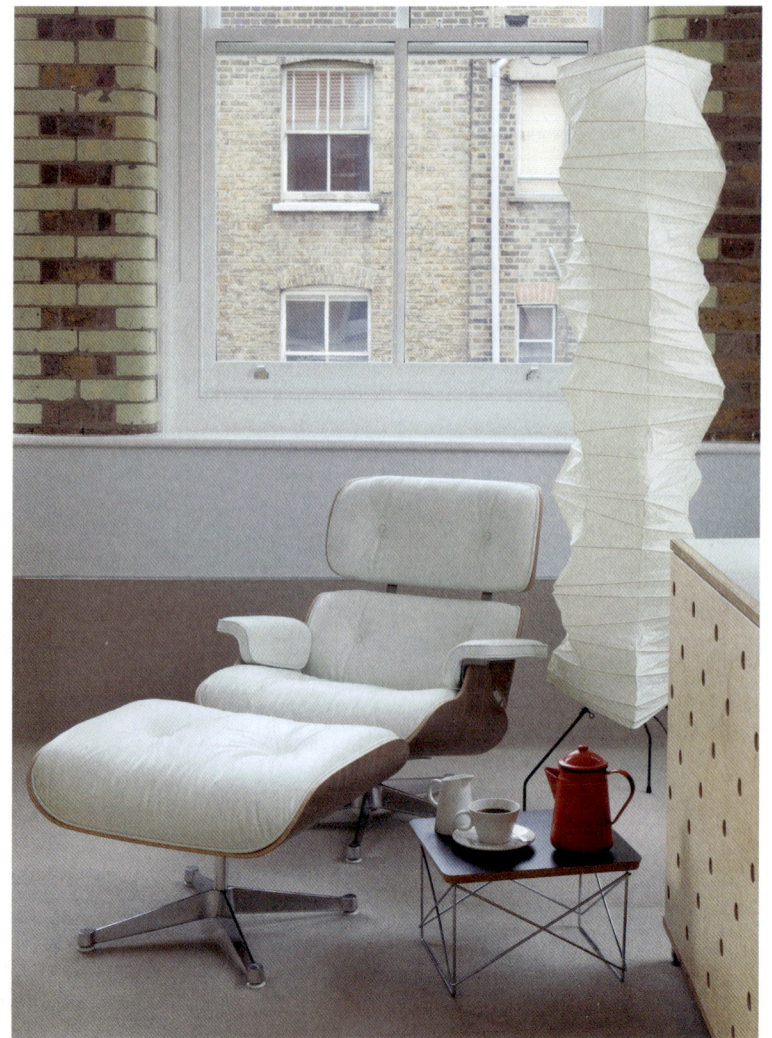

Destination	Location	Rooms	Themes
United Kingdom	London	17	City

Boundary Shoreditch

Housed in a converted Victorian warehouse, Boundary Shoreditch is a boutique hotel with 17 individually designed bedrooms, each inspired by a key designer or design movement of the 20th century. A serene retreat in the heart of Shoreditch, it sits on one of London's most fashionable streets, just minutes from the City. The property includes two restaurants, several bars, a rooftop terrace, and a range of private dining and event spaces. On the ground floor, the light-filled Bar & Brasserie serves seasonal dishes and elevated classics, with a cozy private dining snug tucked behind the bar. Upstairs, the Rooftop Bar and Grill offers a Mediterranean-inspired menu and sweeping views across Shoreditch, the City, and east London. Open year-round, the rooftop features a glass-covered orangery and spacious terrace with parasols for all-weather comfort. Step outside and you're moments from Redchurch Street boutiques, Brick Lane's buzz, and the City's cultural landmarks—whatever your interest, the hotel is your inside guide to East London.

Noa Hotel Beijing

Inspired by Beijing's ancient *hutongs* (narrow alleyways), Noa Hotel Beijing is a sociable ecosystem punctuated by courtyards and public spaces that encourage guests to connect. Thoughtful design links the space to the nearby Longfu Temple, a 600-year-old landmark from the Ming and Qing dynasties that has been reborn as a cultural venue. The hotel's red-walled exterior pays homage to the historic temple complex, while inside, gray bricks, natural wood, and structural steel beams establish a modern aesthetic. A dramatic lighting installation inspired by Chinese lanterns hovers above the dining area, its surface adorned with hand-painted dragon motifs. HK Workshop, the hotel's retail space, crafts handmade leather goods in a retro-inspired setting, while Deck Coffee & Taproom transitions from daytime drip-coffee meetups to craft-beer gatherings once the sun goes down.

Destination	Location	Rooms	Themes
Italy	Laigueglia	25	Beach, Gastronomy

Hotel Windsor

Sitting abandoned for nearly two decades among the winding alleyways and boutique shops of the sleepy seaside town of Laigueglia on the Italian Riviera, **Alessandro Sironi** quickly recognized the charm of this waterfront building. With the help of Studio Blesi and Subitoni, Sironi drew on the heritage of the surrounding area to return the building to its former splendor. Hotel Windsor exudes old world charm, with elegant shuttered windows and iron filigree railings embellishing the sand-colored façade. The designers evoked the building's glamorous past with neutral interiors against which custom-made furniture, sculptures, and iconic pieces of Italian design shine.

The hotel's restaurant capitalizes on fresh local produce and quality seafood, as well as rabbit, sheep, and lamb's meat to reinterpret classic dishes. Nearby hilltops provide space for hiking and mountain biking, while the hotel's private beach boasts pristine waters with comfortable loungers for guests to soak up the sun.

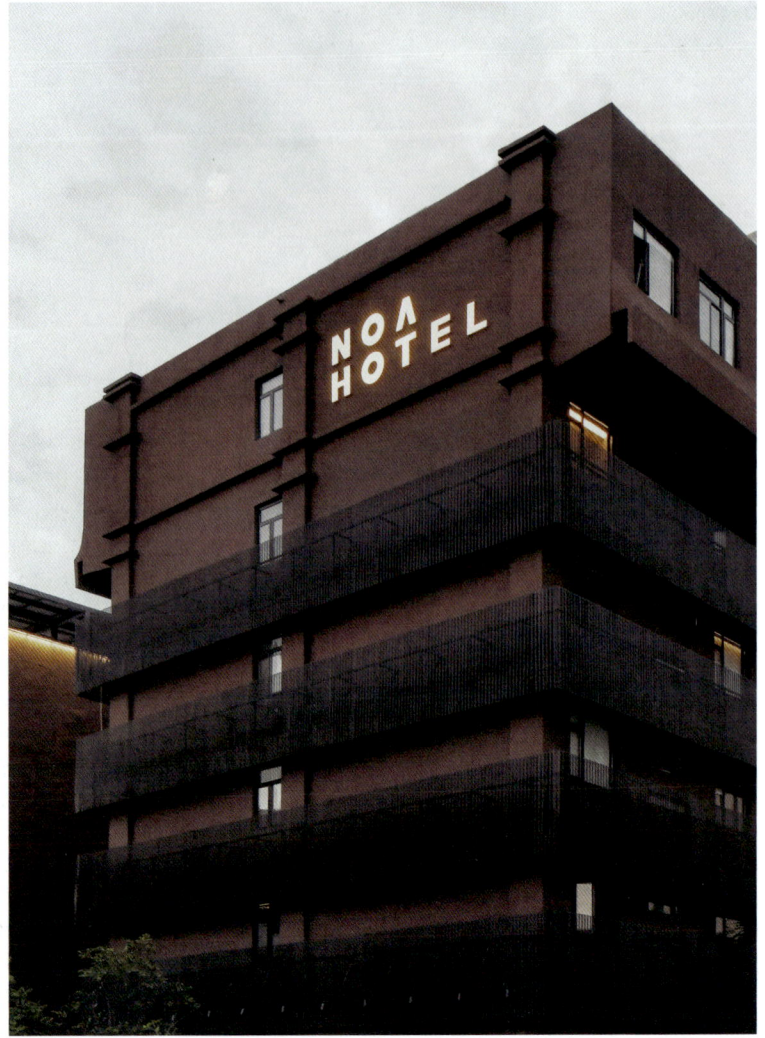

Destination	Location	Rooms	Themes
China	Shenzhen	102	City, History, Offbeat

Noa Hotel Shenzhen

In Shenzhen's Luohu district, **Peter Pan** and **Leo Li** have transformed a former factory into a contemporary retreat inspired by the story of Noah's Ark. The design celebrates the building's industrial past, thoughtfully evoked via raw concrete, stone, and steel. Within the 39 thoughtfully appointed rooms, guests can wake to a traditional American breakfast before exploring curatorial touchpoints integrated throughout the building: an eyewear boutique, the Noa Design Store, contemporary art exhibitions. At Deck Coffee & Taproom, innovative fusion cuisine pairs with specialty coffees and craft brews in a relaxed, sociable atmosphere. Wellness seekers can find respite at AN SPA's therapeutic and aerobics facilities, while the lovely People's Park nearby offers its own, floral-scented respite from the city's thrust. A short walk from Sungang metro station and the iconic Shun Hing Square skyscraper, Noa Hotel Shenzhen is a gathering place for the city's young, dynamic crowd.

Destination
United States

Location
Kingston, NY

Rooms
42

Themes
City, History

Hotel Kinsley

Just over 150 kilometers north of New York City is Kingston, a historic town nestled between the Catskill Mountains and the banks of the Hudson River. Named for its charming location, Hotel Kinsley offers convenient access to the area's beloved nature trails and quaint shops. The hotel is an amalgamation of four architecturally distinct buildings that date from the 17th to the 19th centuries. Studio Robert McKinley brought the interiors to life, restoring distinct architectural details like the original tin ceilings and centuries-old tile work, while introducing watercolor illustrations throughout and retro touches like leather banquettes in the hotel restaurant. Among the buildings is former bank 301 Wall Street, which acts as the hotel's fulcrum. Each of 301's 10 rooms features a different color story, with locally made and individually painted headboards contrasting with the clean lines and pastel walls. The other locations include a 1680s Dutch-settler building, a three-story building complete with a retail store, and a captivating 17th-century cottage.

Destination
Austria

Location
Lech am Arlberg

Rooms
62

Themes
Family-Friendly, Gastronomy,
Mountain, Sustainable

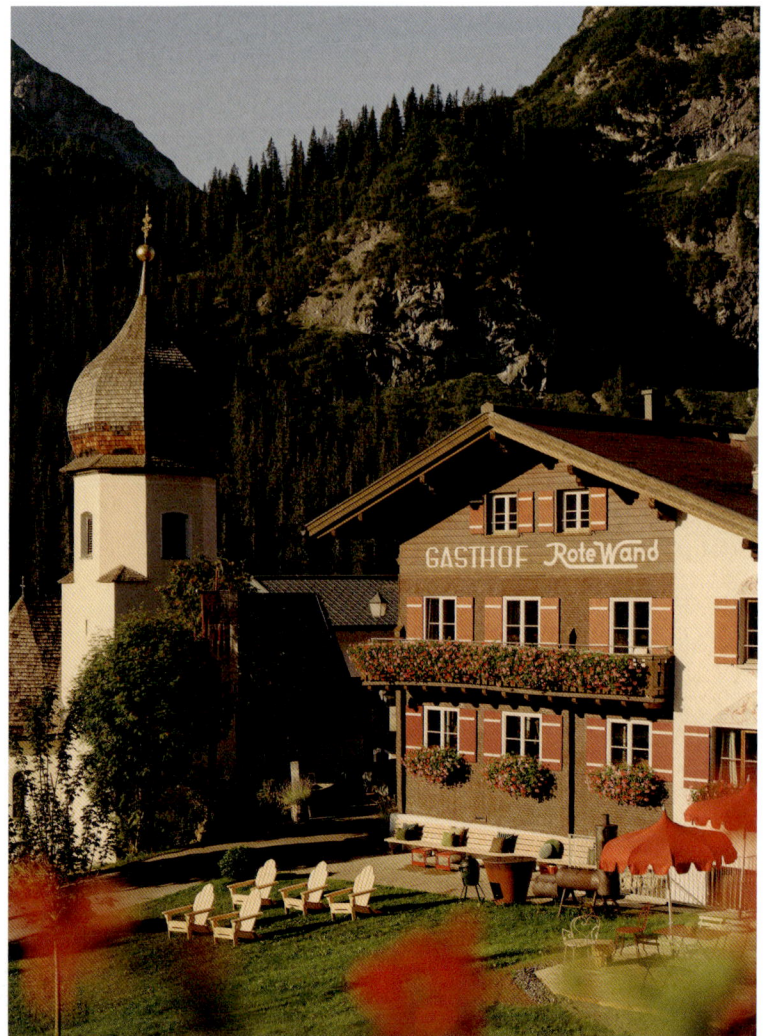

Rote Wand
Gourmet Hotel

Located in the picturesque Lech am Arlberg village is Rote Wand Gourmet Hotel. Owners **Josef Martin** and **Natascha Walch** have created a culinary haven that respects the hotel's traditional Alpine setting with modern indulgences and culinary starpower. Thoughtfully designed by Untertrifaller Architects, the hotel comprises five distinct houses with guest rooms furnished by local artisans using hand-hewn sycamore, ash, and spruce in a subtle palette of white and gray with touches of red. Rote Wand's culinary offerings are the crown jewel of this experience: the celebrated Chef's Table, set in a schoolhouse from the 1780s, is where two-Michelin-starred chef Julian Stieger creates exceptional dishes using the finest regional products. After skiing or hiking, guests can retreat to the spacious Rote Spa, complete with saunas, steam baths, heated pools, and wellness treatments for the ultimate in relaxation.

Hotel J

By the sea in Nacka Strand—and evocative of evokes the charm of nautical New England—Hotel J is just a quick drive from Stockholm's city center. Conceived by **Alessandro Catenacci** and inspired by the sleek J-class yachts of the America's Cup heyday, the 1912 brick building has been reborn in houseboat style, with whitewashed walls, oak furnishings, and cotton textiles. Surrounded by towering oaks and pines, the hotel features its own pier with views of the marina. The interiors reflect those found on a prized yacht—all natural wood, distressed rugs, and Breton stripes that enhance the nautical theme. A 10-minute stroll brings guests to Njuta Spa, perched peacefully on a seaside cliff.

The nearby Tornvillan, a 19th-century landmark, has been transformed into a summer bar. Guests can enjoy seasonal dishes with a focus on Swedish flavors, including—naturally—fresh seafood. Hotel J offers the perfect balance of city and nature, a breezy retreat through which to experience both Stockholm and its beloved archipelago.

Destination	Location	Rooms	Themes
Switzerland	Buchs	14	Countryside, Offbeat

Gasthaus Traube

In the Swiss town of Buchs, a 19th-century brewery-turned-restaurant has been lovingly expanded into a 14-room boutique hotel by **Kathrin** and **Ivan Secli-Schertler.** The new building rises from the bones of a dismantled stable, its natural materials and hand-built details reflecting a deep local lineage. Each room is individually designed, with handcrafted ceramics, timber walls and floors, silk lamps, and, crucially, no televisions—just speakers for music and space to unwind. A natural aesthetic and high-quality finishes unite the discrete spaces. The lush garden oasis connects to dining rooms filled with art nouveau murals, putti motifs, and preserved memorabilia that speaks to the building's past. Culinary offerings are spread across three distinct spaces: the cozy Braustube with comforting classics, the casual fine dining restaurant Traubensaal, and the sunlit Gartenzimmer, which serves brunch and bistro fare. From the rarity-stocked wine cellar to long, languorous meals beneath historic ceilings, every corner channels Buchs's rhythm—quiet, regional, and full of character.

257

Destination	Location	Rooms	Themes
Switzerland	Basel	33	Art&Culture, City, Interior Design, Sustainable

Art House Basel

Situated in Basel's Steinenvorstadt neighborhood, and in a city renowned for its art collections, Art House Basel reimagines the hotel as a canvas for creativity. Under the vision of **Antoine Faeh,** this city sanctuary celebrates contemporary design, culinary innovation, and artistic expression over six floors. An architectural passage connects two streets, with a statement staircase uniting the building's levels. Japanese-inspired materials—onyx stone, raw concrete, black steel, and oak—form a minimalist backdrop for art exhibitions curated with nearby COLAB Gallery. Guestrooms become galleries, showcasing emerging street artists alongside design pieces from Artek and Vitra. The hotel pulses with creative energy, with a rooftop bar and co-working space that invite explorers to connect. Large windows provide a cinematic view onto the neighborhood, reinforcing a sense of dialogue with the local urban landscape and its myriad creatives.

Destination	Location
United States	Palm Springs, CA

Rooms	Themes
39	Art & Culture, City

Drift Palm Springs

At Drift Palm Springs, California cool meets desert serenity and Mexican craftsmanship. Created by **Philip Bates** with interiors by Folklor, this 39-room retreat channels a Baja spirit through minimalist architecture, raw materials like steel, brick, and cedar, and artisanal touches from Mexico City and Oaxaca. Set against a backdrop of clean lines and a monochromatic-stucco exterior, the property balances desert modernist-style with organic, earth-toned luxury. Guests can unwind poolside with craft cocktails, cruise the neighborhood on complimentary bikes, or join a Saturday morning yoga flow class at Sol Studio. The onsite restaurant, Maleza, serves family-style Baja fare and rare mezcals in a vibrant indoor-outdoor setting. Every detail—from the artisanal ceramics to the locally sourced art—celebrates thoughtful design and cultural connection just minutes from Palm Springs' best dining and shopping.

Destination	Location
United States	Los Angeles, CA

Rooms	Themes
147	Art & Culture, City

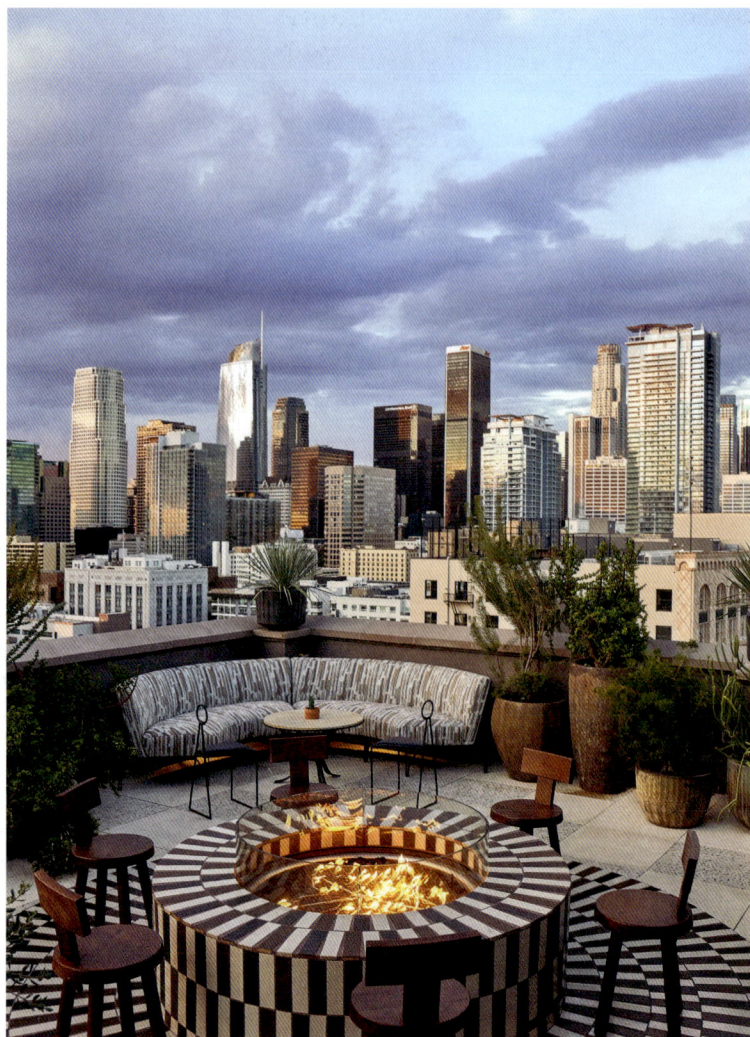

Downtown L.A.
Proper Hotel

Set in a 1920s Renaissance Revival landmark is Downtown L.A. Proper Hotel. With 147 rooms and suites, including an indoor pool suite and a full-size basketball court suite, the hotel channels West Coast cool through the creative lens of acclaimed designer **Kelly Wearstler** and co-owners **Brad Korzen** and **Brian De Lowe.** Wearstler's interiors mix Mexican modernism with French and Moroccan influences, and feature custom works from Los Angeles-based artists like Abel Macias and Ben Medansky. Culinary stars Suzanne Goin and Caroline Styne helm Caldo Verde and rooftop Cara Cara, where panoramic views meet fresh Southern Californian flavors. Once a YWCA and private club, the building's layered history is woven into every detail, from a speakeasy to multilevel pool deck. Proximity to the buzzing Fashion District completes the picture. With rooftop cocktails and curated art, Proper captures downtown Los Angeles's creative heartbeat, drawing travelers and locals alike.

Lo Sereno Casa de Playa

Lo Sereno Casa de Playa is an intimate 10-room retreat where the mountains meet the Pacific Ocean. Situated on the beaches of the world-class surfing destination Troncones, this oceanfront hotel by visionary **Rafael Sainz Skewes** integrates traditional Mexican craftsmanship with contemporary design. Created by Nicolas Sainz, Lo Sereno embraces a contemporary aesthetic infused with locally sourced materials and artisanal details. Each room features handcrafted furniture, spacious terraces, and slatted wooden doors designed to allow natural cross-ventilation. Bathrooms are minimalist yet striking, incorporating just three elements—glass, concrete, and wood—while *palapa*-inspired woven palm leaf artwork and textiles add palpable authenticity and warmth. A beachfront common space brings guests together at the infinity pool, restaurant, and bar, where fresh Mexican cuisine shines. This hideaway offers surfboards, beach essentials, and local treasures to further enhance this immersive coastal experience.

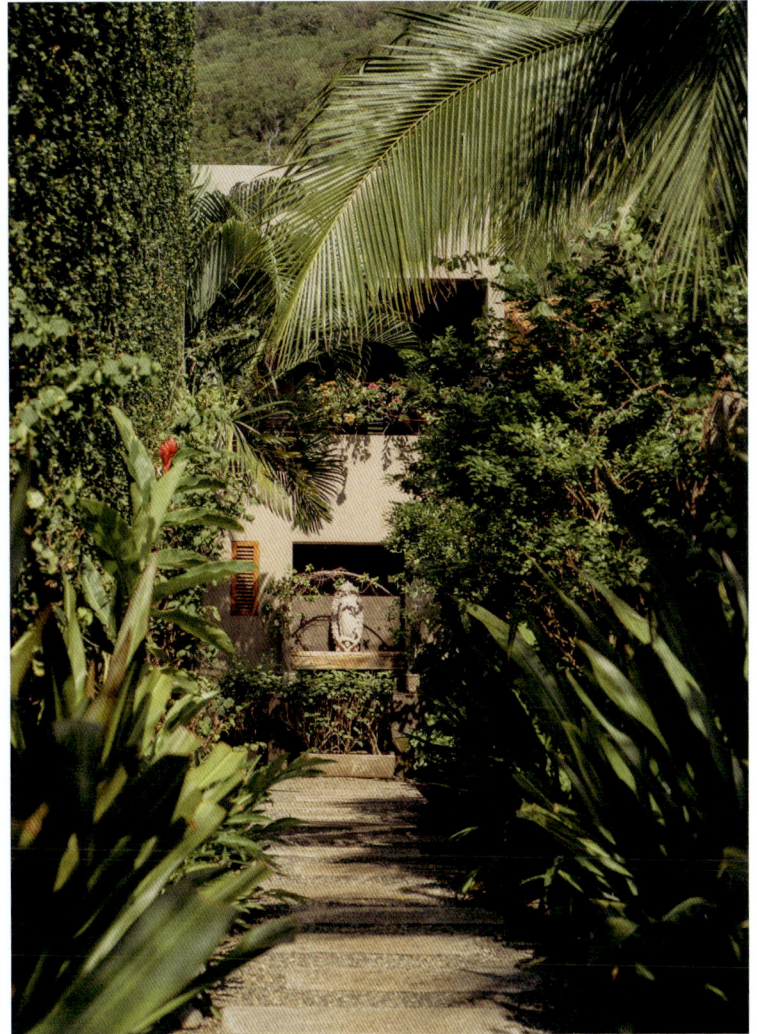

Destination	Location	Rooms	Themes
United States	San Diego, CA	96	City, Interior Design

Granger Hotel
Gaslamp Quarter

Located in a restored 1904 Romanesque landmark, the Granger Hotel embodies San Diego's past and future. With elaborate molding and arched windows, the hotel's historic exterior gives way to interiors where time periods beautifully collide. Inside, 120-year-old doors line wide corridors beneath original tin ceilings. The lobby is bathed in natural light from expansive windows, with a romantic palette of blush, chartreuse, and cerulean, and abundant plant life. Rose-colored marble and handmade tiles make for a sophisticated backdrop to artwork and vintage pieces. The 96 rooms are appealingly homey in navy and espresso tones, while custom ceiling murals featuring abstract depictions of elephants and lions add whimsical touches throughout. Artisanal plaster walls and lime-wash effects complement handcrafted built-ins. Steps away from San Diego's finest restaurants and boutiques, this **Mansour brothers'** creation—with interiors by Erika Baker—provides elevated accommodation in the city's timeless Gaslamp Quarter.

Destination	Location	Rooms	Themes
Germany	Munich	16	Art & Culture, City, History

The Flushing Meadows Hotel & Bar

Set in Munich's vibrant Glockenbach district, The Flushing Meadows Hotel & Bar embodies a vibe that's synonymous with its dynamic, youthful neighborhood. Originally a post office, **Sascha Arnold, Steffen Werner,** and **Niels Jäger** transformed the 1970s building into a loft-like boutique hotel that marries luxury with retro-midcentury style. The owners brought 11 local tastemakers on board to each craft their own light-filled loft studio. Harnessing the high concrete-enforced ceilings and building's industrial style, they developed a variety of unique designs—including a pink boudoir-style room with four-poster bed, a beachy retreat strung with a hammock, and a gloriously

gothic room featuring a record player and a whimsical sculpture of three skeletons rocking out. In shared spaces, Lebanese design firm PSLaB mixed industrial style with modern Scandinavian influences. Kvadrat fabrics soften the spaces, alongside ClassiCon and Thonet furniture. The rooftop bar is the place to go to soak up the local scene.

Destination	Location
Greece	Patras

Rooms	Themes
10	City, Gastronomy, History

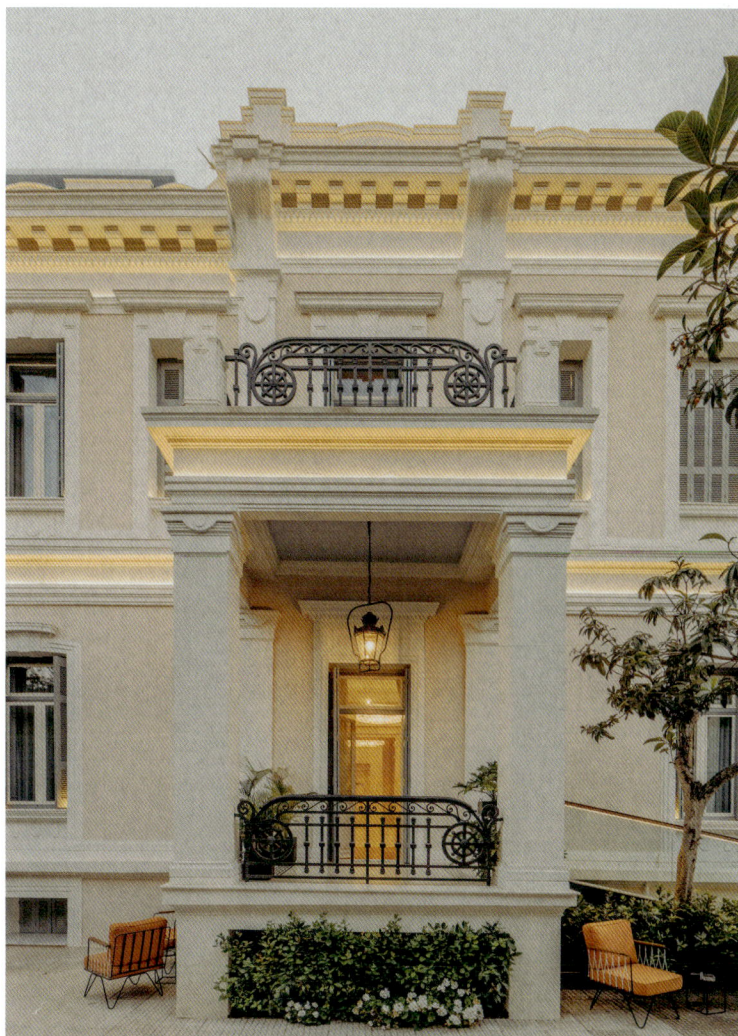

The Bold Type Hotel

In the ancient port city of Patras, a 19th-century mansion has been transformed into the area's only five-star property. Architect Empi Spathi approached the restoration as a work of art, maintaining the original shell's historical integrity with utmost care. A thoughtful three-tone color scheme connects guests to their surroundings—brick-red on the first floor honors the neighboring ancient amphitheater, cobalt blue on the second references the original house, and verdant green on the third complements the lush vegetation which embraces the structure. Soaring ceilings encourage guests to gather and mingle, with restored marble floors, authentic wooden shutters, Calligaris rugs, and Varangis furniture. The heart of the property is a magnificent Mediterranean garden courtyard, where talented chef Christos Spyropoulos serves inspired Greek-Mediterranean fusion cuisine. From the rooftop, guests can marvel at the Medieval Castle, which dates back to 551 AD, and the Roman Odeon, an open-air theater for 2,300 people that now hosts contemporary performances.

Destination	Location
Indonesia	Ekas Bay

Rooms	Themes
7	Beach, Gastronomy, Honeymoon, Offbeat

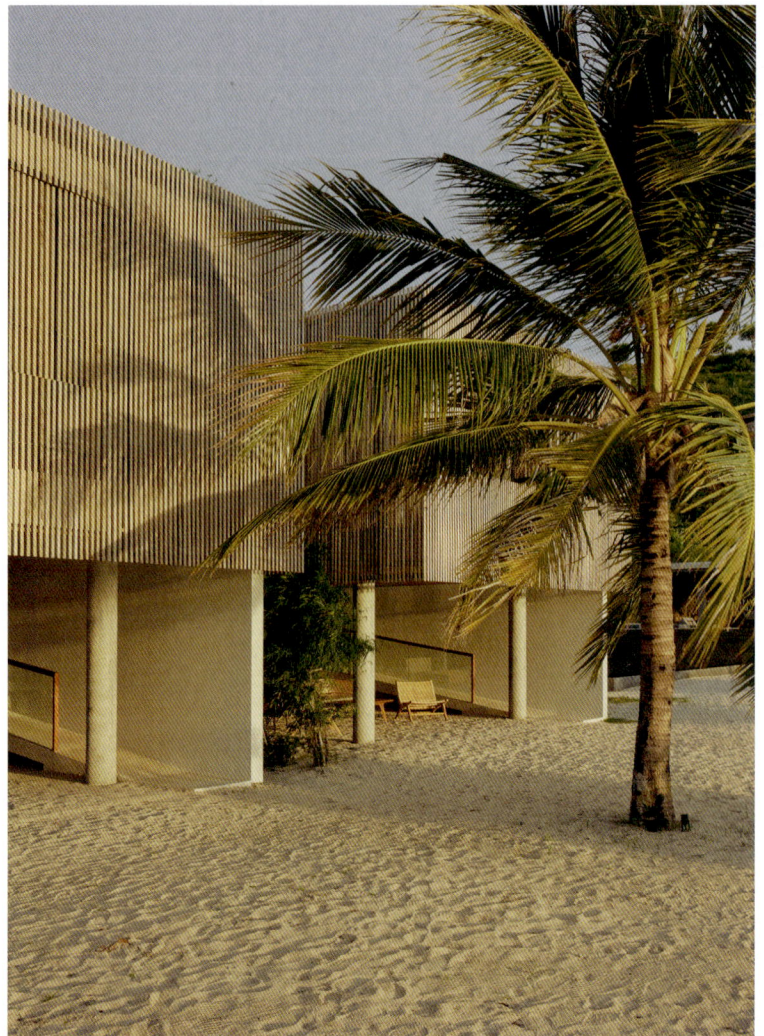

Innit Lombok

Owned by **Michal Tyles** and exquisitely designed by architects Andra Matin, Gregorius Supie Yolodi, and Maria Rosantina, Innit Lombok is a seven-villa sanctuary set along a secluded 250-meter stretch of white sand beach. Framed by a bamboo forest, the property is a poetic homage to Indonesia's architectural heritage, highlighting traditional Lombok Lumbung style alongside contemporary design. Each villa is a carefully crafted showpiece, utilizing local materials like teak, bamboo, and rock. Open-air living spaces and sand-level dining areas create an intimate connection with the landscape. Interiors feature understated, sleek furnishings by local designers, with standout elements like terrazzo bathrooms and handmade concrete surfaces. A culinary destination helmed by Indonesian chef Matthew Angga, Innit serves farm-to-table cuisine and locally caught seafood. From sunset beach barbecues to Michelin-inspired dishes, the experience celebrates the region's rich culinary traditions and natural bounty.

266

Cultural
Infrastructure

Sarah Owen

for the
Connected Age

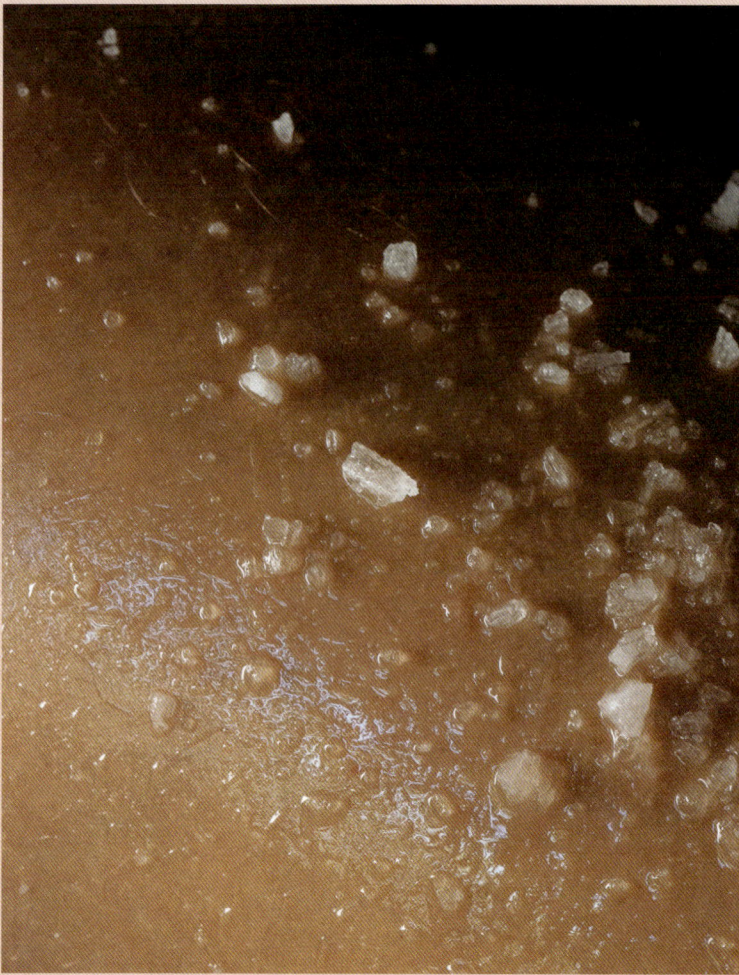

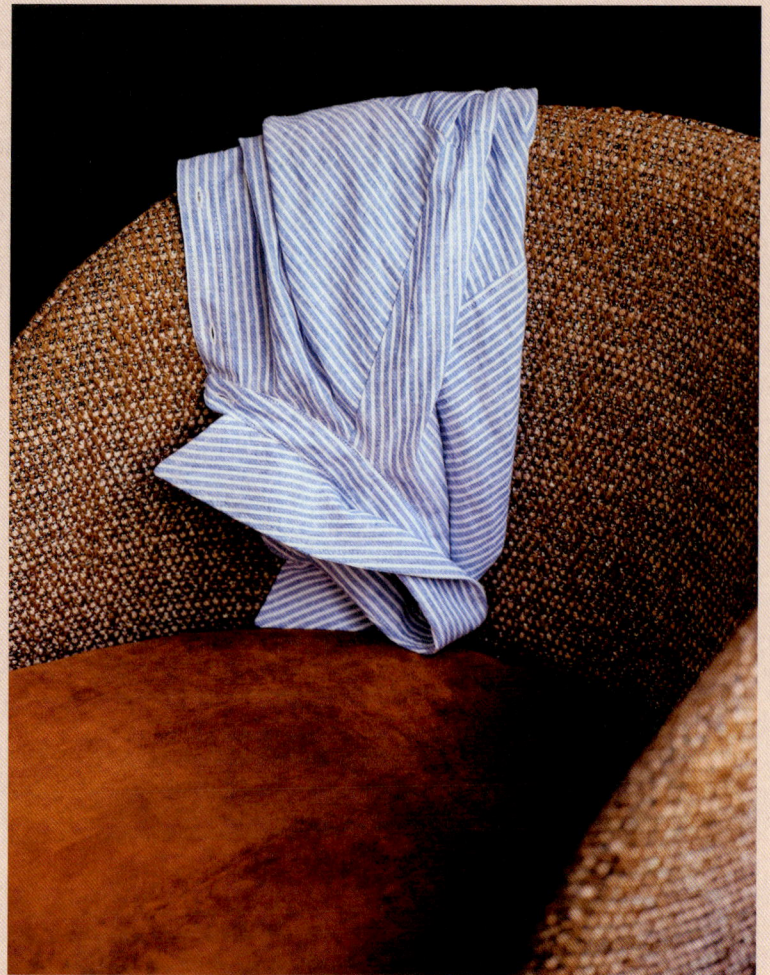

As a futurist and trend forecaster, Sarah Owen considers the shifting role of hospitality—how hotels, once seen as stopovers, have become vital civic spaces that help people feel rooted, seen, and connected.

A hotel is no longer just a place to rest your head. Over the last couple of years, they have emerged as a cultural interface, mediating who we meet, what we feel, and how we make meaning in a place.

In an age defined by social isolation and a relentless pace, the quiet ache for connection has become a near-constant presence, even if most of us have learned to numb or outrun it. Travel, once considered a form of escapism, is now more often a search for a sense of anchorage. Today, people aren't seeking luxury in the way that people used to. Instead, they're looking for resonance, for spaces that feel emotionally attuned, grounded, and human-size.

Nowadays hotels are doing more than hosting bodies: they're hosting meaning, too. Those in taste-making circles know that the most compelling hotels don't just provide amenities. On the contrary, they are shaping atmospheres, projecting values, and cultivating cultural capital by creating environments in which people can connect with one another.

This is simply the world we live in. It's a place filled with hybrid work, frayed relationships, and transient social networks. And what's missing isn't infrastructure but social architecture: Third places, which sit between home and work, are becoming increasingly difficult to find. Think of the bustling café, the rich public realm, or the bookshop with warm lighting and an open invitation to linger. These once-common spaces offered a sense of being seen without requiring performance. Hotels are now uniquely positioned to fill that void—not as stylish stopovers but as emotional landing pads for those navigating fluid identities, dispersed communities, and cultural dislocation.

This shift is also part of something more profound. Experience has become a form of identity work. Modern travelers are looking for alignment rather than just collecting decor ideas or ticking off destinations. The values of a place, its "vibes," and its pace all contribute. What's more, the most resonant hotels understand this, lean into it, and build intentional cultures with clarity and soul. This creates porous

Sarah Owen

boundaries between guests and locals, insiders and outsiders.

What people often want isn't that complicated. Most simply wish to gather, to feel part of something, even if fleetingly. And what nearly everyone wants now is to be welcomed to a space that isn't driven by metrics or the algorithm.

This may be one of hospitality's most overlooked powers: not just to provide comfort but to offer structures of belonging. In an era marked by fragmentation, fatigue, and ambient loneliness, the act of bringing people together is no longer a luxury. It's a form of cultural infrastructure.

If hotels can rise to meet this need, they will become more than destinations. They will evolve into vital civic spaces, not just mirrors of where we are but contributors to where we're going.

Christina Ohly Evans is a futurist, trend forecaster, and social scientist with over a decade of experience helping brands navigate emerging cultural shifts. With a background in strategic foresight and sociology, she has worked across the USA, Australia, and Europe, analyzing behavioral change for companies like WGSN and Protein. As cofounder of Soon Futures, she helps organizations anticipate what's next and make sense of what's happening today. Her writing has appeared in *The New York Times, Kinfolk, i-D,* and *WARC,* and she has spoken at global events including Cannes Lions and World Retail Congress.

When every detail speaks the same language, a guest's stay becomes immersive, intuitive, and lasting.

Destination	Location	Rooms	Themes
Indonesia	Canggu, Bali	6	Beach, Gastronomy

The Bohemian Bali

The Bohemian Bali is a former industrial warehouse turned sanctuary where a relaxed, bohemian spirit infuses Balinese heritage. Shaped by owner **Markus Hofer,** architect Josefina Gruenwald, and designers Nyree McKenzie and Fransisca Simon, this boutique retreat in Canggu unites raw urban aesthetics with the island's lush tropical setting. Indoor-outdoor living defines the space, with expansive sliding doors and windows dissolving boundaries between interiors and the landscape. Midcentury modern and boho-chic influences intertwine with traditional Balinese craftsmanship; natural wood, rattan, and stone for eclectic yet pared-back interiors. The hotel functions as both a retreat and a gallery celebrating local artistic talent, drawing a free-spirited creative crowd. Elsewhere, carefully chosen, atmospheric paintings make striking visual statements on textured walls. An open-kitchen restaurant serves innovative Indonesian cuisine, transforming time-honored recipes into nutritious, contemporary dishes. A pool shaded by palms promises unfettered serenity.

Destination	Location	Rooms	Themes
Japan	Tokyo	1	City, History

TRUNK (HOUSE)

Shibuya local **Yoshitaka Nojiri** decided to open the single-suite residence TRUNK (HOUSE) with the goal of reigniting his beloved neighborhood's creative spirit. The boutique one-suite hotel is tucked away down a secluded, narrow alley of Shinjuku's historic Kagurazaka neighborhood, in a traditional wooden house dating back to the early 20th century. Designers Tripster incorporated the building's past as a *ryōtei* (a traditional restaurant) and geisha practice room into the design, maintaining the original black walls of the ryotei. The designers further embraced tradition by including features like the tatami tearoom alongside more modern aspects of Tokyo life in the miniature karaoke bar—for guests wanting to exercise their vocals. Varied materials like Mortex, terrazzo, stucco, and black wood combine to create a rich, textural palette. Contemporary international furnishings embellish the Japanese design, from a Serge Mouille statement floor lamp to tea sets by Tom Sachs.

Destination	Location	Rooms	Themes
Sweden	Stockholm	49	City, History, Sustainable

Stallmästaregården

On Brunnsviken's shores, **Alessandro Catenacci** has revitalized Stockholm's very first inn into an idyllic retreat rich with royal history. The location for Queen Kristina's midsummer celebration in 1645, this estate has welcomed gourmands through its doors for centuries. Today, the property unites a restored historic structure with a thoughtfully integrated addition from 2000. Inside, 18th-century Swedish decor prevails—clean lines and floral patterns accented by oriental touches for subtle flourishes of stately grandeur. The main restaurant celebrates the hotel's heritage with warm copper tones, while chefs prepare local specialties from an open kitchen.

Versatile gathering spaces range from the courthouse banqueting room, adorned with sweeping chandeliers and murals, to the intimate Queen Kristina Pavilion—a garden-set gazebo with bay views for magical tête-à-têtes in winter and summer. Just a short walk from Stockholm's center, guests can enjoy uplifting vistas across the water in surroundings that continue to honor the legacy begun when Swedish royalty first discovered this exceptional spot.

YORUYA

Set among the willow-lined canals of the Kurashiki Bikan Historical Quarter, Yoruya distills centuries of history inside a restored *machiya,* or traditional townhouse. Once the residence of a Meiji-era merchant and later a beloved *ryokan* (traditional inn), the building is now a Kurashiki City–designated Traditional Building, balanced with contemporary comforts. Japanese lime plaster walls echo those found throughout Kurashiki, while Edo-period features like timber ceiling beams, tatami floors, and *shoji* doors invite quietude. Housed in 110-year-old renovated villas, the suites offer a serene retreat with spacious interiors and semi-open-air baths overlooking private stone gardens. At a cypress-wood counter, guests enjoy a vibrant, micro-seasonal, hyperlocal dinner menu featuring Seto Inland Sea seafood and sun-ripened produce. The intimate Bar Yoruya offers a curated list of sake and wines, including bottles from Okayama vineyard Domaine Tetta. Named after *yoru*—meaning to unite or intertwine—Yoruya weaves history, design, and hospitality into the evolving fabric of Kurashiki life.

Destination
Italy

Location
Panicale

Rooms
17

Themes
Countryside, Honeymoon,
Offbeat, Sustainable

Rastrello

Between Umbria and Tuscany, Rastrello is a meticulously restored 14th-century palazzo located in a picturesque village. This historic gem, brought to life by **Christiane Wassmann,** captures the essence of Italian countryside living with its mix of timeless elegance and contemporary comforts. Each of the 14 rooms and three apartments faces the valley, with calming views of Lake Trasimeno glittering in the distance. Inside, original beams, custom furniture by Pelizzari Studio, travertine marble, and *pietra serena* sandstone create spaces that honor both local heritage and modern sensibilities. At Rastrello Cucina & Giardino, chef Nicola Fanfano crafts farm-to-table cuisine using ingredients harvested daily from the hotel's gardens. The property's namesake— a *rastrello* is a small rake used for picking olives— hints at another treasure: extra-virgin olive oil produced from its own grove. Located in Panicale, recognized as one of Italy's most beautiful villages, Rastrello offers a taste of authentic Italian life while serving as a perfect base for exploring the surrounding countryside.

Destination	**Location**	**Rooms**	**Themes**
Lithuania	Vilnius	104	City, Gastronomy, History, Sustainable

Hotel Pacai

Set in one of Lithuania's most luxurious mansions, Hotel Pacai reenvisions 17th-century baroque opulence through contemporary eyes. Owner **Saulius Mikštas** and YesDesign Architecture executed the building's interiors using traditional materials such as clay, tin, stone, and barn wood to cohere the hotel's multilayered history. The team's goal was to keep the property's history on display, highlighting existing frescoes, vaulted ceilings, and unique wall textures with lighting design. Drawing on Baltic culture, Hotel Pacai hosts a range of art events and dinners, and has established itself as a cultural hub in Vilnius. The soft, deep palette of the interiors reflects the colors of different seasons in the region, with complementing artworks. A spacious courtyard sits at the heart of the property, acting as a convivial center point from which to enjoy Michelin-star dining and an award-winning spa.

Casa Foscolo
Hotel, Istanbul

Nestled in the heart of historic Beyoğlu, Casa Foscolo is a masterful restoration that brings Istanbul's layered past into the present. This early 1900s neoclassical building, reimagined by visionary **Yasemin Vargı Emirdağ** and architect Emre Kuzlu, is more than a hotel—it's a cultural haven where art, heritage, and contemporary life intertwine. The design preserves original stone walls, elegant doorways, and ceiling frescos, layered with refined modern touches. Spacious rooms with high ceilings, warm pastels, and elegant marble, ceramics, and tile mosaics reflect both authenticity and comfort. Art is central to the experience, with hotel walls doubling as exhibition space for the family's collection and commissioned works. A gallery and a branch of independent bookstore Minoa on the ground floor root the hotel in Beyoğlu's creative fabric. Its restored façade—highlighted by brick and travertine—along with revived doors and windows, celebrates neoclassical elegance while embracing a modern sensibility. Atop the building, a rooftop bar offers sweeping views of Istanbul's historic skyline. At Casa Foscolo, history isn't just preserved—it's alive.

Rėja

In a restored building in Klaipėda, Lithuania's only port city, stands Rėja. Set at the mouth of the Danė River on the Baltic Sea, the country's third-largest city is known for its 18th-century German-style timber architecture. A hotel since 1855, Rėja features a gorgeous mint-green façade with period detailing and a name that nods to the city's nautical roots—rėja referring to the beam that supports a ship's mast. Inside, rooms echo the rhythm of the Baltic: a sculpted marble headboard evokes the movement of waves, while soft blankets mimic the shifting coastal dunes. Sculptural mirrors and theatrical lighting play across rich textures and refined finishes—parquet floors, golden accents, and layered details that feel both immersive and elegant. Local craftsmanship is present throughout, from handmade ceramics and unique artworks to natural linen uniforms. Coffee beans are roasted locally in Klaipėda, while jams and preserves come from just 15 kilometers away—deepening the hotel's authentic connection to its surroundings.

Destination	Location
United Kingdom	Edinburgh

Rooms	Themes
98	City, History, Offbeat

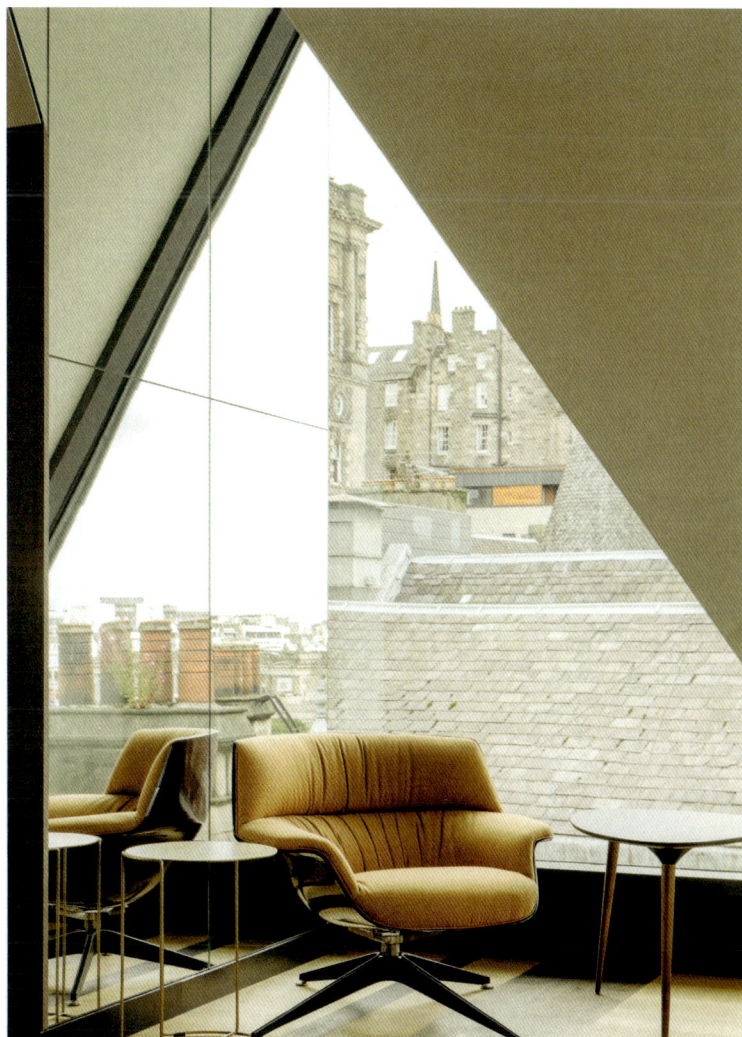

Market Street Hotel

Christa van Camp and **Colin Finnegan** built the Market Street Hotel on a small piece of land that had been neglected for over 50 years. The hotel is perched on the edge of Edinburgh's Old Town, moments from North Bridge, which leads to the city's New Town. This element of linkage inspired the owners to design the hotel around the notion of connection between history, modernity, and people. JM Architects referenced the materials and proportions of the surrounding city for the design and the result is an eight-story sandstone and whinstone building with a rippling roofline. Nor' Loft, the seventh-floor champagne lounge, serves small dishes alongside the largest Champagne list in the city, as well as views across the New Town. Inside, FG Stijl embraced a contemporary aesthetic, deploying Scandinavian-style furniture, sleek lines, and traditional fabrics like tartan on furnishings. The result is a calm, contemporary space that provides direct access to the city's ancient architectural wonders, cultural scene, and culinary offerings.

L'Ovella Negra Mountain Lodge

In a secluded valley in Andorra, L'Ovella Negra Mountain Lodge offers a genuine mountain escape where nature leads the way. The vision of **Prisca Llagostera,** brought to life in collaboration with interior designer Aminda Saludes, turned this former tractor and hay storage building into a community-minded haven that embraces slow hospitality. The lodge combines stone walls, wooden elements, and concrete floors to create a rustic yet refined atmosphere. Inside, natural materials form the backdrop for carefully curated interiors—brass candlesticks, velvet sofas, leather armchairs, and patterned fabrics—all trained around the property's central fireplace. Talented chefs Sergi Simó and Guille serve hearty dishes that complement the cuisine and atmosphere of surrounding glacial Vall d'Incles, where guests can immerse themselves in authentic mountain living through activities such as hiking, heli-skiing, fishing, and foraging.

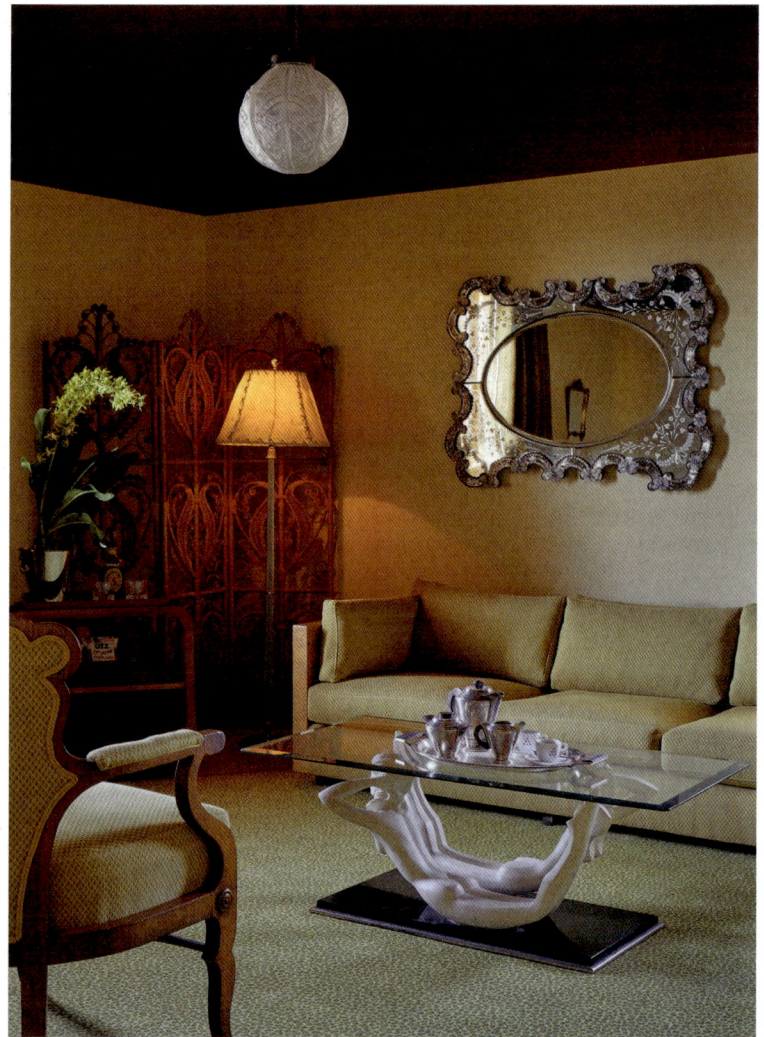

Hotel Ulysses

Canopy beds, plush quilted bedding, and charming vintage pieces combine in this opulent Italian Renaissance Revival building from 1912. Owners **Ari Heckman** and **Jonathan Minkoff** of Ash hotels engaged architect Quinn Evans to transform what were once a series of bachelor pads into an inviting hotel, cafe, and late-night lounge. Ash created a rich, cinematic landscape that takes influence from an eclectic palette including Indian design elements and Baltimore native John Waters's "high camp" style. One-time Baltimore residents Edgar Allan Poe and Billie Holiday also provide design inspiration, while rooms are planned around the four color schemes of cerise, citron, jade, and azure. Set in the historic District of Mount Vernon, Hotel Ulysses is moments away from the city's cultural attractions, restaurants, bars, and shops. Guests can experience an old-world cafe atmosphere at Ash—Bar, designed to resemble an ocean liner, with high-class cocktails and refined, European-inspired food, while the Art Deco-inspired Bloom's bar features a classic menu.

Destination	Location	Rooms	Themes
United States	Healdsburg, CA	55	City, Gastronomy, Offbeat

Hotel Healdsburg

In northern Sonoma, Hotel Healdsburg sits at the crossroads of three wine regions, with the area's finest dining just steps away. This 55-room sanctuary by **Circe Sher** and **Paolo Petrone** embodies wine-country elegance. David Baker Architects created a building where light defines the spaces, flooding French doors and balconies, and illuminating the glass-encased stairwell. Steel corridors are suspended over landscaped grounds that merge with public alleyways, creating a dialogue between the hotel and historic plaza. Inside, soft cloud paintings by Wade Hoefer complement pale blue design accents, ranging from shutters to throws. Custom furnishings from salvaged bay laurel trees bring Northern California's warmth to rooms framing garden views. Chef Charlie Palmer's Dry Creek Kitchen celebrates seasonal bounty, while the spa offers biodynamic treatments. As evening falls, the courtyard bar invites guests to enjoy live music amid trellised vines for an experience defined by relaxed sophistication.

Destination	Location	Rooms	Themes
Italy	Umbertide, Umbria	12	Adults Only, Countryside, History, Honeymoon, Offbeat

Vocabolo Moscatelli

Within Umbria's rolling hills, Vocabolo Moscatelli is a transformed 12th-century monastery, now a 12-room sanctuary. Owned by **Frederik Kubierschky** and **Catharina Lütjens,** and reimagined by architect Jacopo Venerosi Pesciolini, the hotel respectfully breathes new life into ancient stone walls. The property unfolds with a central piazza featuring a restored church (now an event space) and a pergola forged by a century-old blacksmith. Rooms exude historical charm alongside midcentury Italian craftsmanship. Custom furnishings, four-poster beds, and local art enliven spaces that honor the building's monastic roots. Bathrooms showcase tiles from Cotto Etrusco, with some suites featuring cantilevered bathtubs on sun-drenched loggias. A plant-forward restaurant celebrates Umbria's fertile landscape, serving dishes that prioritize local, sustainable ingredients. The travertine pool, surrounded by Paola Lenti furnishings, invites guests to linger between exploration and relaxation.

Destination	Location	Rooms	Themes
Poland	Stawiguda	20	Adults Only, Art & Culture, Countryside, Offbeat

Hotel Galery69

Hotel Galery69 is a living artwork born from the vision of artists **Malgosia** and **Wojtek Zoltowski**—a space where art, design, and lifestyle unfold as one intimate creation. Every detail is original, hand-crafted in their own manufactory, and the furniture is available for those who wish to bring a piece of this world home. Framed by a serene lake visible from every window, the hotel invites quiet moments on loungers and hammocks or gentle adventures by kayak, sail, or board. Inside, hidden nooks and crannies reveal ever-shifting works by artist friends, each visit unveiling new stories and inspirations. The gallery spaces come alive with concerts, exhibitions, and events, weaving art and experience into the very fabric of each stay. The restaurant offers natural cuisine, served à la carte exclusively to guests, while the pool and wellness sanctuary provide a private retreat within an adults-only haven. At 24 years into its planned 30-year life, Galery69 remains an evolving masterpiece—a rare, poetic experience to be lived before the final chapter is written.

Destination	Location	Rooms	Themes
Japan	Kyoto	19	Art & Culture, City

Genji Kyoto

Along the banks of the Kamo River, Genji Kyoto reveals an enchanting world where tradition and innovation intertwine. Designed by **Geoffrey P. Moussas,** this sanctuary celebrates Japanese heritage and craftsmanship through a contemporary architectural lens. The hotel embodies *teioku ichinyo,* the philosophy where garden and architecture become one. Zen gardens dissolve boundaries between interior and exterior, creating a harmony with nature that is both meditative and enlivening. Cedar-imprinted concrete walls, innovative *washi* windows, and custom-crafted furniture complement heritage elements that anchor the property in its cultural context, like a water basin, a small shrine, and antique stones. Each room pays homage to Murasaki Shikibu's *The Tale of Genji,* with artworks interpreting elements of the thousand-year-old novel about court life and the transience of happiness. Stand-alone hinoki bathtubs overlook pocket gardens, continuing Japan's historic bathing traditions. From the communal Genji Bar & Lounge to the Sky Forest Garden with its panoramic views, the hotel offers a modern expression of *omotenashi* (hospitality) that resonates with Kyoto's spirit.

289

Destination	**Location**	**Rooms**	**Themes**
Turkye	Istanbul	62	City, Gastronomy, Interior Design, Sustainable

The Bank Hotel Istanbul

This Neo-Renaissance-style building from 1876 was originally a German-built bank and vault, its stately façade an icon of Istanbul's Banks Street. Named for its history and the area's past as a center for goldsmiths and bankers, the building was purchased in 2010. It was then meticulously converted into a grand 62-room hotel and vibrant cultural meeting point, now known as The Bank Hotel Istanbul. Architect Han Tümertekin and designer Sinan Kafadar led the extensive restoration, prioritizing the preservation of the building's original grandeur. Inside, historical elements like authentic cash registers, elaborate fireplaces, and exquisite tiles seamlessly blend with modern luxury.

A rich color palette, custom-designed Italian furniture, and artworks carefully selected by an in-house curator complete the sophisticated ambiance, offering guests a truly luxe city sojourn.

Destination
United States

Location
Chicago, IL

Rooms
89

Themes
City, Gastronomy

The Robey

Wicker Park and Bucktown are among Chicago's most exciting, arts-engaged neighborhoods. At the intersection of these districts sits The Robey, a hotel steeped in both history and culture. Hotelier duo **Carlos Couturier** and **Moisés Micha**—known for their ability to create hotels that uniquely reflect their locale—opened The Robey as a hip meeting spot for visitors and locals with a sky-high cocktail lounge and modern-American cuisine on the menu. Antunovich Associates designed the hotel from two adjoining historic buildings; one a distinctive triangular prism, among the tallest in the area, and the other a former warehouse. The first, gray limestone structure houses the Tower Rooms, while the second houses 20 Annex Loft guestrooms with an open-plan lobby and a neighborhood-hub feel. Nicolas Schuybroek Architects and Marc Merckx Interiors executed the interior design using hardwood floors, pristine glass, and a palette of terrazzo, natural woods, and red, pink, white and gray tones in communal spaces.

Attuned to
the City

In the heart of the world's busiest cities, these hotels don't retreat from energy—they reshape it. Through rhythm, atmosphere, and sensory intelligence, they create spaces of emotional clarity. Here, presence is carefully composed: not silent but attuned. The city doesn't disappear—it becomes more human.

The Static Performance:

Eleni Petaloti

Designing for Felt Experience

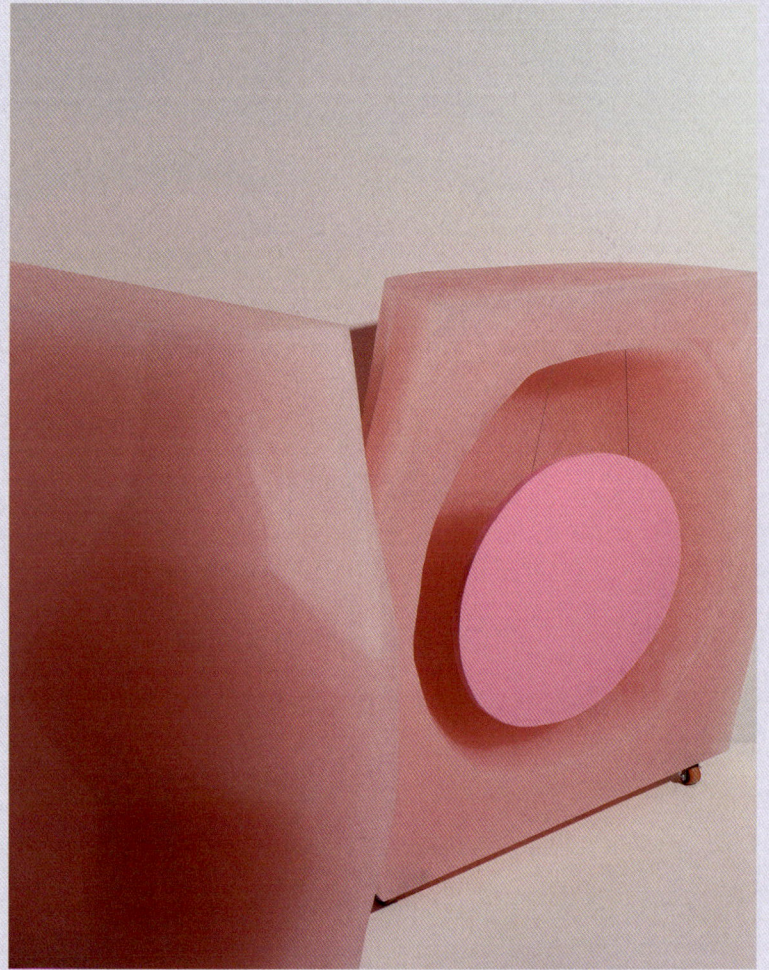

Working at the edge of architecture and sculpture, Eleni Petaloti of Objects of Common Interest explores how softness, ambiguity, and spatial tactility can reorient our perception of hospitality.

Design begins with a quiet provocation: can a space offer more than what first meets the eye? Not a single, instant reading, but a layered experience, how it resonates in the body, how it invites stillness or movement, intimacy or awe. At the core of Objects of Common Interest's practice is thus an exploration of atmosphere, spatial softness, and sculptural form as a tool for emotional orientation. In this way, architecture becomes not a static container but a dynamic field of perception—a choreography of encounters.

We consequently often work in the spaces between disciplines: where furniture becomes architecture, where light becomes material, and where a room becomes a landscape. This ambiguity is purposeful: it creates moments of pause, reflection, and curiosity. It can often arrive via an element that ostensibly offers no clear function yet quietly defines the

space around it nonetheless. This could be a glowing volume that becomes both sculpture and light source, or a soft surface that slows your gait. Whatever it is, such gestures are not merely ornamental, but invitations to inhabit space more consciously and sensorially.

Thus, in our practice, softness, tactility, and ambiguity are not aesthetic choices; they are spatial strategies. They offer a slower rhythm of engagement, introducing not only a sense of comfort but also a touch of unfamiliarity. This contrast encourages presence. Slowness becomes a condition of attention. It enables presence. You are invited not only to see but to feel; to read space with the body rather than just with the eyes. That act demands time, and in that time reflection becomes possible.

In a hotel context, this can create micro-moments of grounding. Such instances could include placing a hand on a textured wall, sitting against a rounded surface, or following the curve of an object with your fingers. But whatever the case, these physical interactions are always subtle yet deeply felt, often bypassing intellectual critique and striking directly at memory and emotion.

Softness, tactility, and ambiguity invite slowness; they encourage reflection rather than reaction.

The objects we design are therefore not fixed in meaning. They exist in dialogue with their environment. We think of them as part of a static performance: carefully placed yet open-ended, encouraging interaction, awareness, and evolving engagement over time. Their stillness is not passive but intentional. They act as anchors of experience, shaping how one moves, sits, rests, or simply notices one's surroundings.

Part of this ethos is informed by the belief that everyone carries a story. Often quiet, even subconscious, it moves beneath the surface like a hidden current—occasionally rising, taking form through memory, gesture, and space. That story, constantly in flux, finds its way into the spaces we shape and inhabit. When revealed, it becomes a gift. A shared narrative. This mode of experiencing design through personal memory and emotion moves beyond critique or competition. It forms relationships, and in so doing it subtly reshapes the stories of others.

When designed according to these principles, hotels can become immersive

Eleni Petaloti

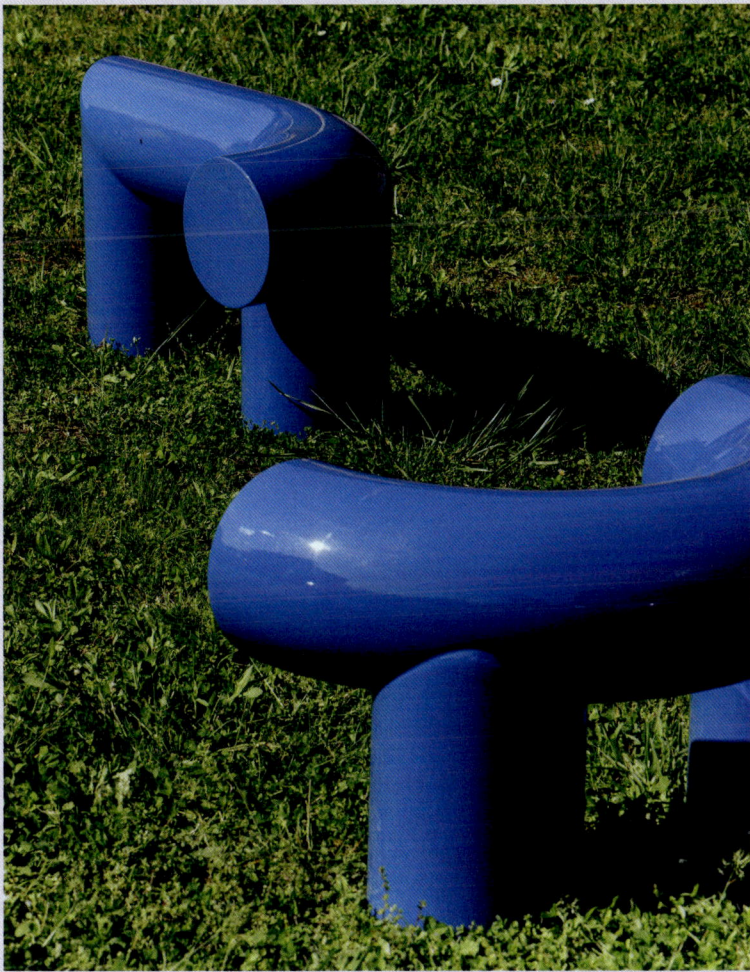

environments that heighten everyday experiences. A hotel's layout, for instance, will guide the rhythm of a guest's stay. Materiality can also create thresholds between public and private, between the active and the introspective. Light can mark time. Tactility can evoke memory. Through this, design becomes a form of storytelling, employing sensation as its primary means of narration.

In our work, we are drawn to elemental forms and raw materials, such as marble, resin, glass, and textiles. These materials are chosen as much for their visual presence as for how they shift with changing light, how they age, and how they invite touch. We believe in the power of ambiguity: soft edges over hard lines, and transitions over divisions. These gestures encourage a slower mode of engagement, where boundaries dissolve and the body takes the lead.

In our Weltanschauung, a hotel is thus a type of landscape. It is not arranged like a stage set, but like a terrain to be explored, where paths are revealed rather than dictated and moments of solitude and collectivity emerge organically. The guest becomes an active participant in shaping the experience, rather than a passive observer. And it is for this reason that we see architecture and design as tools to create presence. That might seem self-evident, but there's a nuance to our philosophy. It's about drawing awareness to the here and now and offering shelter not just from the elements but from noise, speed, and the overwhelming excess of the modern world. As such, a well-designed space doesn't impose itself—it supports, frames, and nurtures. In doing so, design becomes an invisible host. It sets the mood, orchestrates transitions, and shapes memory. And it is this invisible choreography—the interplay of light, form, surface, and time—that allows a space to truly stay with you.

Eleni Petaloti is an architect, designer, and cofounder of the transdisciplinary studio Objects of Common Interest. Working between New York and Athens, her practice blends spatial design, sculpture, and material research to create emotionally resonant environments. With a background in architecture from the University of Thessaloniki and Columbia GSAPP, she explores the poetics of form and tactility at the intersection of art and design.

Destination
United States

Location
New York City, NY

Rooms
207

Themes
Art & Culture, City, History

11 Howard

In 11 Howard, hotelier and real estate legend **Aby Rosen's** goal was to create a hotel that felt timeless, while paying homage to modernist architect Philip Johnson. Anda Andrei Design and Space Copenhagen—the pioneers behind Noma restaurant—collaborated on the design, gutting the 1961 building to execute a minimalist, Scandinavian aesthetic, with simple, midcentury-style furniture, natural materials, and pale timbers in rooms with high ceilings and substantial windows. A suite of works by international artists graces the hotel, reinforcing its air of timeless elegance: a poetic Alexander Calder mobile hanging from the soaring lobby ceiling;

ceramics by Taiwanese American artist Katie Yang; atmospheric prints by Hiroshi Sugimoto; and hand-painted murals by English artist Holly Fowler. Sweeping views from the hotel's rooftop pool invite guests to soak up the downtown atmosphere from on high. In the restaurant Le Coucou, Michelin star-holder Daniel Rose collaborates with restaurateur Stephen Starr on classic French dishes.

Destination
Portugal

Location
Lisbon

Rooms
50

Themes
City, Gastronomy

Altis Belém Hotel & Spa

On the Tagus River, **Raul Martins** and **Maria Júlia Valente-Rodrigues's** award-winning Altis Belém continues their family's tradition of Portuguese hospitality, alive since 1973. Architect João Almeida created two intersecting structures enhanced by self-described "waves of lace"—movable shutters shading rooms from the sun's rays. Inside, each space evokes the Age of Discovery, with glass walls softening a minimalist aesthetic. The ethos is simple: work with local materials and staff to bring local character to the hotel. The Michelin-starred Feitoria Restaurant & Wine Bar embodies this philosophy, blending traditional Portuguese gastronomy with exotic world cuisines, while Gastrobar 38°41 offers jazz nights and cocktails on its riverside terrace. The exclusive BSpa by Karin Herzog—the Swiss brand's only Portuguese outpost—provides ancient oriental relaxation traditions in its Thermo Garden. Marking the spot where 15th-century explorers once departed, this sophisticated property welcomes guests to Belém's palatial parks and cultural landmarks.

Destination	Location	Rooms	Themes
Italy	Rome	32	Art & Culture, City, Gastronomy

Palazzo Velabro

Nestled between the Palatine Hill and Tiber Island, and curated by **Cristina Paini,** Palazzo Velabro is a place where time seems to pause. Housed in an 18th-century palazzo reimagined in the 1960s by architect Luigi Moretti, it still carries his signature curves, now reawakened in tones of sage, brick, and cobalt. Inside, a quiet alchemy of walnut, marble, glazed ceramics, and velvet creates a tactile sense of comfort and depth. In the lobby, a work by Ettore Spalletti sets the tone for a space where art is more than decoration. A site-specific fresco by Edoardo Piermattei and rotating exhibitions offer an evolving dialogue with contemporary creativity. A secluded terrace frames fleeting views of ruins and Roman rooftops. The hotel's library and cinema feel like two chapters of the same story: by day, Patricia Urquiola armchairs invite quiet reading; by night, the space transforms into an intimate screening room. At Apicio 16, Roman culinary heritage is distilled into contemporary expressions. With pieces by Moroso and handcrafted floors by Garbellotto, every detail contributes to a quiet, immersive experience where history and design meet in a uniquely Roman rhythm.

Destination
Germany

Location
Berlin

Rooms
158

Themes
City, Gastronomy,
Sustainable, Well-Being

The Mandala Hotel

Intimately linked to the redevelopment of Potsdamer Platz, Lutz Hesse and Christian Andresen launched The Mandala Hotel in 1999, where it quickly became a hub for visitors wanting to explore the newly updated precinct. Architects Lauber + Wöhr designed the hotel (alongside two other Potsdamer Platz projects), while Hesse executed the interiors with Donghia furnishings, cherry-wood floors, and raw-silk curtains paired with hand-picked Chinese antiques. On the fifth-floor courtyard, the hotel restaurant Facil boasts two Michelin Stars in an oasis of greenery, while first-floor Qiu Bar & Restaurant provides a calm vantage on the city below. The 600-square-meter, top-floor Ono Spa offers respite with hot stone massage, saunas, and metabolism-stimulating infrared couch.

Drift Santa Barbara

Housed in a reimagined 1920s Spanish building, Drift Santa Barbara brings raw, natural materials to Baja minimalism—dark walls, concrete textures, oak mill-work, and repurposed California redwood—for a sleek, design-forward experience. Just blocks away from the beach and pier, the property invites exploration by day and connection by night, with Dawn coffee shop offering brews and pastries and Dusk bar serving tequila, tapas, and a sheltering ambiance beneath soft, atmospheric lighting. Architecture and interiors by Anacapa embrace both the city's heritage and an urban edge, with brass accents, black-painted walls, and sculptural built-in furniture. The rooms feel simultaneously grounded and elevated, balancing moody tones with warm details. Throughout, subtle design choices nod to local surf culture, art scene, and overall laid-back rhythms. With street-facing venues designed to foster community and a restrained yet inviting aesthetic, Drift challenges the expected Santa Barbara experience, grounded by a bold creative vision from founder **Philip Bates.**

Destination
Italy

Location
Bergamo

Rooms
15

Themes
City, History, Offbeat

Destination
Spain

Location
Madrid

Rooms
42

Themes
City, History

GombitHotel

Galeotti Nadia's GombitHotel offers an experience of cultural and epicurean discovery. Its original 13th-century stone walls and wooden beams provide a canvas for designer Giò Pozzi's vision. Twelve rooms and three suites feature a restrained palette complemented by handmade linens. Local artist Steven Cavagna incorporated salvaged materials into his additions, while two mezzanine suites feature views of the hotel's tower. Here, guests can enjoy a vibrant community of artisans, unparalleled fine dining, and vistas of the Alps and renaissance domes.

Hospes Puerta de Alcalá

In 2008, José Maria de Aguilar updated this red-brick building from 1883—once a royal estate, no less—into a stately hotel with dark woods, rich textures, and gold, silver, and white accents. Designer Tomás Alía struck a delicate balance between honoring the building's history—enhanced with ornate bedframes and luxe jacquard fabrics—and modernizing the setting with Eero Saarinen Tulip chairs and tables, and spacious in-room bathtubs. Guests can enjoy innovative tapas overlooking the Puerta de Alcalá in the hotel's Terraza Malvar.

Destination
Czech Republic

Location
Prague

Rooms
109

Themes
City

Destination
Spain

Location
Seville

Rooms
41

Themes
City, History, Sustainable

Hotel Josef

Architect Eva Jiřičná brings her distinctive aesthetic to Prague's Hotel Josef. Streetside, geometric awnings exaggerate the hotel's façade, while a statement staircase in glass and steel spirals in a double helix. Meanwhile, Baleri armchairs, Philippe Starck fittings, and limestone floors contrast with contemporary angles. **Markus** and **Michael Ploberger's** hotel in the city's famous fairytale Old Town exemplifies modern Czech design. A rooftop gym, verdant garden, and wellness center invites guests to unwind after sampling Prague's many pleasures.

Hospes Las Casas del Rey de Baeza

Housed in an 18th-century dwelling, this 41-room retreat fuses Arabian and Andalusian influences. Whitewashed walls feature ochre accents and wooden balconies overlooking a tranquil courtyard scented with the perfume of flowering orange trees. Inside, natural textures like esparto carpets and riverbed rock paths are paired with dark wood furnishings and beech paneling for a warm, earthy feel. From the rooftop terrace, guests can take in sweeping views of the city, while a plunge pool and sunbeds provide the perfect spot to enjoy the Spanish sun.

Destination
United Kingdom

Location
London

Rooms
86

Themes
City, Well-Being, Sustainable

Inhabit Southwick Street

Nadira Lalji's second London sanctuary takes a holistic approach to wellbeing, shaped by Caitlin Henderson Design's sensorially attuned interiors. Holland Harvey Architects have reimagined six Georgian townhouses into contemplative environments that invoke calm. A plant-filled atrium offers space for quiet reflection, while a former drawing room houses a modern library stocked with literary classics, contemporary novels, and design volumes. English limestone floors help guests feel grounded, as fiddle-leaf fig trees and planters of rosemary and thyme scent the air. Furnishings by Hans Wegner, EOOS for Carl Hansen & Søn, and GamFratesi for Gubi are paired with sustainably crafted pieces by Burmese artisans. Miya Ando's fine art prints and Nur Mut's nature photography impart stillness, while dedicated wellness areas offer restorative programs. From a pantry filled with goods from local makers and organic farms to Yeotown's kitchen serving plant-based dishes, cold-pressed juices, and specialty coffees, wellbeing here feels intuitive and ingrained.

Le Roch Hotel & Spa

Nestled in the ultimate sweet spot between Place Vendôme, Palais Garnier, and the Louvre, Le Roch Hotel & Spa is a soft-lit, pastel-hued escape in Paris's prestigious 1st arrondissement. The hotel's 37 refined rooms seamlessly blend timeless luxury with contemporary flair. Interior designer Sarah Lavoine has thoughtfully curated spaces that showcase clean lines, rich walnut wood, and Carrara marble, creating a sophisticated yet welcoming atmosphere. Guests are invited to relax in the plush lounge or the cozy library, where shelves are lined with carefully selected books and art pieces. The gastronomic experience shines at Maison 28, a casual dining spot serving delicate French classics made with fresh, local ingredients. For a restorative escape, the serene spa features a striking black-lava rock pool bathed in natural light, complemented by a leafy, plant-shaded garden—a rare sanctuary in the heart of bustling Paris.

The Prestige

In George Town's UNESCO-listed heart, **Tommy Koay** combines Victorian-era romance with modern design at The Prestige. The 162-room hotel is styled like a garden conservatory, with black-and-white tiled floors, rattan, and lush planting echoing Penang's Botanical Gardens. A delicately etched bronze wall reflects scenes of Penang past and present. Optical illusions make for magical settings: beds appear to levitate, rooms are hidden from view, and rotating corridor lights animate intricate lattices of shadow for guests to walk through. Rest and relaxation await at the rooftop infinity pool with quayside views or the serene wellness spa, where treatments draw on centuries-old Malaysian healing practices.

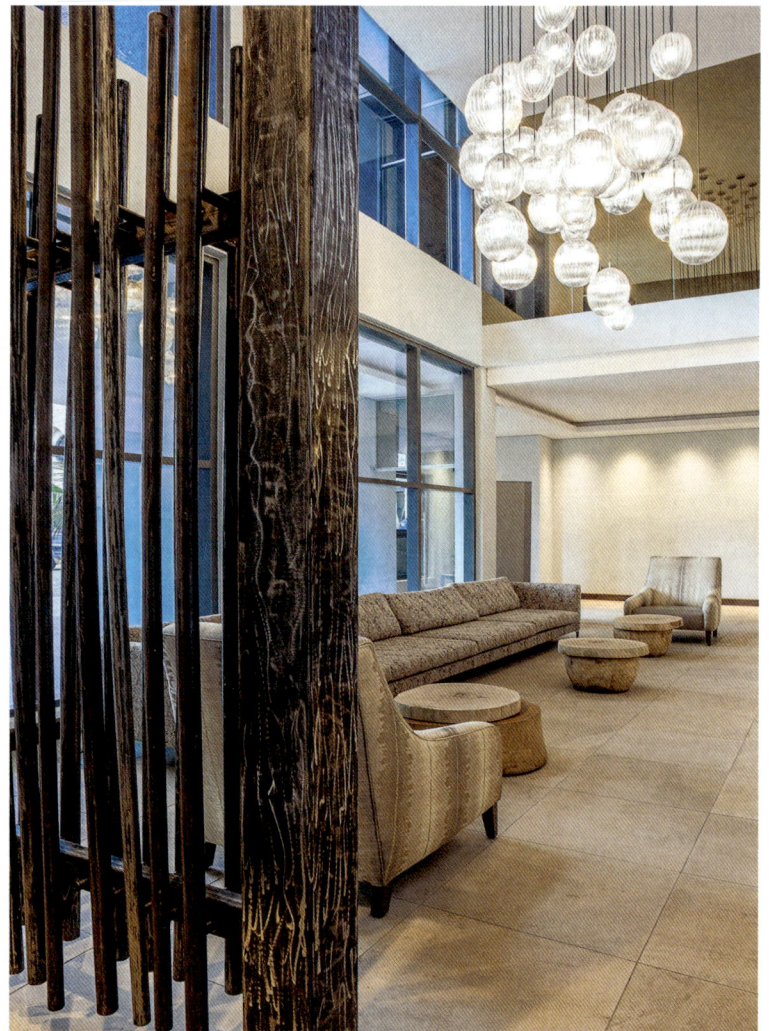

Destination
Turkey

Location
Istanbul

Rooms
18

Themes
City

Destination
Kenya

Location
Nairobi

Rooms
215

Themes
City

Witt Istanbul Hotel

Witt Istanbul Hotel invites guests to step into a stylish, immersive space. Designed by Autoban, **Tuncel Toprak's** hotel blends monochromatic tones, polished black tiles, and marble. French balconies decorate the sandstone façade, enticing passersby with a peaceful retreat and framing views of the Bosphorus. Inside, leather sofas and rocking chairs create an atmosphere perfect for socializing, while subtle floral motifs appear throughout. Enveloped by the area's creative tempo, guests are encouraged to feel like residents of this artistic neighborhood.

Trademark Hotel

Shamim Ehsani's Trademark Hotel offers a fresh take on modern design, featuring pillars that create airy spaces and a sense of flow between rooms. Expansive windows bring the outside in, connecting guests to the surrounding city, while tans and yellows evoke the local landscape. Situated within the Village Market shopping complex, the hotel is also close to the stunning, expansive Karura Forest. With the rooftop pool and gym offering sweeping views of Nairobi's skyline, guests can seamlessly transition from the city's pulse to a peaceful retreat.

Destination
Italy

Location
Milan

Rooms
124

Themes
Art & Culture, City, Gastronomy,
Interior Design, Sustainable

Hotel Viu Milan

In Milan's evolving Porta Volta neighborhood, **Antonio** and **Tommaso Viscardi**
have created a striking destination for
creative, sustainably minded travelers.
The standout feature: a tower partially
cloaked in lush vertical gardens. Natural
light pours through the glass façade,
illuminating interiors where a Gio Ponti–
inspired fireplace anchors the lobby and
sets the tone for inviting spaces framed
by floor-to-ceiling windows, parquet
oak floors, rich wood accents, and timeless Italian furnishings by Molteni in
calm, earthy hues. Michelin-starred chef
Giancarlo Morelli brings his infectious,
innovative energy to three distinct dining
concepts: his eponymous restaurant
featuring signature Milanese cuisine, the
vibrant Bulk Mixology Food Bar, and
the Friends' Table—a special experience
inside the heart of the kitchen, where
guests can immerse themselves in the
artistry of cooking. On the eighth floor,
the Viu Terrace opens up to panoramic
views of the Milan skyline. Here, the rooftop pool and bar create the perfect spot
to swim, sip, and unwind above the city.

Destination	Location	Rooms	Themes
Thailand	Bangkok	78	City, Interior Design

Public House Bangkok

Public House Bangkok offers an inclusive, modern take on the traditional British gentlemen's club, dreamed up by husband-and-wife team **Paul** and **Angie Sachdev.** A social hub in the vibrant Sukhumvit district, the hotel is designed to make guests feel they belong, while serving as a launchpad to explore Bangkok's shopping, dining, and entertainment scene. Interiors feature a stylish mix of industrial and midcentury modern elements, with 78 well-appointed rooms designed for comfort and practicality. Custom-made furniture, imported tiles, and a curated mix of local and international art give each space a fresh, refined character. SWD, the hotel's flagship restaurant, celebrates global comfort-food classics, with flame-cooked dishes using Binchōtan charcoal. The communal, relaxed atmosphere encourages new connections and shared experiences over memorable meals or by the rooftop pool, which offers stunning views of the surrounding neighborhood.

21 Carpenter

Richard Hassell, cofounder of award-winning firm WOHA, reimagined a heritage 1930s shophouse as 21 Carpenter—connecting Singapore's architectural past with its design-forward present. Nestled between Boat Quay and Clarke Quay, the building once served as a remittance house for migrants—personal histories are etched into the façade as a quiet tribute to its past. Hassell preserves the soul of the original structure while adding modern sophistication. Reclaimed materials, original emblems, and historic inscriptions are woven throughout, alongside bespoke elements by Hassell—like headboards featuring fragments of the Chinese character for "home" and carpets with flowing calligraphic patterns. Interiors balance warmth and modernity, with soft palettes, tactile finishes, and custom furnishings. A perforated aluminium façade envelops the hotel, diffusing daylight, reducing heat gain, and boosting sustainability. Anchoring the culinary offering is Kee's, a neo-bistro and bar led by Michelin-starred director Andrew Walsh, serving refined European classics and pan-Asian favourites.

Destination
Bulgaria

Location
Sofia

Rooms
35

Themes
City, Gastronomy

Junó Hotel Sofia

Tucked away among Sofia's architectural treasures, **George** and **Rumi Chopev's** Junó Hotel Sofia is a striking new arrival in the city's dynamic downtown area. The hotel pairs a bold limestone façade made from local marine fossils with soft minimalism inside, where floor-to-ceiling windows, warm wood, and natural fabrics set the tone. Oak and teak flooring, woven carpets, and bespoke furniture from various acclaimed studios ground the earth-hued interiors, while artworks from sculptor Pavel Koychev and street artist Nasimo deepen the connection to local creatives. At street level, the hotel center's around the restaurant Cookó Kitchen:Drinks, where chef Valery Rusanov prepares seasonal dishes inspired by Balkan and Mediterranean traditions. Open to the street through sliding glass doors, the eatery blurs the line between inside and out, mirroring the hotel's larger vision—where light, art, food, and design come together in an atmosphere rooted in heritage while being refreshingly forward-looking.

Destination
Austria

Location
Vienna

Rooms
43

Themes
City

Destination
Germany

Location
Frankfurt am Main

Rooms
50

Themes
City

DO & CO Hotel Vienna

Set within Hans Hollein's visionary Haas Haus, DO & CO Hotel fuses modern design with Austrian tradition. Overlooking St. Stephen's Cathedral, this urban retreat offers luxury, bold architecture, and unforgettable views. Each room is crafted with natural materials like teak and stone. Gastronomic wizard **Attila Dogudan** brings culinary excellence to three floors of dining, including the Onyx Bar and the Temple pavilion. Guests can unwind in the lounge, sip cocktails at the rooftop bar, or step outside to explore. This is Vienna at its most vibrant.

The Pure

Owned by **Alex Urseanu** and **Micky Rosen,** and designed by Scharnberger Architekten and Rosen Architekten, The Pure embodies Frankfurt's cosmopolitanism. In it, Rosen and Urseanu have combined white leather, marble, and clean-lined furnishings with ambient light and music. Guestrooms feature high ceilings, zebrawood, parquet, and open living rooms. A timber patio offers outdoor relaxation, while the 24-hour gym and sauna make for a rejuvenating retreat. Artist Stefan Strumbel's work explores the idea of home—a contemplative motif in this serene sanctuary.

Destination
Spain

Location
Valencia

Rooms
67

Themes
City, Sustainable, Well-Being

Destination
Italy

Location
Rome

Rooms
35

Themes
Art & Culture, City

Hospes Palau de la Mar

Hospes Palau de la Mar reimagines two 19th-century palaces as a modernist retreat. Collaborating with Hospes Design Team, interior designer Tomás Alía infused the property with contemporary textures and tonal contrasts while preserving the original architecture of these stately homes. With its carved bannister, the loggia stairway lends the space drama. The rooftop Spa Bodyna offers curated wellness treatments and breathtaking views, while Ampar restaurant presents elevated Valencian dishes paired with regional Spanish wines.

Elizabeth Unique Hotel

Once a historic palazzo, Elizabeth Unique Hotel is now a gateway to the past. Designed by Studio Marincola Architects, its interiors mix antique references and modern lines. With arched doorways, canopy beds, and lacquered wood, the hotel's 35 rooms epitomize elegance. The lobby welcomes visitors with curated artworks. Many of the rooms feature restored elements and custom furnishings too. Set off Via del Corso on charming Frezza Street, the hotel is near the Spanish Steps, high-end shopping, and Rome's inimitable culinary scene.

Destination	Location
Finland	Helsinki

Rooms	Themes
153	Art & Culture, City, History, Sustainable

Hotel St. George

In Helsinki, Hotel St. George reimagines hospitality within a landmark structure whose walls once housed the Finnish Literature Society and the country's first newspaper. **Mirkku Kullberg** converted this architectural treasure—with parts dating to the 1840s, and whose best-known sections were designed by architect Onni Tarjanne in 1890—into a 153-room escape honoring its heritage. The hotel's artistic vision is manifested immediately through Ai Weiwei's whimsical silk and bamboo dragon floating above the lobby. The commitment to culture extends throughout, from a six-meter-long brass bird sculpture by Finnish artist Pekka Jylhä to the hand-crafted furnishings in the rooms. Culinary excellence thrives at Boon Nam, where chef Tomi Björck combines subtly captivating Thai flavors. Meanwhile, the property houses the Nordic region's first holistic luxury spa. Unostentatious, but undoubtedly luxurious, Hotel St. George reimagines the hotel experience as an intersection of the arts, wellness, and design.

Destination
Spain

Location
Granada

Rooms
42

Themes
City, History, Offbeat, Sustainable

Destination
Vietnam

Location
Ho Chi Minh City

Rooms
36

Themes
City

Hospes Palacio de los Patos

Hospes Palacio de los Patos provides a masterclass in continuity. The original structure has been preserved; its proportions honored as contemporary materials quietly intervene. Inside, coconut leather, stainless steel, and pale wood play against white walls and original stonework. This transformation reflects an evolution and a sensory experience, spotlighting regionally rooted cuisine, including Mozarabic-inflected tapas, and ancestral techniques practiced in the modern rooftop Spa Bodyna. At every turn, the past is thoughtfully reimagined.

Bach Suites Saigon

Bach Khanh Hoa's hotel draws on Ho Chi Minh City's French colonial heritage. Designed in 2018 by Felice Iacobellis and Lam Nguyen, its white, Hausmann-style façade features rounded corners, steel-window accents, and embellished niches. The monochrome aesthetic is reflected in the interiors, where wainscoting lines the walls, alongside parquet floors, stately lamps, tiles, and lounge chairs. Guest rooms are sumptuously outfitted, with seven suites featuring king-size beds and kitchenettes. A gym and outdoor rooftop pool crown this elegant hotel.

The Dominican

Situated in central Brussels, The Dominican is a luxurious tribute to its former life as a 15th-century Dominican abbey. With architecture by Lens°Ass and interiors conceived by FG Stijl, the hotel takes modern sophistication to medieval grandeur. Soaring ceilings, original stone floors, and pointed arches build a sense of cloistered drama, while elegant guest rooms open onto a peaceful inner courtyard. The Grand Lounge—richly furnished in velvet and leather—and The Courtyard patio are refined, plant-shaded spaces in which to dine on delicious Belgian cuisine. Located near La Monnaie opera house, The Dominican is a veritable sanctuary where ancient charm meets contemporary luxury in the heart of bustling Brussels.

The Pulse of
a Place:

Arman Naféei

Why Ambiance Is
the Secret Sauce

Drawing on over a decade of experience mastering the sensory identities of both boutique and renowned hospitality franchises alike, Arman Naféei reveals how atmosphere and emotional intelligence transform hotels into cultural institutions—and why true hospitality is always a matter of feeling.

Hotels aren't just places where we sleep. They're multifaceted institutions, home to restaurants, bars, leisure, wellness, and fitness facilities, performance halls, retail experiences; and other inspiring spaces that transport guests to other realms. Of course, such notions are hardly new. In the late 19th and early 20th centuries, grand hotels were social hubs where conversations unfolded, aesthetics were shaped, and cultural codes were exchanged. Figures like César Ritz understood this intuitively, designing hotels not only as places of rest but as stages for life. In the postwar years, that sensibility shifted when hospitality became more democratic and utilitarian. Suddenly, hotels had become places to pass through, not dwell in.

Indeed, it wasn't until the 1980s that we witnessed a return to hotels as curated, experiential spaces. During this decade, pioneers like Steve Rubell and Ian Schrager, co-owners of Studio 54, began to reimagine what hospitality could be—particularly in cities like New York, where public life often takes precedence over private space. Through their iconic Royalton Hotel—which opened its doors in 1988 and is commonly regarded as the first design hotel—the hotel lobby evolved from a purely functional threshold into a hybrid environment. Restaurants, nightclubs, boutiques, and bars became part of the hotel's offering, creating an ecosystem that extended far beyond the guest room.

In effect, the Royalton laid the foundation for what we now call lifestyle hospitality. Today, a successful hotel is expected to have a point of view. Cultural programming, art direction, and collaborations with local creatives are no longer added value; they are the baseline. I spent a decade working alongside André Balazs, whose influence on this evolution cannot be overstated. His approach was not driven solely by visual styling but by spatial flow, emotional tone, and a commitment to hospitality as a cultural medium.

Arman Naféei

To be sure, his philosophy helped shape the trajectory of my own work. What began as a tongue-in-cheek title—"director of ambiance"—ultimately became central to how I operate, capturing the ineffable qualities of atmosphere that define my approach. In fact, it became so important that we even trademarked it. The idea is to articulate and take ownership of the curatorial decisions that shape how a space feels—viscerally, sensorially, and socially. It's what I describe as sensory branding: a layered orchestration of lighting, scent, acoustics, and materiality. These elements operate below the level of conscious attention but have an outsized impact on how people remember and relate to a space.

But it wasn't always quite like this. The turning point was arguably my early role as music director at The Standard in New York. Prior to this, no one quite knew what a hotel music director was meant to do. And in truth, neither did I. But I quickly learned that music could calibrate mood with remarkable precision. It set the pace, shifted the energy, and helped express the hotel's identity in ways that language or visuals could not. That realization broadened my focus to include other intangible aspects of experience design—the elements you can't capture in a blueprint but ultimately define a space's atmosphere. Naturally, there are technical components to consider as well: acoustics, lighting schemes, and floor plans. But experience is shaped as much by instinct as by specification. I often compare this process to cooking. You can give two chefs the same ingredients, but the dish they produce will depend entirely on their intuition, taste, and ability to balance flavors. The same is true when composing a space. It's not just about what goes into the design. It's also about how it's arranged, how it flows, and how it interacts with human behavior.

A good example of this is a large project that I recently worked on. In that case, we simply—and relentlessly—rearranged furniture to test how guests might feel in the space. It was a physical, collaborative process, almost like choreography. The work lies in observing, responding, and iterating in real-time, based not on metrics but on emotion, intuition, and flow.

In this sense, I believe that personalization—that is, ensuring the layout of rooms, including fittings and furniture, is optimally configured—will define the next phase of the hospitality industry. Generic experiences no longer satisfy. Guests want to feel seen. They want spaces that respond to their preferences, moods, and values. For younger audiences, especially Gen Z, identity and experience are closely intertwined. The smallest gestures, such as a personalized playlist, a preferred drink waiting at the bar, or an handwritten note, can create lasting emotional resonance.

Of course, technology will play a part in this evolution, but only when it is used to create a sense of connectedness between humans. When integrated thoughtfully, AI can help anticipate needs and refine the guest's journey. Its function is not to automate hospitality but to elevate it. Used well, it doesn't replace a space's emotional intelligence but enhances it. At the same time, there are conventions in hospitality that should be challenged. I've always been wary of institutional language, such as those empty, pre-scripted phrases like "How was your journey?" or "Can I get you another glass of tap water?" They reduce human interaction to performance. Authenticity, by contrast, is imperfect. It allows for spontaneity and nuance. Hospitality should never feel like a transaction; it should feel like care.

In this sense, the simplest proof of this wisdom is that people will always remember how you made them feel, not whether you executed the script flawlessly. This distinction is critical. The most successful hotels I've worked with understand that tone matters more than polish. They don't aim for perfection but for presence. They create environments that invite people to stay longer than they planned, to engage more deeply, and to carry the memory with them.

Memories, after all, are the bricks and mortar of our lives. They are what make us unique, and that is why this simple principle is so vital. For me, I've a few ambitions that, if fulfilled, I'll be able to look back on proudly.

In a world that often favors the fast and forgettable, it's a space for slow, thoughtful conversation. And, of course, if Wes Anderson ever calls and asks me to score a film, I'll be ready.

Arman Naféei of Studio Neu in Los Angeles is a pioneering "director of ambiance"—a title he famously trademarked—working at the intersection of hospitality, fashion, and media. Known for his transformative role in shaping the sonic and experiential identity of spaces like The Standard Hotels, he's also famous for his cult-favorite podcast *Are We On Air?*, where he's hosted such cultural titans as Björk, Frank Ocean, André 3000, and Jeff Goldblum, among others. His work explores how music, atmosphere, and compelling storytelling converge to define cultural relevance in contemporary hospitality.

Destination	Location	Rooms	Themes
United States	New York, NY	81	City, Interior Design

The Moore

Situated in the heart of Manhattan's Chelsea neighborhood, The Moore is a refined urban retreat envisioned by **Eric Freitas Orford.** With 81 elegantly appointed rooms, the hotel mixes historic charm with contemporary hospitality. Its classic façade, left untouched, pays homage to the area's storied architectural past, while interiors by Vanessa Guilford of design studio Tocci make for a warm, homey atmosphere. Guests enter a space that feels more like a welcoming neighborhood gathering spot than a traditional lobby, with a coffee shop encouraging casual connection. Luxurious yet understated, rooms are accented with rich oak-wood flooring, brass-inlaid furniture, and deep charcoal velvet drapery. Named after Clement Clarke Moore, the renowned writer and scholar behind Chelsea's development in the 1880s, The Moore is a fine balance of heritage and modernity—an experience that feels less like a hotel, and more like home in the heart of New York City.

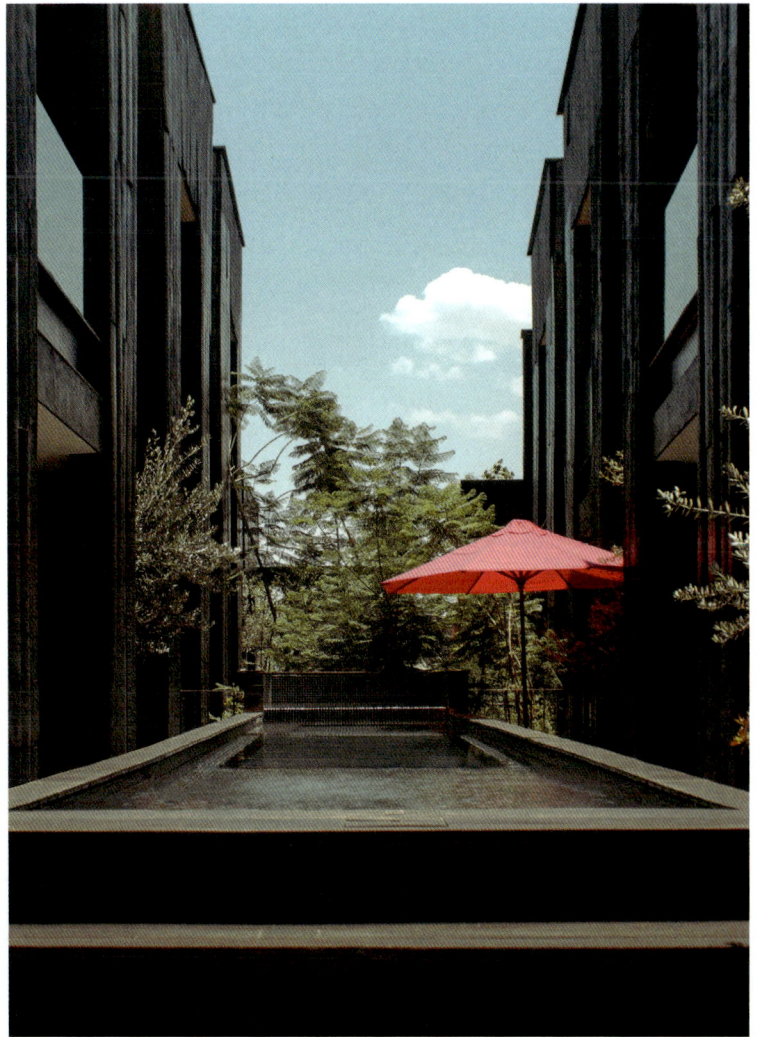

Destination
Turkey

Location
Istanbul

Rooms
67

Themes
City

Destination
Mexico

Location
León, Gto.

Rooms
19

Themes
City, Gastronomy, History

Gezi Hotel Bosphorus

Can Atay's Gezi Hotel Bosphorus is a curved zinc-and-titanium sanctuary. A green-certified property, it represents METEX Design Group's signature fusion of timeless design and eco-technology. Inside, bold color-blocking enlivens cream and chocolate spaces, while wood and leather furnishings create warmth. Windows frame panoramic Bosphorus views, each room a tranquil refuge fitted with modern comforts. Beyond aesthetics, this practically zero-emissions hotel features a relaxing hammam, spa, and a restaurant where guests can watch ships sail the strait.

Elena de Cobre

Elena de Cobre's links past, present, and future. Guided by his mantra "the more you do, the more you learn," **Mario Plasencia** created a Brutalist-style copper structure floating above a 19th-century mansion. In turn, the design maintains many of the building's original elements while incorporating hydraulic floors and Japanese wood-charring techniques. Inside, authentic mosaics and wood beams meet clean contemporary angles. At Luciérnaga Restaurant, old family recipes make for authentic Mexican cuisine that draws guests to the glass-ceilinged bar.

Destination	Location	Rooms	Themes
United States	West Hollywood, CA	23	Adults Only, City, History

Hotel 850 SVB

Hotel 850 SVB resonates with a lived-in, timeless elegance. Hotelier **Jeff Klein** envisioned a boutique hotel that combines residential living with luxury design. From the street, the West Hollywood bungalow resembles a beautiful house, and this homeliness carries through the property, encouraging guests to unwind. English interior designer and journalist Rita Konig combines eclectic items including artworks, hardwood floors, luxury linens, weathered armchairs, and marble bathrooms for an artfully undone feel. Konig's color palette takes inspiration from the California sun to add light to the space, with warm, uplifting tones. The open-air roof deck is inviting and relaxed, with views across the city, padded deck chairs, and a fireplace for year-round comfort, while the reception area doubles as an intimate lounge and wine bar ideal for relaxing or working.

Destination
United Kingdom

Location
London

Rooms
115

Themes
Art & Culture, City,
Interior Design, Well-Being

Ham Yard Hotel

The vivid and vivacious design style of Ham Yard Hotel mingles easily with the atmosphere of London's West End. Following interior designer **Kit Kemp's** idiosyncratic style, the hotel, owned by Tim and Kit Kemp, has art at its core, with pieces such as a Tony Cragg bronze sculpture located in the hotel's tree-filled garden thoroughfare. London-based architectural design firm Woods Bagot designed the hotel as a contemporary building that's equal to the scale of its surroundings. The village-style hotel is expansive, with a restaurant and bar, state-of-the-art theater, 13 specialist shops, and an antique 1950s bowling alley imported from Texas. Raised railway sleepers and picket fences frame herb and vegetable gardens, whose produce features on the Ham Yard Bar and Restaurant menu. Kit Kemp's meticulous eye for detail—from the undulating form of a headboard to the particular style of a valance—cultivates a truly unique hotel experience.

Destination	Location	Rooms	Themes
Poland	Warsaw	47	Art & Culture, City, History

H15 Boutique Hotel

Occupying a 19th-century building on one of Warsaw's most historic streets, H15 Boutique Hotel's central location has borne silent witness to the upheavals of European history. Architect Mariola Tomczak preserved its neoclassical socialist façade while opening the interior out with glass walls, natural oak floors, and a tranquil palette. A black-and-white checkered courtyard conservatory, serving as both the lobby and a cultural venue, leads into calm spaces where high ceilings and original works by Rita Zimmermann lend each suite their own character. Select rooms, including the Penthouse and Signature Junior Suite, feature spacious terraces with views over the city, while the restaurant serves fittingly modern European fare.

Destination	Location	Rooms	Themes
Germany	Cologne	39	Art & Culture, City, History

The Qvest Hotel

In the heart of Cologne's Old Town, The Qvest occupies a 1897 neo-Gothic treasure on a tranquil square between the city's cathedral and Belgian Quarter. This contemporary refuge marries historical architecture—pointed arches, stained glass windows—with museum-worthy art and modern design. Owner and art collector **Michael Kaune** preserved the cross-vault ceilings, original stucco, and windows during renovation, while ensuring each of the rooms and suites holds individual character. Some boast six-meter-high cross vaults, while the Salon Suite showcases a handpainted medieval wooden ceiling dating back to 1390. Throughout the property there are vintage and midcentury masterpieces: Verner Panton's playful Living Tower takes advantage of the building's grand scale, Greta Grossman's Grasshopper floor lamps illuminate bathrooms lined with Parisian Metro tiles, and a striking brass and Belgian bluestone desk dominates the lobby. The Qvest functions as a kind of cultural nucleus, with each room featuring a small library of books on art, design, photography, and fashion.

Destination	Location	Rooms	Themes
Germany	Berlin	44	Art & Culture, City, Sustainable

Sir Savigny Hotel

Located in Berlin's elegant Charlotten-burg district, Sir Savigny Hotel channels the creative pulse of Savigny Platz with a refined, artistic vibe. Designed by Baranowitz + Kronenberg, and owned by **Liran Wizman,** the hotel unites art nouveau elegance with modern touches in the form of leather, metal, and curated works of art by local artists. Guests can mingle in The Kitchen Library or savor gourmet burgers from The Butcher, even via an in-room dial-a-burger service. Interiors by Saar Zafrir feature custom-made furniture and inventive displays of art objects, making each room feel like a collector's hideaway, with inspiration lingering long after check-out. A courtyard decorated with an enormous mural of a woman reading sets the tone for relaxed cultural immersion in this corner of Berlin.

Kruisherenhotel Maastricht

In Maastricht, **Camille Oostwegel** has transformed a 15th-century Gothic monastery into an architectural marvel with modern, airy interiors by designer Henk Vos and lighting master Ingo Maurer. Guests enter directly into the monastery's inner sanctum, where stained-glass windows cast colored light across wall paintings and contemporary furnishings. The rooms pair age-old construction techniques with modern amenities, while mural-sized artworks and splashes of color on drapery, glassware, and upholstery appear throughout. The former church houses the reception, library, and boutique, and connects to the erstwhile monastery area by way of an innovative glass elevator. Spencer's Restaurant serves French cuisine with a creative twist on the mezzanine within the chancel, while food and drinks can be enjoyed in the lobby, lounge, and courtyard. Guests can also select wines from a glass-vaulted cellar, offering them relaxed drinks in a magnificent, soaring setting.

Destination	Location	Rooms	Themes
Germany	Berlin	172	City, Interior Design

KPM Hotel & Residences

In Berlin's leafy Tiergarten district, KPM Hotel & Residences is an elegant homage to the city's industrial design heritage. Designed by architects Annette Axthelm and Henner Rolvien, Original **Jürgen Groth's** property offers 172 accommodations, ranging from hotel rooms to full-service apartments designed for extended stays. The hotel's identity is linked to its historic neighbor, the renowned KPM porcelain factory that has been crafting exquisite tableware and objets since the 18th century. The connection comes through in minimalist interiors decorated with porcelain light fixtures, artistic installations, and decorative items. Even the restaurant showcases KPM's craftsmanship through its fine tableware, providing an elegant canvas for mouth-watering Asian cuisine. Other amenities include a gym, sauna, bar, and a rooftop terrace with views across the city for an immersive stay in the heart of Berlin.

Destination	Location	Rooms	Themes
Mexico	Mexico City	36	City

Habita

Sheltered behind a glowing sheath of frosted glass, Habita—the vision of **Carlos Couturier** and **Moisés Micha**—sparked a design revolution when it debuted in Mexico City's upscale Polanco district. Originally a 1950s building, the five-story structure was transformed by TEN Arquitectos into a minimalist icon, its floating glass façade providing both privacy and ambient light. Inside, Joseph Dirand's interiors are equally spare and striking, with cantilevered glass desks, Eames chairs, and paneled walls concealing storage to maintain purity of form. The rooftop boasts a lap pool and mezzanine bar, where guests can sip cocktails amid panoramic views. A celebration of modernist restraint, Habita balances creative energy with architectural elegance. The interplay of polished surfaces, geometric lines, and translucent materials creates an immersive, dreamlike sanctuary.

Destination	Location	Rooms	Themes
United Kingdom	London	158	City, Sustainable, Well-Being

Inhabit Queen's Gardens

Nadira and **Rahim Lalji** transformed seven connecting Victorian townhouses into this sustainability-minded sanctuary in west London, close to the tranquil expanses of Hyde Park. Elements of Scandinavian minimalism and Zen design infuse the buildings' ostensibly British character, with calm, restful spaces anchored by a bespoke terrazzo reception desk. Timber floors, jute rugs, Carl Hansen and Søn chairs, and woven rope furnishings combine to create a comfortable, homey tactility. Culture A curates a selection of work by over 30 artists across painting, photography, textiles, and AI. At Yeotown restaurant, plant-centric, Californian-inspired cuisine nourishes body and mind with high-quality ingredients, superfood smoothies, and cold-pressed juices. Treatment rooms include a wood-paneled fitness center with Peloton bikes, a yoga studio, and an infrared sauna—each space designed to slow the pace and shift perspective, offering a quiet reminder that wellbeing is its own kind of wealth.

Memmo Príncipe Real

High above the rooftops of Lisbon, **Rodrigo Machaz's** Memmo Príncipe Real brings quiet elegance to the city's most vibrant quarter. Architect Samuel Torres de Carvalho designed a geometric, minimal edifice that appears to levitate atop a hill off a main square, offering breathtaking 180-degree views of the surrounding city. Entering via the glass-fronted ground floor, guests move through spaces where interior and exterior blur, creating the impression that the reception, restaurant, and terrace are part of the public square. Portuguese and international dishes are served in the hotel's restaurant and cocktail bar, while an outdoor pool and curated walking tours spark moments of leisure and connection with local culture. The same limestone found in Lisbon's royal palaces creates continuity with the surrounding cityscape, while interiors thoughtfully preserve a sense of place in what feels like a blissfully tucked-away enclave in this nonstop city.

Destination
South Africa

Location
Cape Town

Rooms
32

Themes
Art & Culture, City, History,
Interior Design

Gorgeous George

Set in the center of Cape Town, Gorgeous George is an upbeat, joyful hotel that simultaneously connects visitors with the heart of the city and provides a serene escape from the hustle and bustle. While looking after the interior design himself, **Tristan du Plessis** contracted Urbane Citizen Architecture to design the building. The architects formed the hotel from two buildings—one art deco and the other New Edwardian—incorporating 18th-century Victorian, industrial, and African elements. Timber floors, high ceilings, and subtle wall colors provide a backdrop for bright upholstery, floral rugs, and lush greenery reflecting the city's temperate climate. Local design and art are everywhere, including pieces from David Krynauw, Gregor Jenkin, and Egg studio and artworks by David Brits and Porky Hefer. Gigi Rooftop restaurant embraces seasonal, local produce and is served beside the pool, which flows from a decorated indoor space to the outside, where guests can soak up the sun.

Destination
Guatemala

Location
Antigua Guatemala

Rooms
22

Themes
City, History, Interior Design, Offbeat

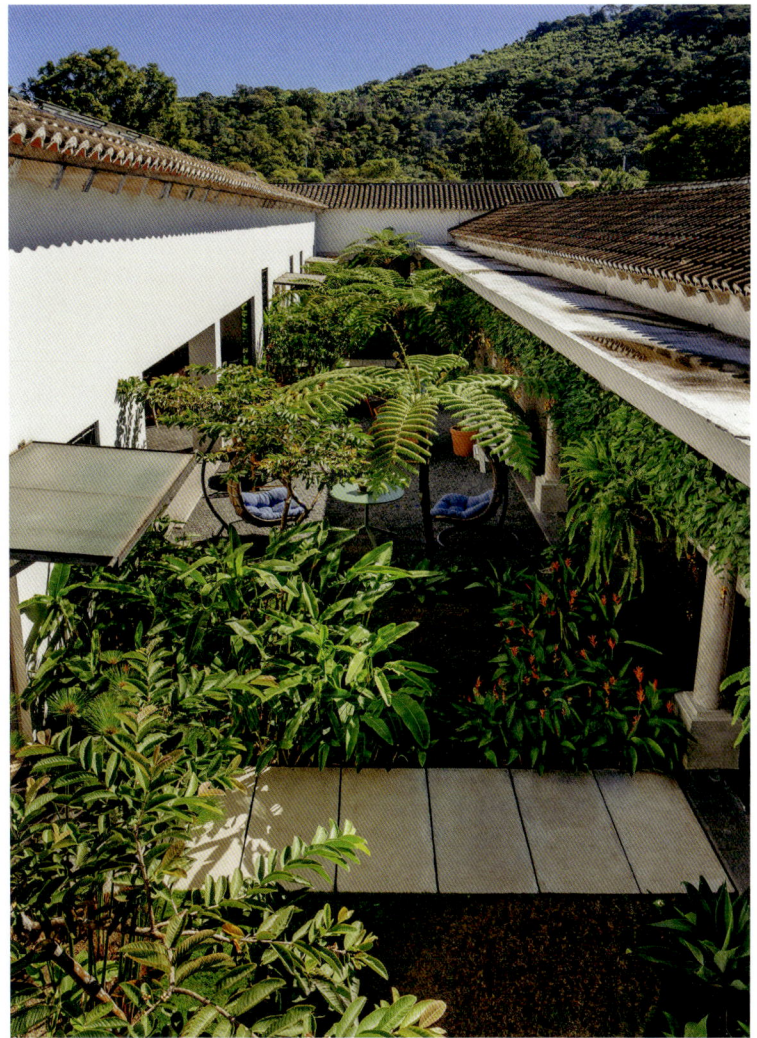

Good Hotel Antigua

Good Hotel, in the historic Guatemalan town of Antigua, offers a meaningful stay in a mansion-like setting. Founded by **Marten Dresen,** whose vision for social business is underpinned by a deep commitment to long-term community impact, the hotel's profits support the charity Niños de Guatemala, which provides education for over 550 children. A single night's stay covers a child's education for one week. The overall experience was crafted by a team that blends local wisdom (Inés Guzmán of Taller KEN and architect Tino Iraheta) with Dutch design vision (Remko Verhaagen and Jeroen Vester of Studio Ninetynine), resulting in thoughtfully sourced local materials paired with timeless, elegant design. Pared-back rooms offer a peaceful retreat with tranquil views of lush courtyards and gardens. At its restaurant, in partnership with local restaurant Saúl, Mediterranean-inspired dishes shine with homegrown ingredients at the fore. Sustainable materials and Dutch design principles are threaded throughout— from bespoke furnishings to locally made toiletries—for a truly community-minded experience that is *good* in every sense of the word.

Destination	Location	Rooms	Themes
Georgia	Tbilisi	119	City, Offbeat

Rooms Tbilisi

In the hillside neighborhood of Vera, **Temur Ugulava** has transformed a former Soviet publishing house into a chic hotel for the creative set. Behind a façade of salvaged wood and Bauhaus-style windows, guests encounter a layered interior shaped by Collective Development. Handmade wallpaper, rich wooden floors, and claw-foot tubs define the 119 rooms and suites, where a rough yet refined sensibility introduces 1930s New York edge to traditional Georgian style. In the lounge, moody lighting, leather armchairs, and curated soundtracks invite lingering beside the fire or at the cocktail bar. Daylight floods gallery-like atriums, where artworks by local artists echo the city's creative pulse. At The Kitchen, chef Levan Buadze offers refined, seasonal cuisine in a setting that nods to Parisian cafe culture, while sister venue Lolita brings together Italian and American flavors in a more casual atmosphere. Rooms Tbilisi is a contemporary cultural node, where restored materials, bold design, and a sense of place converge.

Destination	Location
Spain	Palma de Mallorca

Rooms	Themes
31	City, Gastronomy, History, Interior Design

Concepció by Nobis

On the edge of Palma's historic Old Town, not far from the former fishing barrio of Santa Catalina, is Concepció by Nobis, a refreshed 16th-century building nestled among historic properties, boutique cafes, and museums. Italian **Alessandro Catenacci's** hospitality empire Nobis is based in Sweden and Denmark, and he contracted architects Gert Wingårdh and Helena Toresson to bring a touch of Scandinavia to this Balearic island hotel. The designers employed a mix of natural fibers, pared-back decor, and black timber beams to provide a contrast with striking green and white Huguet-tile floors and crisp white walls. The palette references Mediterranean sea blues and the greens of the surrounding mountains, while the layout puts focus on the unusually spacious lobby and crystalline pool. Chef Xema Álvarez draws on his Mallorcan heritage to present a celebration of local food and regional wines in the hotel's ground floor Restaurant Xalest.

Destination	Location	Rooms	Themes
Germany	Hamburg	125	Art & Culture, City, Gastronomy, Sustainable

The George

Set in Hamburg's vibrant St. Georg district, The George Hotel brings timeless elegance into a distinctly contemporary frame. Conceived by **Kai** and **Lea Hollmann**, with interiors by Sibylle von Heyden and Tom Schlotfeld, the hotel features 125 rooms and suites in warm tones punctuated by pleated lampshades, custom-made furniture, and carefully selected artworks. Guests can retreat to the atmospheric library or take in panoramic views of Alster Lake from the rooftop terrace, spa, and select rooms. For meetings, four rooms with dark timber flooring offer refined, functional space. Culinary highlights include DaCaio, a sleek Italian restaurant known for its Mediterranean menu and deep wine list. The adjoining bar flows onto a generous outdoor terrace—ideal for cocktails or quiet conversation. Anchored in one of Hamburg's most diverse neighborhoods, The George offers a stay that feels polished, personal, and perfectly in step with the city's creative rhythm.

Destination
France

Location
Paris

Rooms
45

Themes
Art & Culture, City, History

Destination
France

Location
Paris

Rooms
105

Themes
Art & Culture, City, History

Hôtel Wallace

Hôtel Wallace channels the glamour of an Italian Riviera motel; a place where glossy headboards, fringed sconces, and terrazzo bathrooms are in every room. Behind the hotel's white façade, Tuco's terrace serves *aperitivi.* The bar's marble and wood counter hosts bartenders working the taps like seasoned maestros, while locally sourced breakfasts to sunset drinks round out the experience. Ideally situated on a quiet street near the Seine and within walking distance of the Champ de Mars, Wallace offers a stylish base for exploring the Left Bank.

Hôtel Rochechouart

Since 1929, this Art Deco establishment has been a Parisian landmark. Recently redesigned by architecture duo Festen, it leans into its period style. Rooms feature splendor—plush mattresses, soft materials, warm hues—typical of the City of Light. Citrons et Huîtres, designed by architect Marion Mailaender, serves oysters and crudo platters, while on the ninth floor, Maggie Rooftop offers panoramic views. Maggie keeps the boulevard's tempo, while in the basement there's a bar where DJs spin their sets beneath disco balls and Japanese lanterns.

Destination
United Kingdom

Location
London

Rooms
97

Themes
City, Gastronomy, History

Town Hall Hotel

Loh Lik Peng's hotel unites East End Edwardian architecture and contemporary design. Inside the former Bethnal Green Town Hall, Rare Architecture blends preserved features with glass partitions and bespoke furniture. A rooftop extension adds a contemporary touch. The rooms offer refined comfort, with the De Montfort Suite boasting triple-height ceiling and art deco details. Guests can soak up the relaxed yet vibrant energy of Ellis Restaurant or savor a more elevated experience at Da Terra, the hotel's acclaimed two-Michelin-starred restaurant.

Destination
United Arab Emirates

Location
Dubai

Rooms
136

Themes
City, Sustainable

FORM Hotel Dubai

FORM Hotel Dubai is a refined alternative to anonymous luxury. Designed by Architecture-Studio, it speaks to health-conscious, connected travelers. Color and light provide evolving moods, and public spaces open to the urban landscape. Guestrooms offer unique vistas, framed by white plaster, stone, and walnut. Other sophisticated flourishes include black aluminum, marble countertops, and wood paneling. Alongside its clean-eating restaurant, rooftop pool and gym, in-house retailer, and bespoke leisure experiences, FORM delivers a dynamic experience.

Sir Prague Hotel

A dramatic escape in the heart of the Czech capital, Sir Prague Hotel is housed in a 19th-century Gothic landmark overlooking the Vltava River. Originally built in 1884 as the Ministry of Coal headquarters, guests now enter through a courtyard dressed in trelliswork and greenery, with glowing light softening the original stonework and intricate ceilings. Interior designer Linda Boronkay preserved this historical tapestry while introducing playful geometric forms and bold graphic patterns inspired by Czech cubism. In the 76 rooms and suites, a mood-setting color palette of butter cream, soft greens, and rust reds, alongside whimsical artworks, patterned headboards, and dark wood furniture, speak to the multifaceted character of this storied city. The surrounding New Town, a mix of Gothic, baroque, renaissance, and art nouveau, adds further layers that enhance the overall experience. After catching a ballet or opera at the National Theater—incidentally designed by the same architect as Sir Prague—guests can return to the hotel's wellness area for rest and reflection.

Destination	Location	Rooms	Themes
Japan	Tokyo	25	City, Sustainable

TRUNK (HOTEL)
Yoyogi Park

TRUNK (HOTEL) Yoyogi Park sits just across Inokashira-Dori Street from Yoyogi Park, one of Tokyo's most expansive green spaces. Under the concept of "urban recharge," the hotel provides a luxurious and distinctive stay for travelers. The harmony of solace and stimulus is reflected throughout the guest experience. Designed through a collaboration between Keiji Ashizawa Design, Norm Architects, and Trunk, the hotel blends traditional Japanese materials and spatial sensibility with Scandinavian modernism and a nature-focused approach, creating an elegant, one-of-a-kind environment that integrates naturally into the Tomigaya neighborhood. On the rooftop, Trunk

Pool Club awaits with its stunning infinity pool overlooking the park—a tranquil retreat reserved exclusively for hotel guests. Meanwhile, on the ground floor, Pizzeria e Trattoria L'Ombelico invites guests to savor authentic Neapolitan pizza baked in a wood-fired oven imported from Italy, along with timeless Italian dishes in a relaxed, welcoming setting.

OCEANIA

This book was conceived, edited, and designed by Design Hotels and gestalten.

Managing Director
Stijn Oyen

Global Brand Leader
Sarah Doyle

Creative Director
Nina Zywietz

Editorial Director
Iris Hempelmann

Commissioning Editor
François-Luc Giraldeau

Senior Project Managers
Tasya Kudryk and
Lars Pietzschmann

Lead Editors
Laura Allsop and Steph Wade

Editors
Ken Baron, Allison Reiber DiLiegro,
Vidula Kotian

Art Director
Alexandra Bruns

Designers
Inês Chambel, Lucy Deverall,
Raquel D'Oliveira, Jonathan von Holst,
Hy-Ran Kilian, Linda Kunnath,
Marcin Liwarski, Stefan Morgner,
Vivian Nebelin, Melanie Ullrich

Hotel Features
Laura Allsop, Laura Box, Hayley Dean,
Amy Everett, Rachel Ingram,
Alisa Kotmair, Victorine Lamothe,
Emma Love, Ananda Pellerin,
and Maisie Skidmore

Features
Kissa Castañeda, Alexis Dornier,
Oliver Jahn, Arman Naféei,
Christina Ohly Evans, Sarah Owen,
Nicola Leigh Stewart

Photo Editors
Madeline Dudley-Yates,
Marvyn Emmons, Alina Soare Rada

Cover Artwork
Monja Gentschow

Production Manager
Vincent Illner

Featured Photographers
Bastian Achard (p. 11, 270 left)
Jonas Bjerre-Poulsen/Norm Architects (p. 45)
Daniel Farò (p. 95)
Khoo Guo Jie (p. 239, 269, 323)
Yiorgos Kaplanidis (p. 300 right, 301 right)
KIE, kiearch.com (p. 167-199)
Ian Lanterman (p. 46)
Maximilian Mair (p. 12)
Alejandro Ramirez Orozco (p. 299)
Michal Rzepecki (p. 324)
Danilo Scarpati (p. 238)
Piergiorgio Sorgetti (p. 300 left, 301 left)
Vivek Vadoliya (p. 271)

Typefaces
Plantin by Monotype and
Suisse Int'l by Swiss Typefaces

Paper
Cover material: Gmund Moonlight,
White Shadow
Inside: Sappi Magno Volume

Printing
Schleunungdruck GmbH,
Marktheidenfeld
Made in Germany

Publisher
Die Gestalten Verlag GmbH & Co. KG

ISBN 978-3-96704-194-1 (Trade Edition)
1st printing, 2025

Special Thanks
To all the contributors, including so
many behind the scenes, from our
partner hotels and beyond.

© Die Gestalten Verlag GmbH & Co. KG,
Berlin 2025

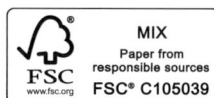

Design Hotels

Design Hotels is a global collection of 300+ independently owned hotels with an unrivalled community of design, architecture, and original hospitality experiences. From the pioneering hotels of New York and London to the rising stars of Shanghai and Mexico City, from mountaintops to off-the-beaten-path escapes, each is the unique creative expression of our hoteliers, or "Originals", as we call them. It's what makes our hotels not just a place to stay, but an experience that lives on in memory.

Design Hotels GmbH
Rummelsburger Seeblick 1
10317 Berlin, Germany

@design_hotels
designhotels.com

Marriott Bonvoy®

A number of Design Hotels properties are available to book with Marriott Bonvoy, one of the most widely recognized travel programs in the hospitality industry. Since joining Marriott Bonvoy's portfolio in 2019, we've continued to ensure the hotels under our wing are the very best. You can earn, redeem, and enjoy Marriott Bonvoy member benefits with Design Hotels venues around the globe. To find out more and to see our participating hotels, visit designhotels.com.

For more information and to order books, please visit www.gestalten.com

Die Gestalten Verlag GmbH & Co. KG
Mariannenstrasse 9–10
10999 Berlin, Germany

Bibliographic information published by the Deutsche Nationalbibliothek The Deutsche Nationalbibliothek lists this publication in the Deutsche Nationalbibliografie; detailed bibliographic data is available online at www.dnb.de

DESIGN HOTELS™   MARRIOTT BONVOY®   gestalten   GMUND